PRAISE FOR it's complicated

"An exhaustively researched study of how teens use technology . . . and a manifesto on how parents as individuals and society as a whole let young people down when they insist on protection and paternalism over media literacy and critical thinking. Even readers who are not parents, or teens, may well find this one of the most interesting books of the year."—Amy Benfer, *Los Angeles Times*

"boyd has done her homework and listened well. She is a high-tech medium translating the language and meaning of teenagers and social networking." —Eve Ensler, author of *The Vagina Monologues* and *In the Body of the World*

"A persuasive anti-alarmist polemic that should help ease parents' concerns about all sorts of Internet bogeymen."—Randye Hoder, *TIME* Health & Family

"Students, parents, and educators will find this a comprehensive study of how technology impacts teens' lives and how adults can help balance rather than vilify its inevitable use."—*Publishers Weekly*

"A truly enlightening read."—Jane Mulkerrins, *Sunday Telegraph*

"*It's Complicated* . . . places today's smartphones, iPads and laptops in the context of this perennial power struggle between adolescents and parents. In doing so, it adds much to our understanding of a young generation of hyper-connected, hybrid consumer-producers—a cohort whose behaviour often unites parents, educators and investors in collective bewilderment." —Gautam Malkani, *Financial Times*

"boyd's extensive research illuminates the oft-misunderstood world of teens today, where social media is an extension of life. . . . Thorough information interwoven with common-sense advice from teens and the author enable readers, particularly parents, to relax a bit regarding this new media age. . . . Comprehensive new research that illuminates why and how social media is important to teens."—*Kirkus Reviews*

"If you want to understand the digital worlds inhabited by today's young people, this is *the* book to read."—Howard Gardner, coauthor of *The App Generation*

P9-BYG-613

"I want to get this publication into the hands of every teacher, parent, policy maker, and journalist. Thoughtful in her analysis and adept at skewering the most common misunderstandings and anxieties about teens' online lives, boyd is the best possible person to write a book like this, and this book does not disappoint in any way."—Henry Jenkins, coauthor of *Spreadable Media: Creating Meaning and Value in a Networked Culture*

"Astute, nuanced, provocative and hopeful, boyd does it all in this must-read treatise on teens and their digital lives."—Stephen Balkam, Founder and CEO, Family Online Safety Institute

"Impeccably researched, written and argued, danah boyd's *It's Complicated* is essential reading for anyone with even the slightest interest in teens or social media."—Justine Larbalestier, author of *Liar* and *Zombies vs. Unicorns*

"Crucial reading for anyone who wants to understand the nuances and hard realities of being a teenager in our networked world. (I'm looking at you, parents, policy makers, and YA writers.)"—Scott Westerfeld, author of *Uglies*

"Finally, a book about youth and social media that actually gives youth a voice! The insights here offer unprecedented perspective for parenting and teaching in this networked world of ours."—Anne Collier, codirector of ConnectSafely.org, writer at NetFamilyNews.org

"For the price of two grande frappucinos, you can buy this book . . . and young people will make sense."—Nancy Lublin, CEO, DoSomething.org

"A rare teens'-eye view into the often mystifying changes to our everyday communication, boyd's book offers a voice of reason in the often heated debates over young people and technology."—Mizuko Ito, University of California, Irvine

"boyd always moves beyond conventional wisdom when it comes to understanding teen online behavior. It's invaluable to have here the results of her years of study."—Elisa Camahort Page, cofounder, BlogHer

"There is something marvellously sensible about boyd's resolutely academic style. . . . boyd's anatomy of teenage life is penetrating."—Jane Shilling, *Sunday Telegraph*

"*It's Complicated* champion[s] a rich, complex idea of what youth is about, and view[s] with horror the way adult discussions so often reduce the young to mute metrics."—Simon Ings, *New Scientist*

it's
complicated

the social lives of
networked teens

danah boyd

Yale UNIVERSITY PRESS

new haven + london

Published with assistance from the foundation established in memory of Philip Hamilton McMillan of the class of 1894, Yale College.

Yale University Press books may be purchased in quantity for educational, business, or promotional use. For information, please e-mail sales.press@yale.edu (US office) or sales@yaleup.co.uk (UK office).

Designed by Lindsey Voskowsky.
Set in Avenir LT STD and Adobe Garmond type by IDS Infotech, Ltd.
Printed in the United States of America.

The Library of Congress has cataloged the hardcover edition as follows:

boyd, danah (danah michele), 1977–
    It's complicated : the social lives of networked teens / danah boyd.
        pages   cm
    Includes bibliographical references and index.
    ISBN 978-0-300-16631-6 (clothbound : alk. paper)
    1. Internet and teenagers.   2. Online social networks.
3. Teenagers—Social life and customs—21st century.
4. Information technology—Social aspects. I. Title.
    HQ799.2.I5B68 2014
    004.67'80835—dc23

                                            2013031950

    ISBN 978-0-300-19900-0 (pbk.)

A catalogue record for this book is available from the British Library.

10 9 8 7 6 5 4 3 2 1

For Peter Lyman (1940–2007), who took a
chance on me and helped me find solid ground

contents

preface

The year was 2006, and I was in northern California chatting with teenagers about their use of social media. There, I met Mike, a white fifteen-year-old who loved YouTube.[1] He was passionately describing the "Extreme Diet Coke and Mentos Experiments" video that had recently gained widespread attention, as viewers went to YouTube in droves to witness the geysers that could be produced when the diet soda and mint candy were combined. Various teens had taken to mixing Mentos and Diet Coke just to see what would happen, and Mike was among them. He was ecstatic to show me the homemade video he and his friends had made while experimenting with common food items. As he walked me through his many other YouTube videos, Mike explained that his school allowed him to borrow a video camera for school assignments. Students were actively encouraged to make videos or other media as part of group projects to display their classroom knowledge. He and his friends had taken to borrowing the camera on Fridays, making sure to tape their homework assignment before spending the rest of the weekend making more entertaining videos. None of the videos they made were of especially high quality, and while they shared them publicly on YouTube, only their friends watched them. Still, whenever they got an additional view—even if only because they forced a friend to watch the video—they got excited.

As we were talking and laughing and exploring Mike's online videos, Mike paused and turned to me with a serious look on his face. "Can you do me a favor?" he asked, "Can you talk to my mom? Can you tell her that I'm not doing anything wrong on the internet?" I didn't immediately respond, and so he jumped in to clarify. "I mean, she thinks that everything online is bad, and you seem to get it, and you're an adult. Will you talk to her?" I smiled and promised him that I would.

This book is just that: my attempt to describe and explain the networked lives of teens to the people who worry about them—parents, teachers, policy makers, journalists, sometimes even other teens. It is the product of an eight-year effort to explore various aspects of teens' engagement with social media and other networked technologies.

To get at teens' practices, I crisscrossed the United States from 2005 to 2012, talking with and observing teens from eighteen states and a wide array of socioeconomic and ethnic communities. I spent countless hours observing teens through the traces they left online via social network sites, blogs, and other genres of social media. I hung out with teens in physical spaces like schools, public parks, malls, churches, and fast food restaurants.

To dive deeper into particular issues, I conducted 166 formal, semi-structured interviews with teens during the period 2007–2010.[2] I interviewed teens in their homes, at school, and in various public settings. In addition, I talked with parents, teachers, librarians, youth ministers, and others who worked directly with youth. I became an expert on youth culture. In addition, my technical background and experience working with and for technology companies building social media tools gave me firsthand knowledge about how social media was designed, implemented, and introduced to the public. Together, these two strains of expertise allowed me to enter into broader policy conversations, serve on commissions focused on youth practices, and help influence public conversations about networked sociality.

As I began to get a feel for the passions and frustrations of teens and to speak to broader audiences, I recognized that teens' voices rarely shaped the public discourse surrounding their networked lives. So many people talk about youth engagement with social media, but very few of them are willing to take the time to listen to teens, to hear them, or to pay attention to what they have to say about their lives, online and off. I wrote this book to address that gap. Throughout this book, I draw on the voices of teens I've interviewed as well as those I've observed or met more informally. At times, I also pull stories from the media or introduce adults' perspectives to help provide context or offer additional examples.

I wrote this book to reflect the experiences and perspectives of the teens that I encountered. Their voices shape this book just as their stories shaped my understanding of the role of social media in their lives. My hope is that this book will shed light on the complex and fascinating practices of contemporary American youth as they try to find themselves in a networked world.

As you read this book, my hope is that you will suspend your assumptions about youth in an effort to understand the social lives of networked teens. By and large, the kids are all right. But they want to be understood. This book is my attempt to do precisely that.

it's
complicated

introduction

One evening, in September 2010, I was in the stands at a high school football game in Nashville, Tennessee, experiencing a powerful sense of déjà vu. As a member of my high school's marching band in the mid-1990s, I had spent countless Friday nights in stands across central Pennsylvania, pretending to cheer on my school's football team so that I could hang out with my friends. The scene at the school in Nashville in 2010 could easily have taken place when I was in high school almost two decades earlier. It was an archetypical American night, and immediately legible to me. I couldn't help but smile at the irony, given that I was in Nashville to talk with teens about how technology had changed their lives. As I sat in the stands, I thought: the more things had changed, the more they seemed the same.

I recalled speaking to a teen named Stan whom I'd met in Iowa three years earlier. He had told me to stop looking for differences. "You'd actually be surprised how little things change. I'm guessing a lot of the drama is still the same, it's just the format is a little different. It's just changing the font and changing the background color really." He made references to technology to remind me that technology wasn't changing anything important.

Back in Nashville, the cheerleaders screamed, "Defense!" and waved their colorful pom-poms, while boys in tuxes and girls in formal gowns lined up on the track that circled the football field, signaling that halftime was approaching. This was a Homecoming game, and at halftime the Homecoming Court paraded onto the field in formal attire to be introduced to the audience before the announcer declared the King and Queen. The Court was made up of eight girls and eight boys, half of whom were white and half of whom were black. I reflected on the lack of Asian or Hispanic representation in a town whose demographics were changing. The announcer introduced each member to the audience, focusing on their extracurricular activities, their participation in one of the local churches, and their dreams for the future.

Meanwhile, most of the student body was seated in the stands. They were decked out in the school colors, many even having painted their faces in support. But they were barely paying attention to what was happening on the field. Apart from a brief hush when the Homecoming Court was presented, they spent the bulk of the time facing one another, chatting, enjoying a rare chance to spend unstructured time together as friends and peers.

As in many schools I've visited over the years, friendships at this school in Nashville were largely defined by race, gender, sexuality, and grade level, and those networks were immediately visible based on whom students were talking to or sitting with. By and large, the students were cordoned off in their own section on the sides of the stands while parents and more "serious" fans occupied the seats in the center. Most of the students in the stands were white and divided by grade: the upperclassmen took the seats closest to the field, while the freshmen were pushed toward the back. Girls were rarely alone with boys, but when they were, they were holding hands. The teens who swarmed below and to the right of the stands represented a different part of the school. Unlike their peers in the stands, most of the students milling about below were black. Aside from the Homecoming Court, only one group was racially mixed, and they were recognizable mainly for their "artistic" attire—unnaturally colorful hair, piercings, and black clothing that I recognized from the racks of Hot Topic, a popular mall-based chain store that caters to goths, punks, and other subcultural groups.

Only two things confirmed that this was not 1994: the fashion and the cell phones. Gone were the 1980s-inspired bangs, perms, and excessive use of hair gel and hairspray that dominated my high school well into the 1990s. And unlike 1994, cell phones were everywhere. As far as I could tell, every teen at the game that day in Nashville had one: iPhones, Blackberries, and other high-end smartphones seemed to be especially popular at this upper-middle-class school. Unsurprisingly, the phones in the hands of the white students were often more expensive or of more elite brands than those in the hands of the black students.

The pervasiveness of cell phones in the stands isn't that startling; over 80 percent of high school students in the United States had a cell phone in 2010.[1] What was surprising, at least to most adults, was how little the teens actually used them as phones. The teens I observed were not making calls. They whipped out their phones to take photos of the Homecoming Court, and many were texting frantically while trying to find one another in the crowd. Once they connected, the texting often stopped. On the few occasions when a phone did ring, the typical response was an exasperated "Mom!" or "Dad!" implying a parent calling to check in, which, given the teens' response to such calls, was clearly an unwanted interruption. And even though many teens are frequent texters, the teens were not directing most of their attention to their devices. When they did look at their phones, they were often sharing the screen with the person sitting next to them, reading or viewing something together.

The parents in the stands were paying much more attention to their devices. They were even more universally equipped with smartphones than their children, and those devices dominated their focus. I couldn't tell whether they were checking email or simply supplementing the football game with other content, being either bored or distracted. But many adults were staring into their devices intently, barely looking up when a touchdown was scored. And unlike the teens, they weren't sharing their devices with others or taking photos of the event.

Although many parents I've met lament their children's obsession with their phones, the teens in Nashville were treating their phones as no more than a glorified camera plus coordination device. The reason was clear: their friends were right there with them. They didn't need anything else.

I had come to Nashville to better understand how social media and other technologies had changed teens' lives. I was fascinated with the new communication and information technologies that had emerged since I was in high school. I had spent my own teen years online, and I was among the first generation of teens who did so. But that was a different era; few of my friends in the early 1990s were interested in computers at all. And my own interest in the internet was related to my dissatisfaction with my local community. The internet presented me with a bigger world, a world populated by people who shared my idiosyncratic interests and were ready to discuss them at any time, day or night. I grew up in an era where going online—or "jacking in"—was an escape mechanism, and I desperately wanted to escape.

The teens I met are attracted to popular social media like Facebook and Twitter or mobile technologies like apps and text messaging for entirely different reasons. Unlike me and the other early adopters who avoided our local community by hanging out in chatrooms and bulletin boards, most teenagers now go online to connect to the people in their community. Their online participation is not eccentric; it is entirely normal, even expected.

The day after the football game in Nashville, I interviewed a girl who had attended the Homecoming game. We sat down and went through her Facebook page, where she showed me various photos from the night before. Facebook hadn't been on her mind during the game, but as soon as she got home, she uploaded her photos, tagged her friends, and started commenting on others' photos. The status updates I saw on her page were filled with references to conversations that took place at the game. She used Facebook to extend the pleasure she had in connecting with her classmates during the game. Although she couldn't physically hang out with her friends after the game ended, she used Facebook to stay connected after the stands had cleared.

Social media plays a crucial role in the lives of networked teens. Although the specific technologies change, they collectively provide teens with a space to hang out and connect with friends. Teens' mediated interactions sometimes complement or supplement their face-to-face encounters. In 2006, when MySpace was at the height of its popularity, eighteen-year-old Skyler told her mother that being on MySpace was utterly essential to her social life. She explained, "If you're not on MySpace, you don't exist." What Skyler meant is simply that social acceptance depends on the ability to socialize with one's peers at the "cool" place. Each cohort of teens has a different space that it decides is cool. It used to be the mall, but for the youth discussed in this book, social network sites like Facebook, Twitter, and Instagram are *the* cool places. Inevitably, by the time this book is published, the next generation of teens will have inhabited a new set of apps and tools, making social network sites feel passé. The spaces may change, but the organizing principles aren't different.

Although some teens still congregate at malls and football games, the introduction of social media does alter the landscape. It enables youth to create a cool space without physically transporting themselves anywhere. And because of a variety of social and cultural factors, social media has become an important public space where teens can gather and socialize broadly with peers in an informal way. Teens are looking for a place of their own to make sense of the world beyond their bedrooms. Social media has enabled them to participate in and help create what I call *networked publics*.

In this book, I document how and why social media has become central to the lives of so many American teens and how they navigate the networked publics that are created through those technologies.[2] I also describe—and challenge—the anxieties that many American adults have about teens' engagement with social media. By illustrating teens' practices, habits, and the tensions between teens and adults, I attempt to provide critical insight into the networked lives of contemporary youth.

What Is Social Media?

Over the past decade, social media has evolved from being an eso-teric jumble of technologies to a set of sites and services that are at the heart of contemporary culture. Teens turn to a plethora of popular services to socialize, gossip, share information, and hang out. Although this book addresses a variety of networked technologies—including the internet broadly and mobile services like texting specifically—much of it focuses on a collection of services known as social media. I use the term *social media* to refer to the sites and services that emerged during the early 2000s, including social network sites, video sharing sites, blogging and microblogging platforms, and related tools that allow participants to create and share their own content. In addition to referring to various communication tools and platforms, social media also hints at a cultural mindset that emerged in the mid-2000s as part of the technical and business phenomenon referred to as "Web2.0."[3]

The services known as social media are neither the first—nor the only—tools to support significant social interaction or enable teenagers to communicate and engage in meaningful online com-munities. Though less popular than they once were, tools like email, instant messaging, and online forums are still used by teens. But as a cultural phenomenon, social media has reshaped the information and communication ecosystem.

In the 1980s and 1990s, early internet adopters used services like email and instant messaging to chat with people they knew; they turned to public-facing services like chatrooms and bulletin boards when they wanted to connect with strangers. Although many who participated in early online communities became friends with people they met online, most early adopters entered these spaces without knowing the other people in the space. Online communities were organized by topic, with separate spaces for those interested in dis-cussing Middle East politics or getting health advice or finding out how various programming languages worked.

Beginning around 2003, the increased popularity of blogging and the rise of social network sites reconfigured this topically oriented landscape. Although the most visible blogging services helped people connect based on shared interests, the vast majority of bloggers were blogging for, and reading blogs of, people they knew.[4] When early social network sites like Friendster and MySpace launched, they were designed to enable users to meet new people—and, notably, friends of friends—who might share their interests, tastes, or passions. Friendster, in particular, was designed as a matchmaking service. In other words, social network sites were designed for social network*ing*. Yet what made these services so unexpectedly popular was that they also provided a platform for people to connect with their friends. Rather than focusing on the friends of friends who could be met through the service, many early adopters simply focused on socializing with their friends. At the height of its popularity, MySpace's tagline was "A Place for Friends," and that's precisely what the service was for many of its users.

Social network sites changed the essence of online communities. Whereas early online community tools like Usenet and bulletin boards were organized around interests, even if people used them to engage with friends, blogs, like homepages, were organized around individuals. Links allowed people to highlight both their friends and those who shared their interests. Social network sites downplayed the importance of interests and made friendship the organizing tenant of the genre.

Early adopters had long embraced internet technologies to socialize with others, but in more mainstream culture, participating in online communities was often viewed as an esoteric practice for geeks and other social outcasts. By the mid-2000s, with the mainstreaming of internet access and the rise of social media—and especially MySpace, Facebook, and Twitter—sharing information and connecting to friends online became an integrated part of daily life for many people, and especially the teens who came of age during this period. Rather than being seen as a subcultural practice, participating in social media became normative.

Although teens have embraced countless tools for communicating with one another, their widespread engagement with social media has been unprecedented. Teens who used Facebook or Instagram or Tumblr in 2013 weren't seen as peculiar. Nor were those who used Xanga, LiveJournal, or MySpace in the early to mid-2000s. At the height of their popularity, the best-known social media tools aren't viewed with disdain, nor is participation seen to be indicative of asocial tendencies. In fact, as I describe throughout this book, engagement with social media is simply an everyday part of life, akin to watching television and using the phone. This is a significant shift from my experiences growing up using early digital technologies.

Even though many of the tools and services that I reference throughout this book are now passé, the core activities I discuss—chatting and socializing, engaging in self-expression, grappling with privacy, and sharing media and information—are here to stay. Although the specific sites and apps may be constantly changing, the practices that teens engage in as they participate in networked publics remain the same. New technologies and mobile apps change the landscape, but teens' interactions with social media through their phones extend similar practices and activities into geographically unbounded settings. The technical shifts that have taken place since I began this project—and in the time between me writing this book and you reading it—are important, but many of the arguments made in the following pages transcend particular technical moments, even if the specific examples used to illustrate those issues are locked in time.

The Significance of Networked Publics

Teens are passionate about finding their place in society. What is different as a result of social media is that teens' perennial desire for social connection and autonomy is now being expressed in *networked publics*. Networked publics are publics that are restructured by networked technologies. As such, they are simultaneously (1) the space constructed through networked technologies and (2) the imagined community that emerges as a result of the intersection of people, technology, and practice.[5]

Although the term *public* has resonance in everyday language, the construct of a public—let alone publics—tends to be more academic in nature. What constitutes a public in this sense can vary. It can be an accessible space in which people can gather freely. Or, as political scientist Benedict Anderson describes, a public can be a collection of people who understand themselves to be part of an *imagined community.*[6] People are a part of multiple publics—bounded as audiences or by geography—and yet, publics often intersect and intertwine. Publics get tangled up in one another, challenging any effort to understand the boundaries and shape of any particular public. When US presidents give their State of the Union speeches, they may have written them with the American public in mind, but their speeches are now accessible around the globe. As a result, it's never quite clear who fits into the public imagined by a president.

Publics serve different purposes. They can be political in nature, or they can be constructed around shared identities and social practices. The concept of a public often invokes the notion of a state-controlled entity, but publics can also involve private actors, such as companies, or commercial spaces like malls. Because of the involvement of media in contemporary publics, publics are also interconnected to the notion of audience. All of these constructs blur and are contested by scholars. By invoking the term *publics*, I'm not trying to take a position within the debates so much as to make use of the wide array of different interwoven issues signaled by that term. Publics provide a space and a community for people to gather, connect, and help construct society as we understand it.

Networked publics are publics both in the spatial sense and in the sense of an imagined community. They are built on and through social media and other emergent technologies. As spaces, the networked publics that exist because of social media allow people to gather and connect, hang out, and joke around. Networked publics formed through technology serve much the same functions as publics like the mall or the park did for previous generations of teenagers. As social constructs, social media creates networked publics that allow people to see themselves as a part of a broader community. Just as shared TV consumption once allowed teens to see themselves as connected through mass media, social media allows contemporary teens to envision themselves as part of a collectively imagined community.

Teens engage with networked publics for the same reasons they have always relished publics; they want to be a part of the broader world by connecting with other people and having the freedom of mobility. Likewise, many adults fear networked technologies for the same reasons that adults have long been wary of teen participation in public life and teen socialization in parks, malls, and other sites where youth congregate. If I have learned one thing from my research, it's this: social media services like Facebook and Twitter are providing teens with new opportunities to participate in public life, and this, more than anything else, is what concerns many anxious adults.

Although the underlying structure of physical spaces and the relationships that are enabled by them are broadly understood, both the architecture of networked spaces and the ways they allow people to connect are different. Even if teens are motivated to engage with networked publics to fulfill desires to socialize that predate the internet, networked technologies alter the social ecosystem and thus affect the social dynamics that unfold.

To understand what is new and what is not, it's important to understand how technology introduces new social possibilities and how these challenge assumptions people have about everyday interactions. The design and architecture of environments enable certain types of interaction to occur. Round tables with chairs make chatting with someone easier than classroom-style seating. Even though students can twist around and talk to the person behind them, a typical classroom is designed to encourage everyone to face the teacher. The particular properties or characteristics of an environment can be understood as *affordances* because they make possible—and, in some cases, are used to encourage—certain types of practices, even if they do not determine what practices will unfold.[7] Understanding the affordances of a particular technology or space is important because it sheds light on what people can leverage or resist in achieving their goals. For example, the affordances of a thick window allow people to see each other without being able to hear each other. To communicate in spite of the window, they may pantomime, hold up signs with written messages, or break the glass. The window's affordances don't predict how people will communicate, but they do shape the situation nonetheless.

Because technology is involved, networked publics have different characteristics than traditional physical public spaces. Four affordances, in particular, shape many of the mediated environments that are created by social media. Although these affordances are not in and of themselves new, their relation to one another because of networked publics creates new opportunities and challenges. They are:

- persistence: the durability of online expressions and content;
- visibility: the potential audience who can bear witness;
- spreadability: the ease with which content can be shared; and
- searchability: the ability to find content.

Content shared through social media often sticks around because technologies are designed to enable *persistence*. The fact that content often persists has significant implications. Such content enables interactions to take place over time in an asynchronous fashion. Alice may write to Bob at midnight while Bob is sound asleep; but when Bob wakes up in the morning or comes back from summer camp three weeks later, that message will still be there waiting for him, even if Alice had forgotten about it. Persistence means that conversations conducted through social media are far from ephemeral; they endure. Persistence enables different kinds of interactions than the ephemerality of a park. Alice's message doesn't expire when Bob reads it, and Bob can keep that message for decades. What persistence also means, then, is that those using social media are often "on the record" to an unprecedented degree.

Through social media, people can easily share with broad audiences and access content from greater distances, which increases the potential *visibility* of any particular message. More often than not, what people put up online using social media is widely accessible because most systems are designed such that sharing with broader or more public audiences is the default. Many popular systems require users to take active steps to limit the visibility of any particular piece of shared content. This is quite different from physical spaces, where people must make a concerted effort to make content visible to sizable audiences.[8] In networked publics, interactions are often public by default, private through effort.

Social media is often designed to help people spread information, whether by explicitly or implicitly encouraging the sharing of links, providing reblogging or favoriting tools that repost images or texts, or by making it easy to copy and paste content from one place to another. Thus, much of what people post online is easily *spreadable* with the click of a few keystrokes.[9] Some systems provide simple buttons to "forward," "repost," or "share" content to articulated or curated lists. Even when these tools aren't built into the system, content can often be easily downloaded or duplicated and then forwarded along. The ease with which everyday people can share media online is unrivaled, which can be both powerful and problematic. Spreadability can be leveraged to rally people for a political cause or to spread rumors.

Last, since the rise of search engines, people's communications are also often *searchable*. My mother would have loved to scream, "Find!" and see where my friends and I were hanging out and what we were talking about. Now, any inquisitive onlooker can query databases and uncover countless messages written by and about others. Even messages that were crafted to be publicly accessible were not necessarily posted with the thought that they would reappear through a search engine. Search engines make it easy to surface esoteric interactions. These tools are often designed to eliminate contextual cues, increasing the likelihood that searchers will take what they find out of context.

None of the capabilities enabled by social media are new. The letters my grandparents wrote during their courtship were persistent.

Messages printed in the school newspaper or written on bathroom walls have long been visible. Gossip and rumors have historically spread like wildfire through word of mouth. And although search engines certainly make inquiries more efficient, the practice of asking after others is not new, even if search engines mean that no one else knows. What is new is the way in which social media alters and amplifies social situations by offering technical features that people can use to engage in these well-established practices.

As people use these different tools, they help create new social dynamics. For example, teens "stalk" one another by searching for highly visible, persistent data about people they find interesting. "Drama" starts when teens increase the visibility of gossip by spreading it as fast as possible through networked publics. And teens seek attention by exploiting searchability, spreadability, and persistence to maximize the visibility of their garage band's YouTube video. The particular practices that emerge as teens use the tools around them create the impression that teen sociality is radically different even though the underlying motivations and social processes have not changed that much.

Just because teens can and do manipulate social media to attract attention and increase visibility does not mean that they are equally experienced at doing so or that they automatically have the skills to navigate what unfolds. It simply means that teens are generally more comfortable with—and tend to be less skeptical of—social media than adults. They don't try to analyze how things are different because of technology; they simply try to relate to a public world in which technology is a given. Because of their social position, what's novel for teens is not the technology but the public life that it enables. Teens are desperate to have access to and make sense of public life; understanding the technologies that enable publics is just par for the course. Adults, in contrast, have more freedom to explore various public environments. They are more likely—and more equipped—to compare networked publics to other publics. As a result, they focus more on how networked publics seem radically different from other publics, such as those that unfold at the local bar or through church.

Because of their experience and stage in life, teens and adults are typically focused on different issues. Whereas teens are focused on what it means to be in public, adults are more focused on what it means to be networked.

Throughout this book, I return to these four affordances to discuss how engagement with networked publics affects everyday social practices. It's important to note, however, this is not how teenagers themselves would describe the shifts that are under way. More often than not, they are unaware of why the networked publics they inhabit are different than other publics or why adults find networked publics so peculiar. To teens, these technologies—and the properties that go with them—are just an obvious part of life in a networked era, whereas for many adults these affordances reveal changes that are deeply disconcerting. As I return to these issues throughout the book, I will juxtapose teens' perspectives alongside adults' anxieties to highlight what has changed and what has stayed the same.

New Technologies, Old Hopes and Fears

Any new technology that captures widespread attention is likely to provoke serious hand wringing, if not full-blown panic. When the sewing machine was introduced, there were people who feared the implications that women moving their legs up and down would affect female sexuality.[10] The Walkman music player was viewed as an evil device that would encourage people to disappear into separate worlds, unable to communicate with one another.[11] Technologies are not the only cultural artifacts to prompt these so-called moral panics; new genres of media also cause fearful commentary. Those who created comic books, penny arcades, and rock-and-roll music have been seen as sinister figures bent on seducing children into becoming juvenile delinquents.[12] Novels were believed to threaten women's morals, a worry that Gustave Flaubert's *Madame Bovary* dramatizes brilliantly. Even Socrates is purported to have warned of the dangers of the alphabet and writing, citing implications for memory and the ability to convey truth.[13] These fears are now laughable, but when these technologies or media genres first appeared, they were taken very seriously.

Even the most fleeting acquaintance with the history of information and communication technologies indicates that moral panics are episodic and should be taken with a grain of salt. So too with utopian visions, which prove just as unrealistic. A popular T-shirt designed by John Slabyk and sold on the website Threadless sums up the disillusionment with failed technological utopias:

> they lied to us
> this was supposed to be the future
> where is my jetpack,
> where is my robotic companion,
> where is my dinner in pill form,
> where is my hydrogen fueled automobile,
> where is my nuclear-powered levitating house,
> where is my cure for this disease

Technologies are often heralded as the solution to major world problems. When those solutions fail to transpire, people are disillusioned. This can prompt a backlash, as people focus on the terrible things that may occur because of those same technologies.

A great deal of the fear and anxiety that surrounds young people's use of social media stems from misunderstanding or dashed hopes.[14] More often than not, what emerges out of people's confusion takes the form of utopian and dystopian rhetoric. This issue will reappear throughout the book. Sometimes, as in the case of sexual predators and other online safety issues, misunderstanding results in a moral panic. In other cases, such as the dystopian notion that teens are addicted to social media or the utopian idea that technology will solve inequality, the focus on technology simply obscures other dynamics at play.

Both extremes depend on a form of magical thinking scholars call *technological determinism*.[15] Utopian and dystopian views assume that technologies possess intrinsic powers that affect *all* people in *all* situations the same way. Utopian rhetoric assumes that when a particular technology is broadly adopted it will transform society in magnificent ways, while dystopian visions focus on all of the terrible things that will happen because of the widespread adoption of a particular technology that ruins everything. These extreme rhetorics are equally unhelpful in understanding what actually happens when new technologies are broadly adopted. Reality is nuanced and messy, full of pros and cons. Living in a networked world is complicated.

Kids Will Be Kids

If you listen to the voices of youth, the story you'll piece together reveals a hodgepodge of opportunities and challenges, changes and continuity. As with the football game in Nashville, many elements of American teen culture remain unchanged in the digital age. School looks remarkably familiar, and many of the same anxieties and hopes that shaped my experience are still recognizable today. Others are strikingly different, but what differs often has less to do with technology and more to do with increased consumerism, heightened competition for access to limited opportunities, and an intense amount of parental pressure, especially in wealthier communities.[16] All too often, it is easier to focus on the technology than on the broader systemic issues that are at play because technical changes are easier to see.

Nostalgia gets in the way of understanding the relation between teens and technology. Adults may idealize their childhoods and forget the trials and tribulations they faced. Many adults I meet assume that their own childhoods were better and richer, simpler and safer, than the digitally mediated ones contemporary youth experience. They associate the rise of digital technology with decline—social, intellectual, and moral. The research I present here suggests that the opposite is often true.

Many of the much-hyped concerns discussed because of technology are not new (for example, bullying) but rather may be misleading (for example, a decline in attention) or serve as distractions for real risks (for example, predators). Most myths are connected to real incidents or rooted in data that are blown out of proportion or are deliberately exaggerated to spark fear. Media culture exaggerates this dynamic, magnifying anxieties and reinforcing fears. For adults to hear the voices of youth, they must let go of their nostalgia and suspend their fears. This is not easy.

Teens continue to occupy an awkward position between childhood and adulthood, dependence and independence. They are struggling to carve out an identity that is not defined solely by family ties. They want to be recognized as someone other than son, daughter, sister, or brother. These struggles play themselves out in familiar ways, as teens fight for freedoms while not always being willing or able to accept responsibilities. Teens simultaneously love and despise, need and reject their parents and other adults in their lives. Meanwhile, many adults are simultaneously afraid of teens and afraid for them.

Teens' efforts to control their self-presentation—often by donning clothing or hairstyles their parents deem socially unacceptable or engaging in practices that their parents deem risky—are clearly related to their larger effort at self-fashioning and personal autonomy. By dressing like the twenty-somethings they see celebrated in popular culture, they signal their desire to be seen as independent young adults. Fashion choices are one of many ways of forging an identity that is cued less to family and more to friends.

Developing meaningful friendships is a key component of the coming of age process. Friends offer many things—advice, support, entertainment, and a connection that combats loneliness. And in doing so, they enable the transition to adulthood by providing a context beyond that of family and home. Though family is still important, many teens relish the opportunity to create relationships that are not simply given but chosen.

The importance of friends in social and moral development is well documented.[17] But the fears that surround teens' use of social media overlook this fundamental desire for social connection. All too often, parents project their values onto their children, failing to recognize that school is often not the most pressing concern for most teens. Many parents wonder: Why are my kids tethered to their cell phones or perpetually texting with friends even when they are in the same room? Why do they seem compelled to check Facebook hundreds of times a day? Are they addicted to technology or simply wasting time? How will they get into college if they are constantly distracted? I encounter these questions from concerned adults whenever I give public lectures, and these attitudes figure prominently in parenting guides and in journalistic accounts of teens' engagement with social media.

Yet these questions seem far less urgent and difficult when we acknowledge teens' underlying social motivations. Most teens are not compelled by gadgetry as such—they are compelled by friendship. The gadgets are interesting to them primarily as a means to a social end. Furthermore, social interactions may be a distraction from school, but they are often not a distraction from learning. Keeping this basic social dynamic firmly in view makes networked teens suddenly much less worrisome and strange.

Consider, for example, the widespread concern over internet addiction. Are there teens who have an unhealthy relationship with technology? Certainly. But most of those who are "addicted" to their phones or computers are actually focused on staying connected to friends in a culture where getting together in person is highly constrained. Teens' preoccupation with their friends dovetails with their desire to enter the public spaces that are freely accessible to adults. The ability to access public spaces for sociable purposes is a critical component of the coming of age process, and yet many of the public spaces where adults gather—bars, clubs, and restaurants—are inaccessible to teens.

As teens transition from childhood, they try to understand how they fit into the larger world. They want to inhabit public spaces, but they also look to adults, including public figures, to understand what it means to be grown-up. They watch their parents and other adults in their communities for models of adulthood. But they also track celebrities like Kanye West and Kim Kardashian to imagine the freedoms they would have if they were famous. For better or worse, media narratives also help construct broader narratives for how public life works. "Reality" TV shows like *Jersey Shore* signal the potential fun that can be had by young adults who don't need to appease parents and teachers.

Some teens may reject the messages of adulthood that they hear or see, but they still learn from all of the signals around them. As they start to envision themselves as young adults, they begin experimenting with the boundaries of various freedoms, pushing for access to cars or later curfews. Teens' determination to set their own agenda can be nerve-racking for some parents, particularly those who want to protect their children from every possible danger. Coming of age is rife with self-determination, risk taking, and tough decision-making.

Teens often want to be with friends on their own terms, without adult supervision, and in public. Paradoxically, the networked publics they inhabit allow them a measure of privacy and autonomy that is not possible at home where parents and siblings are often listening in. Recognizing this is important to understanding teens' relationship to social media. Although many adults think otherwise, teens' engagement with public life through social media is not a rejection of privacy. Teens may wish to enjoy the benefits of participating in public, but they also relish intimacy and the ability to have control over their social situation. Their ability to achieve privacy is often undermined by nosy adults—notably their parents and teachers—but teens go to great lengths to develop innovative strategies for managing privacy in networked publics.

Social media enables a type of youth-centric public space that is often otherwise inaccessible. But because that space is highly visible, it can often provoke concerns among adults who are watching teens as they try to find their way.

A Place to Call Their Own

Sitting in a cafeteria in a small town in Iowa in 2007, I was talking with Heather, a white sixteen-year-old, when the topic of adult attitudes toward Facebook came up. Heather had recently heard that politicians were trying to prohibit teen access to social network sites, and she was incensed. "I'm really mad about it. It's social networking. It really is a way to communicate, and if they ban that, it's really hard to communicate with other people you don't see that much." I asked her why she didn't just get together with her friends in person. The rant that followed made clear that I had touched a nerve.

> I can't really go see people in person. I can barely hang out with my friends on the weekend, let alone people I don't talk to as often. I'm so busy. I've got lots of homework, I'm busy with track, I've got a job, and when I'm not working and doing homework I'm hanging out with the good friends that I have. But there's some people I've kind of lost contact with and I like keeping connected to them because they're still friends. I just haven't talked to them in a while. I have no means of doing that. If they go to a different school it's really hard and I don't exactly know where everyone lives, and I don't have everyone's cell phone numbers, and I don't have all of their AIM screen names either, so Facebook makes it a lot easier for me.

For Heather, social media is not only a tool; it is a social lifeline that enables her to stay connected to people she cares about but cannot otherwise interact with in person. Without the various sites and services she uses, Heather—like many of her peers—believes that her social life would significantly shrink. She doesn't see Facebook as inherently useful, but it's where everyone she knows is hanging out. And it's the place to go when she doesn't know how to contact someone directly.

The social media tools that teens use are direct descendants of the hangouts and other public places in which teens have been congregating for decades. What the drive-in was to teens in the 1950s and the mall in the 1980s, Facebook, texting, Twitter, instant messaging, and other social media are to teens now. Teens flock to them knowing they can socialize with friends and become better acquainted with classmates and peers they don't know as well. They embrace social media for roughly the same reasons earlier generations of teens attended sock hops, congregated in parking lots, colonized people's front stoops, or tied up the phone lines for hours on end. Teens want to gossip, flirt, complain, compare notes, share passions, emote, and joke around. They want to be able to talk among themselves—even if that means going online.

Heather's reliance on Facebook and other tools registers an important change in teen experience. This change is not rooted in social media but instead helps explain the popularity of digital technologies. Many American teens have limited geographic freedom, less free time, and more rules. In many communities across the United States, the era of being able to run around after school so long as you are home by dark is long over.[18] Many teens are stuck at home until they are old enough to drive themselves. For younger teens, getting together with friends after school depends on cooperative parents with flexible schedules who are willing or able to chauffeur and chaperone.

Socializing is also more homebound. Often, teens meet in each other's homes rather than public spaces. And no wonder: increasing regulation means that there aren't as many public spaces for teens to gather. The mall, once one of the main hubs for suburban teens, is much less accessible now than it once was.[19] Because malls are privately owned spaces, proprietors can prohibit anyone they wish, and many of them have prohibited groups of teenagers from entering. In addition, parents are less willing to allow their children to hang out in malls, out of fear of the strangers teens may encounter. Teens simply have far fewer places to be together in public than they once did.[20] And the success of social media must be understood partly in relation to this shrinking social landscape. Facebook, Twitter, and MySpace are not only new public spaces: they are in many cases the only "public" spaces in which teens can easily congregate with large groups of their peers. More significantly, teens can gather in them while still physically stuck at home.

Teens told me time and again that they would far rather meet up in person, but the hectic and heavily scheduled nature of their day-to-day lives, their lack of physical mobility, and the fears of their parents have made such face-to-face interactions increasingly impossible. As Amy, a biracial sixteen-year-old in Seattle, succinctly put it: "My mom doesn't let me out of the house very often, so that's pretty much all I do, is sit on MySpace and talk to people and text and talk on the phone, cause my mom's always got some crazy reason to keep me in the house." Social media may seem like a peculiar place for teens to congregate, but for many teens, hanging out on Facebook or Twitter is their only opportunity to gather en masse with friends, acquaintances, classmates, and other teens. More often than not, their passion for social media stems from their desire to socialize.

Just because teens are comfortable using social media to hang out does not mean that they're fluent in or with technology. Many teens are not nearly as digitally adept as the often-used assumption that they are "digital natives" would suggest. The teens I met knew how to get to Google but had little understanding about how to construct a query to get quality information from the popular search engine. They knew how to use Facebook, but their understanding of the site's privacy settings did not mesh with the ways in which they configured their accounts. As sociologist Eszter Hargittai has quipped, many teens are more likely to be digital naives than digital natives.[21]

The term *digital native* is a lightning rod for the endless hopes and fears that many adults attach to this new generation. Media narratives often suggest that kids today—those who have grown up with digital technology—are equipped with marvelous new superpowers. Their multitasking skills supposedly astound adults almost as much as their three thousand text messages per month. Meanwhile, the same breathless media reports also warn the public that these kids are vulnerable to unprecedented new dangers: sexual predators, cyberbullying, and myriad forms of intellectual and moral decline, including internet addiction, shrinking attentions spans, decreased literacy, reckless oversharing, and so on. As with most fears, these anxieties are not without precedent even if they are often overblown and misconstrued. The key to understanding how youth navigate social media is to step away from the headlines—both good and bad—and dive into the more nuanced realities of young people.

My experience hanging out with teenagers convinced me that the greatest challenges facing networked teens are far from new. Some challenges are rooted in this country's long history of racial and social inequality, but economic variability is increasingly noticeable. American teens continue to live and learn in radically uneven conditions. I visited schools with state-of-the-art facilities, highly credentialed and specialized faculty, and students hell-bent on going to Ivy League colleges. At the other extreme, I also visited run-down schools with metal detectors, a stream of "substitute" teachers standing in for full-time educators, and students who smoked marijuana during class. The explanations for these variations are complex and challenging, and the disparity is unlikely to be addressed in the near future.

Although almost all teens have access to technology at this point, their access varies tremendously. Some have high-end mobile phones with unlimited data plans, their own laptop, and wireless access at home. Others are constrained to basic phones with pay-per-text plans and access the internet only through the filtered lens of school or library computers. Once again, economic inequality plays a central role. But access is not the sole divide. Technical skills, media literacy, and even basic English literacy all shape how teens experience new technologies. Some teens are learning about technology from their parents while other teens are teaching their parents how to construct a search query or fill out a job application.

One of the great hopes for the internet was that it would serve as the great equalizer. My research into youth culture and social media—alongside findings of other researchers—has made it obvious that the color-blind and disembodied social world that the internet was supposed to make possible has not materialized. And this unfortunate reality—the reality of racial tensions and discrimination that long predates the rise of digital media—often seems to escape our public attention.

Meanwhile, we hear a lot about how the online spaces that teens frequent are sinister worlds populated by sexual predators or bullies. But we rarely if ever hear that many teenagers are scarred by the same experiences offline. Bullying, racism, sexual predation, slut shaming, and other insidious practices that occur online are extraordinarily important to address even if they're not new. Helping young people navigate public life safely should be of significant public concern. But it's critical to recognize that technology does not create these problems, even if it makes them more visible and even if news media relishes using technology as a hook to tell salacious stories about youth. The very sight of at-risk youth should haunt all of us, but little is achieved if we focus only on making what we see invisible.

The internet mirrors, magnifies, and makes more visible the good, bad, and ugly of everyday life. As teens embrace these tools and incorporate them into their daily practices, they show us how our broader social and cultural systems are affecting their lives. When teens are hurting offline, they reveal their hurt online. When teens' experiences are shaped by racism and misogyny, this becomes visible online. In making networked publics their own, teens bring with them the values and beliefs that shape their experiences. As a society, we need to use the visibility that we get from social media to understand how the social and cultural fault lines that organize American life affect young people. And we need to do so in order to intervene in ways that directly help youth who are suffering.

Ever since the internet entered everyday life—and particularly since the widespread adoption of social media—we have been bombarded with stories about how new technologies are destroying our social fabric. Amid a stream of scare stories, techno-utopians are touting the amazing benefits of online life while cyber-dystopians are describing how our brains are disintegrating because of our connection to machines. These polarizing views of technology push the discussion of youth's engagement with social media to an extreme binary: social media is good *or* social media is bad. These extremes—and the myths they perpetuate—obscure the reality of teen practices and threaten to turn the generation gap into a gaping chasm. These myths distort the reality of teen life, sometimes by idealizing it, but more frequently by demonizing it.

How to Read This Book

The chapters that follow are dedicated to different issues that underpin youth engagement with social media. Many are organized around concerns about youth practices that persist in American society. Each chapter offers a grounded way of looking at an issue. Although the chapters can be read independently, they are collectively organized to flow from individual and familial challenges to broader societal issues. A conclusion summarizes my arguments and offers a deeper analysis of what networked publics mean for contemporary youth.

As a researcher passionate about the health and well-being of young people, I wrote this book in an effort to create a nuanced portrait of everyday teen life in an era in which social media has become mainstream. The questions I ask are simple: What is and isn't new about life inflected by social media? What does social media add to the quality of teens' social lives, and what does it take away? And when we as a society don't like the outcomes of technology, what can we do to change the equation constructively, making sure that we take advantage of the features of social media while limiting potential abuse?

It is much easier to understand myths retrospectively than it is to dismantle them as they are being perpetuated, but this book aims to do the latter. That said, some of the most pervasive anxieties about social media have begun to subside in recent years, as adults have started participating in social media and, especially, Facebook. I am cautiously hopeful that adult engagement will calm some of the most anxious panics. And yet the tropes and stories that I use throughout the book tend to be resurrected with each new technology, while others endure in the face of quite overwhelming evidence to the contrary. As many adults have grown comfortable with Facebook, the media's narratives switched to focusing on the scariness of mobile apps like Snapchat and Kik. The story remains the same, even if the site of panic has shifted.

Social media has affected the lives and practices of many people and will continue to play a significant role in shaping many aspects of American society. There are many who lament these developments or wax nostalgic about the pre-internet world. That said, I would be surprised to find anyone who still believes that the internet is going away. Along with planes, running water, electricity, and motorized transportation, the internet is now a fundamental fact of modern life. This does not mean that access to the internet is universal, and some people will always opt out.[22] Even in a country as wealthy as the United States, many lack access to sanitation, and some choose to live without electricity. Just because the internet—and social media—is pervasive in American society does not mean that everyone will have access, will want access, or will experience access in the same way.

Contemporary youth are growing up in a cultural setting in which many aspects of their lives will be mediated by technology and many of their experiences and opportunities will be shaped by their engagement with technology. Fear mongering does little to help youth develop the ability to productively engage with this reality. As a society, we pay a price for fear mongering and utopian visions that ignore more complex realities. In writing this book, I hope to help the public better understand what young people are doing when they engage with social media and why their attempts to make sense of the world around them should be commended.

This book is written with a broad audience in mind—scholars and students, parents and educators, journalists and librarians. Although many sections draw on academic ideas, I do not expect the reader to be familiar with the scholarly literature invoked. When necessary for understanding the argument, I provide background in the text. More often than not, I've provided numerous touchstones and references in endnotes and an extensive bibliography that can enable those who wish to go deeper or to understand the relevant debates to do so.

Throughout this book, I draw on qualitative and ethnographic material that I collected from 2003 to 2012—and interview data conducted from 2007 to 2010—to provide a descriptive portrait of the different issues that I discuss.[23] Given the context in which I'm writing and the data on which I'm drawing, most of the discussion is explicitly oriented around American teen culture, although some of my analysis may be relevant in other cultures and contexts.[24] I also take for granted, and rarely seek to challenge, the capitalist logic that underpins American society and the development of social media. Although I believe that these assumptions should be critiqued, this is outside the scope of this project. By accepting the cultural context in which youth are living, I seek to explain their practices in light of the society in which they are situated.

The networked technologies that were dominant when I began researching this book are different than those that were popular when I was finishing the manuscript. Even MySpace—once the dominant social network site among youth and referred to throughout this book—is barely a shadow of its former self in 2013. Quite probably, what's popular when you're reading this book is different still. As I write this, Facebook is losing its allure as new apps and services like Instagram, Tumblr, and Snapchat gain hold. Social media is a moving landscape; many of the services that I reference throughout this book may or may not survive. But the ability to navigate one's social relationships, communicate asynchronously, and search for information online is here to stay. Don't let my reference to outdated services distract you from the arguments in this book. The examples may feel antiquated, but the core principles and practices I'm trying to describe are likely to persist long after this book is published.

Not everyone has equal access to the internet, nor do we all experience it in the same way. But social media is actively shaping and being shaped by contemporary society, so it behooves us to move beyond punditry and scare tactics to understand what social media is and how it fits into the social lives of youth.

As a society, we often spend so much time worrying about young people that we fail to account for how our paternalism and protectionism hinders teens' ability to become informed, thoughtful, and engaged adults. Regardless of the stories in the media, most young people often find ways to push through the restrictions and develop a sense of who they are and how they want to engage in the world. I want to celebrate their creativity and endurance while also highlighting that their practices and experiences are not universal or uniformly positive.

This book is not a love letter to youth culture, although my research has convinced me that young people are more resilient than I initially believed. Rather, this book is an attempt to convince the adults that have power over the lives of youth—including parents and teachers, journalists and law enforcement officers, employers and military personnel—that what teens are doing as they engage in networked publics makes sense. At the same time, coming to terms with life in a networked era is not necessarily easy or obvious. Rather, it's complicated.

1 identity
why do teens seem strange online?

In 2005, an Ivy League university was considering the application of a young black man from South Central Los Angeles. The applicant had written a phenomenal essay about how he wanted to walk away from the gangs in his community and attend the esteemed institution. The admissions officers were impressed: a student who overcomes such hurdles is exactly what they like seeing. In an effort to learn more about him, the committee members Googled him. They found his MySpace profile. It was filled with gang symbolism, crass language, and references to gang activities. They recoiled.

I heard this story when a representative from the admissions office contacted me. The representative opened the conversation with a simple question: Why would a student lie to an admissions committee when the committee could easily find the truth online? I asked for context and learned about the candidate. Stunned by the question, my initial response was filled with nervous laughter. I had hung out with and interviewed teens from South Central. I was always struck by the challenges they faced, given the gang dynamics in their neighborhood. Awkwardly, I offered an alternative interpretation: perhaps this young man is simply including gang signals on his MySpace profile as a survival technique.

Trying to step into that young man's shoes, I shared with the college admissions officer some of the dynamics that I had seen in Los

Angeles. My hunch was that this teen was probably very conscious of the relationship between gangs and others in his hometown. Perhaps he felt as though he needed to position himself within the local context in a way that wouldn't make him a target. If he was anything like other teens I had met, perhaps he imagined the audience of his MySpace profile to be his classmates, family, and community—not the college admissions committee. Without knowing the teen, my guess was that he was genuine in his college essay. At the same time, I also suspected that he would never dare talk about his desire to go to a prestigious institution in his neighborhood because doing so would cause him to be ostracized socially, if not physically attacked. As British sociologist Paul Willis argued in the 1980s, when youth attempt to change their socioeconomic standing, they often risk alienating their home community.[1] This dynamic was often acutely present in the communities that I observed.

The admissions officer was startled by my analysis, and we had a long conversation about the challenges of self-representation in a networked era.[2] I'll never know if that teen was accepted into that prestigious school, but this encounter stayed with me as I watched other adults misinterpret teens' online self-expressions. I came to realize that, taken out of context, what teens appear to do and say on social media seems peculiar if not outright problematic.[3]

The intended audience matters, regardless of the actual audience. Unfortunately, adults sometimes believe that they understand what they see online without considering how teens imagined the context when they originally posted a particular photograph or comment. The ability to understand how context, audience, and identity intersect is one of the central challenges people face in learning how to navigate social media. And, for all of the mistakes that they can and do make, teens are often leading the way at figuring out how to navigate a networked world in which collapsed contexts and imagined audiences are par for the course.

Taken Out of Context

In his 1985 book *No Sense of Place*, media scholar Joshua Meyrowitz describes the story of Stokely Carmichael, an American civil rights activist. In the 1960s, Carmichael regularly gave different talks to different audiences. He used a different style of speaking when he addressed white political leaders than when he addressed southern black congregations. When Carmichael started presenting his ideas on television and radio, he faced a difficult decision: which audience should he address? No matter which style of speaking he chose, he knew he'd alienate some. He was right. By using a rolling pastoral voice in broadcast media, Carmichael ingratiated himself with black activists while alienating white elites.

Meyrowitz argues that electronic media like radio and television easily collapse seemingly disconnected contexts. Public figures, journalists, and anyone in the limelight must regularly navigate disconnected social contexts simultaneously, balancing what they say with how their diverse audiences might interpret their actions. A context collapse occurs when people are forced to grapple simultaneously with otherwise unrelated social contexts that are rooted in different norms and seemingly demand different social responses. For example, some people might find it quite awkward to run into their former high school teacher while drinking with their friends at a bar. These context collapses happen much more frequently in networked publics.

The dynamics that Meyrowitz describes are no longer simply the domain of high-profile people who have access to broadcast media. When teens interact with social media, they must regularly contend with collapsed contexts and invisible audiences as a part of everyday life.[4] Their teachers might read what they post online for their friends, and when their friends from school start debating their friends from summer camp, they might be excited that their friend groups are combining—or they might find it discomforting. In order to stabilize the context in their own minds, teens do what others before them have done: just like journalists and politicians, teens imagine the audience they're trying to reach.[5] In speaking to an unknown or invisible audience, it is impossible and unproductive to account for the full range of plausible interpretations. Instead, public speakers consistently imagine a specific subset of potential readers or viewers and focus on how those intended viewers are likely to respond to a particular statement. As a result, the imagined audience defines the social context. In choosing how to present themselves before disconnected and invisible audiences, people must attempt to resolve context collapses or actively define the context in which they're operating.

Teens often imagine their audience to be those that they've chosen to "friend" or "follow," regardless of who might actually see their profile. In theory, privacy settings allow teens to limit their expressions to the people they intend to reach by restricting who can see what. On MySpace and Twitter—where privacy settings are relatively simple—using settings to limit who can access what content can be quite doable. Yet, on Facebook, this has proven to be intractable and confusing, given the complex and constantly changing privacy settings on that site.[6] Moreover, many teens have good reasons for not limiting who can access their profile. Some teens want to be accessible to peers who share their interests. Others recognize that privacy settings do little to limit parents from snooping or stop friends from sharing juicy messages. Many teens complain about parents who look over their shoulders when they're on the computer or friends who copy and paste updates and forward them along.

To complicate matters, just because someone is a part of a teen's imagined audience doesn't mean that this person is actually reading what's posted. When social media sites offer streams of content—as is common on Twitter, Facebook, and Instagram—people often imagine their audience to be the people they're following. But these people may not be following them in return or see their posts amid the avalanche of shared content. As a result, regardless of how they use privacy settings, teens must grapple with who can see their profile, who actually does see it, and how those who do see it will interpret it.

Teens' mental model of their audience is often inaccurate, but not because teens are naive or stupid. When people are chatting and sharing photos with friends via social media, it's often hard to remember that viewers who aren't commenting might also be watching. This is not an issue unique to teens, although teens are often chastised for not accounting for adult onlookers. But just as it's easy to get caught up in a conversation at a dinner party and forget about the rest of the room, it's easy to get lost in the back-and-forth on Twitter. Social media introduces additional challenges, particularly because of the persistent and searchable nature of most of these technical systems. Tweets and status updates aren't just accessible to the audience who happens to be following the thread as it unfolds; they quickly become archived traces, accessible to viewers at a later time. These traces can be searched and are easily reposted and spread. Thus, the context collapses that teens face online rarely occur in the moment with conflicting onlookers responding simultaneously. They are much more likely to be experienced over time, as new audiences read the messages in a new light.

When teens face collapsing contexts in physical environments, their natural response is to become quiet. For example, if a group of teens are hanging out at the mall and a security guard or someone's mother approaches them, they will stop whatever conversation they are having, even if it's innocuous. While they may be comfortable having strangers overhear their exchange, the sudden appearance of someone with social authority changes the context entirely. Online, this becomes more difficult. As Summer, a white fifteen-year-old from Michigan, explains, switching contexts online is more challenging than doing so in the park because, in the park, "you can see when there's people around you and stuff like that. So you can like quickly change the subject." Online, there's no way to change the conversation, both because it's virtually impossible to know if someone is approaching and because the persistent nature of most social exchanges means that there's a record of what was previously said. Thus, when Summer's mother looks at her Facebook page, she gains access to a plethora of interactions that took place over a long period of time and outside the social and temporal context in which they were produced. Summer can't simply switch topics with her friends at the sight of her mother approaching. The ability to easily switch contexts assumes an ephemeral social situation; this cannot be taken for granted in digital environments.

Because social media often brings together multiple social contexts, teens struggle to effectively manage social norms. Some expect their friends and family to understand and respect different social contexts and to know when something is not meant for them. And yet there are always people who fail to recognize when content isn't meant for them, even though it's publicly accessible. This is the problem that Hunter faces when he posts to Facebook.

Hunter is a geeky, black fourteen-year-old living in inner-city Washington, DC, who resembles a contemporary Steve Urkel, complete with ill-fitting clothes, taped-together glasses, and nerdy mannerisms. He lives in two discrete worlds. His cousins and sister are what he describes as "ghetto" while his friends at his magnet school are all academically minded "geeks." On Facebook, these two worlds collide, and he regularly struggles to navigate them simultaneously. He gets especially frustrated when his sister interrupts conversations with his friends.

> When I'm talking to my friends on Facebook or I put up a status, something I hate is when people who I'm not addressing in my statuses comment on my statuses. In [my old school], people always used to call me nerdy and that I was the least black black person that they've ever met, some people say that, and I said on Facebook, "Should I take offense to the fact that somebody put the ringtone 'White and Nerdy' for me?" and it was a joke. I guess we were talking about it in school, and [my sister] comes out of nowhere, "Aw, baby bro," and I'm like, "No, don't say that, I wasn't talking to you."

When I asked Hunter how his sister or friends are supposed to know who is being talked to on specific Facebook updates, he replied,

I guess that is a point. Sometimes it probably is hard, but I think it's just the certain way that you talk. I will talk to my sister a different way than I'll talk to my friends at school or from my friends from my old school, and I might say, "Oh, well, I fell asleep in Miss K's class by accident," and they'll say, "Oh, yeah, Miss K is so boring," and [my sister's] like, "Oh, well, you shouldn't fall asleep. You should pay attention." I mean, I think you can figure out that I'm not talking to you if I'm talking about a certain teacher.

Hunter loves his sister, but he also finds her take on social etiquette infuriating. He wants to maintain a relationship with her and appreciates that she's on Facebook, although he also notes that it's hard because of her priorities, values, and decisions. He doesn't want to ostracize her on Facebook, but he's consistently annoyed by how often she tries to respond to messages from his friends without realizing that this violates an implicit code of conduct.

To make matters worse, Hunter's sister is not the only one from his home life who he feels speaks up out of turn. Hunter and his friends are really into the card game Pokémon and what he calls "old skool" video games like the Legend of Zelda. His cousins, in contrast, enjoy first-person shooters like Halo and think his choice of retro video games is "lame." Thus, whenever Hunter posts messages about playing with his friends, his cousins use this as an opportunity to mock him. Frustrated by his family members' inability to "get the hint," Hunter has resorted both to limiting what he says online and trying to use technical features provided by Facebook to create discrete lists and block certain people from certain posts. Having to take measures to prevent his family from seeing what he posts saddens him because he doesn't want to hide; he only wants his family to stop "embarrassing" him. Context matters to Hunter, not because he's ashamed of his tastes or wants to hide his passions, but because he wants to have control over a given social situation. He wants to post messages without having to articulate context; he wants his audience to understand where he's coming from and respect what he sees as unspoken social conventions. Without a shared sense of context, hanging out online becomes burdensome.

The ability to understand and define social context is important. When teens are talking to their friends, they interact differently than when they're talking to their family or to their teachers. Television show plotlines leverage the power of collapsed contexts for entertainment purposes, but managing them in everyday life is often exhausting. It may be amusing to watch Kramer face embarrassment when he and George accidentally run into Kramer's mother on *Seinfeld*, but such social collisions are not nearly as entertaining when they occur without a laugh track.[7] Situations like this require significant monitoring and social negotiation, which, in turn, require both strategic and tactical decisions that turn the most mundane social situation into a high-maintenance affair. Most people are uncomfortable with the idea that their worlds might collide uncontrollably, and yet, social media makes this dynamic a regular occurrence. Much of what's at stake has to do with the nuanced ways in which people read social situations and present themselves accordingly.

Identity Work in Networked Publics

In her 1995 book, *Life on the Screen*, psychologist Sherry Turkle began to map out the creation of a mediated future that resembled both the utopian and dystopian immersive worlds constructed in science fiction novels. Watching early adopters—especially children—embrace virtual worlds, she argued that the distinction between computers and humans was becoming increasingly blurred and that a new society was emerging as people escaped the limitations of their offline identities. Turkle was particularly fascinated by the playful identity work that early adopters engaged in online, and with a psychoanalyst's eye, she extensively considered both the therapeutic and the deceptive potential of mediated identity work.[8]

Turkle was critical of some people's attempts to use fictitious identities to harm others, but she also highlighted that much could be gained from the process of self-reflection that was enabled when people had to act out or work through their identity in order to make themselves present in virtual worlds. Unlike face-to-face settings in which people took their bodies for granted, people who went online had to consciously create their digital presence. Media studies scholar Jenny Sundén describes this process as people typing themselves into being.[9] Although Turkle recognized that a person's identity was always tethered to his or her psyche, she left room for arguments that suggested that the internet could—and would—free people of the burdens of their "material"—or physically embodied—identities, enabling them to become a better version of themselves.

I wanted Turkle's vision for the future to be right. When I embraced the internet as a teenager in the mid-1990s, I was going online to escape the so-called real world. I felt ostracized and misunderstood at school, but online I could portray myself as the person that I wanted to be. I took on fictitious identities in an effort to figure out who I was. I wasn't alone. Part of what made chatting fun in those days was that it was impossible to know if others were all that they portrayed themselves to be. I knew that a self-declared wizard was probably not actually a wizard and that the guy who said he had found the cure to cancer most likely hadn't, but embodied characteristics like gender and race weren't always so clear.[10] At the time, this felt playful and freeing, and I bought into the fantasy that the internet could save us from tyranny and hypocrisy. Manifestos like John Perry Barlow's 1996 "Declaration of the Independence of Cyberspace" spoke to me. Barlow told the global leaders at the World Economic Forum that the new "home of the Mind" enabled "identities [that] have no bodies." I was proud to be one of the children he spoke of who appeared "native" in the new civilization.

Twenty years later, the dynamics of identity portrayal online are quite different from how early internet proponents imagined them to be. Although gaming services and virtual worlds are popular among some groups of youth, there's a significant cultural difference between fictional role-playing sites and the more widely embraced social media sites, which tend to encourage a more nonfiction-oriented atmosphere. Even though pseudonymity is quite common in these environments, the type of identity work taking place on social media sites like Facebook is very different from what Turkle initially imagined. Many teens today go online to socialize with friends they know from physical settings and to portray themselves in online contexts that are more tightly wedded to unmediated social communities. These practices, which encourage greater continuity between teens' online and offline worlds, were much less common when I was growing up.

This doesn't mean that identity work is uniform across all online activities. Most teens use a plethora of social media services as they navigate relationships and contexts. Their seemingly distinct practices on each platform might suggest that they are trying to be different people, but this would be a naive reading of the kinds of identity work taking place on and through social media. For example, a teen might use her given name on a video service like Skype while choosing a descriptive screen name on a photo app like Instagram.[11] And when choosing a login for a blogging site like Tumblr, she might choose a name that intentionally signals her involvement with a particular interest-based community.

Quite often, teens respond to what they perceive to be the norms of a particular service. So when a teen chooses to identify as "Jessica Smith" on Facebook and "littlemonster" on Twitter, she's not creating multiple identities in the psychological sense. She's choosing to represent herself in different ways on different sites with the expectation of different audiences and different norms. Sometimes these choices are conscious attempts by individuals seeking to control their self-presentation; more often, they are whimsical responses to sites' requirement to provide a login handle. Although some teens choose to use the same handle across multiple sites, other teens find that their favorite nickname is taken or feel as though they've outgrown their previous identity. Regardless of the reason, the outcome is a hodgepodge of online identities that leave plenty of room for interpretation. And in doing so, teens both interpret and produce the social contexts in which they are inhabiting.

Context matters. While teens move between different social contexts—including mediated ones like those produced by networked publics and unmediated ones like those constructed at school—they manage social dynamics differently. How they interact and with whom they interact in the school lunchroom is different than at afterschool music lessons than via group text messaging services. For many of the teens I interviewed, Facebook was the primary place where friend groups collide. Other services—like Tumblr or Twitter—were more commonly used by teens who were carving out their place in interest-driven communities.[12] For example, there are entire communities of teens on Tumblr who connect out of a shared interest in fashion; collectively, they produce a rich fashion blogging community that has stunned the fashion industry. On Twitter, it's not uncommon to see teens gushing about the celebrities du jour with other fans. These examples illustrate how these particular platforms are used circa 2013; teens' approaches to different sites may have changed by the time you're reading this book, but managing context within a given site and through the use of multiple sites has been commonplace for well over a decade. What matters is not the particular social media *site* but the *context* in which it's situated within a particular group of youth. The sites of engagement come and go, are repurposed, and evolve over time. Some people assume that these ebbs and flows mean radical changes in youth culture, but often the underlying practices stay the same even as the context shifts what is rendered visible and significant.

The context of a particular site is not determined by the technical features of that site but, rather, by the interplay between teens and the site. In sociological parlance, the context of social media sites is socially constructed.[13] More practically, what this means is that teens turn to different sites because they hear that a particular site is good for a given practice. They connect to people they know, observe how those people are using the site, and then reinforce or challenge those norms through their own practices. As a result, the norms of social media are shaped by network effects; peers influence one another about how to use a particular site and then help collectively to create the norms of that site.

Because teens' engagement with social media is tied to their broader peer groups, the norms that get reinforced online do not deviate much from the norms that exist in school. This does not mean that there aren't distinctions. For example, I met a teen girl who was obsessed with a popular boy band called One Direction even though her friends at school were not. She didn't bother talking about her crush on one of the band's members in the lunchroom because she knew her friends wouldn't find such a topic interesting. She didn't hide her passion for One Direction from her friends, but she didn't turn to them to discuss the band members' haircuts or their latest music video. Instead, she turned to Twitter, where she was able to gush about the band with other fans. She first turned to Twitter because the members of One Direction were using that platform to engage with their fans, but as she engaged with the broader fan community, she spent more time talking with other fans than replying to the musicians' tweets. Through this fan community, she began interacting on Tumblr and posting fan-oriented posts on Instagram. Her friends all knew about her obsession—and occasionally teased her for her celebrity crush—but they didn't follow her on Twitter because they weren't interested in that facet of her life. She wasn't hiding her interests, but she had created a separate context— and thus a separate digital persona—for talking with fellow fans. When she wanted to talk with her school friends, she turned to Facebook or text messaging. At the same time, the contexts were not wholly distinct. When she found out that one of her classmates was also a fellow fan, they started engaging on both Facebook and Twitter, talking about school on Facebook and One Direction on Twitter. And she even ended up Facebook friending a few fans she met through Twitter, which created a space for them to talk about a different range of topics.

This young fan is a typical savvy internet user, comfortable navigating her identity and interests in distinct social contexts based on her understanding of the norms and community practices. She moves between Facebook and Twitter seamlessly, understanding that they are different social contexts. She has a coherent understanding of who she is and is comfortable choosing how she presents herself in these different environments. She moves just as seamlessly between these mediated environments as she does between online and offline settings, not because she's cycling through identities—or creating a segmentation between the virtual and the real—but because she's switching social contexts and acting accordingly.

As teens move between different social environments—and interact with different groups of friends, interest groups, and classmates—they maneuver between different contexts that they have collectively built and socially constructed. Their sense of context is shaped—but not cleanly defined—by setting, time, and audience. Although navigating distinct social contexts is not new, technology makes it easy for young people to move quickly between different social settings, creating the impression that they are present in multiple places simultaneously. What unfolds is a complex dance as teens quickly shift between—and often blur—different social contexts.

The popularity of social media in recent years has produced a significant rise in nonfiction or so-called real names identity production, but it is also important to recognize that there continue to be environments where teens gather anonymously or don crafted identities to create a separation between the kinds of social contexts that are viable offline and those that can be imagined online. Most notably, multiplayer online games like World of Warcraft and StarCraft were quite popular among youth I encountered. It is within these spaces—along with virtual worlds like Second Life and Whyville—where teens can and do engage in much of the playful and productive identity work that early internet scholars initially mapped out.[14] The process of creating an avatar and selecting virtual characteristics requires tremendous reflection, and teens often take this seriously.

Although some teens do invest a great deal of time and thought into their avatars, other teens I met were no more invested in their gaming character than in their Twitter handle. Their choices had meaning and were valuable, but not something that they felt needed to be analyzed for significance. When I asked one teen boy why he had chosen to be a particular character in World of Warcraft, he looked at me with a scrunched face. I pressed on to ask if his choice had any particular meaning, and he responded with an eye roll, saying, "It's just a game!" before continuing on to talk about how he had a collection of characters with different skill sets that could be used depending on what he was trying to achieve in the game.

Choosing and designing an avatar is a central part of participation in immersive games and virtual worlds, but youth approach this practice in extraordinarily varied ways. Some teens purposefully construct their avatars in ways that they feel reflect their physical bodies; other teens choose characters based on skills or aesthetics. For some teens, being "in world" is discrete from their school environment, whereas others game with classmates. It may seem that the role-playing elements of these environments imply a significant separation between the virtual and the real; however, these often get blurred in fantasy game worlds as well.[15]

Alongside the identity work done within common social media sites and wildly popular gaming services, a subculture has emerged in which participants outright eschew recognizable identity altogether by proclaiming the virtues of anonymity. Nowhere is this more visible than in the community of individuals who participate in and contribute to the image-based bulletin board site 4chan. 4chan was initially created in 2003 by a fifteen-year-old named Chris Poole, known as "moot," so that he could share pornography and anime with other teens.[16] Often referred to as the underbelly of the internet, 4chan is an active source of internet cultural production as well as malicious prankster activity. It is the birthplace of popular memes such as lolcats: often entertaining, widely distributed pictures of cats portrayed with text captions written in Impact font using an internet dialect referred to as lolspeak.[17] 4chan is also where Anonymous—the "hacktivist" group mostly known for a series of well-publicized political actions—originated.[18] Although it's impossible to know much about the site's contributors, the content typically shared on the site reflects tastes and humor usually associated with teenage boys.

The reason it's hard to get a handle on who participates on 4chan is that most of the content produced on the site is shared anonymously. As I met teen boys who contributed to 4chan, I found that many of them relished the anonymous norms of the site. They felt that anonymity gave them a sense of freedom they didn't feel they could have on sites for which constructing an identity—pseudonymous or "real"—was more typical. Some admitted to using this freedom in problematic or destructive ways—recounting acts of ganging up on girls whom they deemed annoying or using a combination of wits and trickery to manipulate Facebook administrators into providing data. But more often than not, teens talked about wanting to have a space where they weren't constantly scrutinized by adults and peers. By becoming anonymous and being an invisible part of a crowd, these teens knew that they weren't building a reputation within the site. Yet even when they weren't being personally recognized, many relished seeing their posts get traction and attention within the site; this made them feel part of the community. Furthermore, extensive use of in-group language and shared references made it easy to identify other members of 4chan, thereby enabling another mechanism of status and community.[19]

As teens have embraced a plethora of social environments and helped co-create the norms that underpin them, a wide range of practices has emerged. Teens have grown sophisticated with how they manage contexts and present themselves in order to be read by their intended audience. They don't always succeed, but their efforts are phenomenal.

Crafting a Profile, Creating an Identity Performance

Chris was ecstatic when his sixteen-year-old daughter invited him to be her friend on MySpace during the height of the MySpace craze. He had decided not to require that she befriend him on social network sites, so he saw her invitation as a signal of trust and love. He immediately accepted the friend request and logged in to look at her private profile. His heart sank. About halfway down the page, there was a panel with a question, "What Drug Are You?" followed by a picture of a white substance on a mirror with a rolled-up dollar bill; the text below said, "Cocaine." Trying not to panic, he approached his daughter quizzically. She responded with laughter, followed by a drawn-out, "Daaaaad." She explained that what he'd seen was a quiz. Quizzes were all the rage in her school, and this one was currently making its rounds. She explained that whenever there were quizzes, you could easily guess where the quiz was going and answer so that you could get the result you wanted. This did not give Chris any sense of relief, but he reserved judgment and hesitantly asked why she wanted to get cocaine as the result. She proceeded to explain that the kids who smoked marijuana at school were "lame," while those who took mushrooms were "crazy." And then she explained, "But your generation did a lot of cocaine and you came out OK!" Chris burst out laughing, humored by how she perceived him and his peers. He had grown up in a rural white Midwestern community where alcohol and teen pregnancy dominated. Indeed, Chris was only sixteen years older than his daughter. After high school, he had gotten involved in the music scene, but being a single father left little room for partying. Cocaine was not part of his youth at all. Chris then grew serious and asked if she was interested in cocaine; he felt relieved by her exasperated rejection of this idea, and they proceeded to have a long conversation about how an onlooker could easily take what seemed like a funny quiz out of context.

Many teens post information on social media that they think is funny or intended to give a particular impression to a narrow audience without considering how this same content might be read out of context. Much of what seems like inaccurate identity information is simply a misinterpretation of a particular act of self-presentation. This issue was particularly noticeable in early social media genres in which explicit identity information was required for participation.

Consider, for example, MySpace, which required a user to provide age, sex, location, and other fields to create a profile.

When I stumbled on Allie's MySpace profile, I learned from the demographic section that she is ninety-five years old, from Christmas Island, and makes $250,000+ per year. While it is possible that she is nearly a centenarian and logging onto MySpace from a remote, sparsely populated island in the Indian Ocean while running her highly profitable company, this seems unlikely. A quick glance at the rest of Allie's profile reveals other information that suggests that she is more likely to be a teenage girl attending high school in New Jersey. Her photo album includes self-portraits, photographs of Allie with friends, and images of teens goofing around. The majority of her friends indicate that they're from New Jersey, and the high school she lists on her profile is also located in that state. The comments on her profile included messages about homework and parents. I don't know Allie, but I doubt that she is trying to deceive me with demographic outliers.

I met many teens who fabricated answers like name, location, age, and income to profile questions. They thought it was amusing to indicate their relationship status on Facebook as "It's Complicated" whether they were in a relationship or not. A casual viewer scanning Facebook might conclude that an extraordinary number of teens are in same-sex relationships because so many have chosen to list their best friend as the person that they are "In a Relationship" with. In the same vein, Facebook profiles suggest that the US census data must be inaccurate because, at least on Facebook, teens often have dozens of siblings; of course, a little bit of prying makes it clear that these, too, are close friends. These are but a few of the playful ways in which teens responded to social media sites' requests for information by providing inaccurate information that actually contains meaningful signals about friendship and sociality.

When I talked with teens, I learned that there were also numerous ways of repurposing social network site fields for entertainment and humor. Outside of wealthy communities, where talking about money is deemed gauche, I met countless teens who told MySpace that their income was "$250,000+." Choosing a birth year that made the age field depict "69" was also a common, if unsurprising, trend among teenage boys.[20] Searching for social media users in Afghanistan or Zimbabwe offers an additional window into teen life, as many teens select the top or bottom choice in the pull-down menu when they indicate their location. Facebook expected users to provide "real names," but many teens I met offered up only their first name, preferring to select a last name of a celebrity, fictional character, or friend. These were but a few of the ways that teens provided what appeared to be fictitious information on their profiles. These practices allowed them to feel control over their profiles, particularly given how often they told me that it was ridiculous for sites to demand this information.

One way of reading teens' profiles is to assume that they are lying. But marking oneself as rich or from a foreign land is not about deception; it's a simple way to provide entertaining signals to friends while ignoring a site's expectations.[21] Most teens aren't enacting an imagined identity in a virtual world. Instead, they're simply refusing to play by the rules of self-presentation as defined by these sites.[22] They see no reason to provide accurate information, in part because they know that most people who are reading what they post already know who they are. As Dominic, a white sixteen-year-old from Seattle, told me, he doesn't have to provide accurate information "because all my [social media] friends are actually my friends; they'll know if I'm joking around or not." Awareness of the social context helps shape what teens share and don't share. Many teens treat social media requests for information as a recommendation, not a requirement, because they view these sites purely as platforms for interacting with classmates and other people they know from other settings.

Why teens share what they do is neither arbitrary nor dictated by the social media sites where they hang out—nor by the norms that govern adults' use of those same sites. The youth-oriented social context in which teens share matters. Teens don't see social media as a virtual space in which they must choose to be themselves or create an alternate ego. They see social media as a place to gather with friends while balancing privacy and safety with humor and image. When Los Angeles–based Chicano fifteen-year-old Mickey says, "It's not that I lie on [MySpace], but I don't put my real information," he's highlighting that his choice to provide false data allows him to control the social situation. He doesn't want to be easily searchable by his parents or teachers, nor does he want to be found by "creeps" who might be browsing the site looking for vulnerable teenagers. He wants to be in a space with friends, and so he provides just enough information that his friends can find him without increasing his visibility to adults.

Teens fabricate information because it's funny, because they believe that the site has no reason to ask, or because they believe that doing so will limit their visibility to people they don't want to find them. In doing so, they are seeking to control the networked social context.

When teens create profiles through social media, they are simultaneously navigating extraordinarily public environments and more intimate friendship spaces. Media scholars Paul Hodkinson and Siân Lincoln argue that constructing these profiles can be understood through the lens of "bedroom culture."[23] Just as many middle-class teens use different media artifacts—including photographs, posters, and tchotchkes—to personalize their bedrooms, teens often decorate their online self-presentations using a variety of media. Likewise, teens use their bedrooms to create a space for hanging out with friends and they turn to social media to do the same online. Yet because of the properties of social media, creating boundaries around these online spaces is far more difficult. Although teens complain about the impossibility of keeping siblings and parents out of their rooms, achieving privacy in social media is even harder. This, in turn, challenges teens' ability to meaningfully portray the nuances of who they are to different and conflicting audiences.

Impression Management in a Networked Setting

In *The Presentation of Self in Everyday Life*, sociologist Erving Goffman describes the social rituals involved in self-presentation as "impression management." He argues that the impressions we make on others are a product of what is *given* and what is *given off*. In other words, what we convey to others is a matter of what we choose to share in order to make a good impression and also what we unintentionally reveal as a byproduct of who we are and how we react to others. The norms, cultural dynamics, and institutions where giving and giving off happen help define the broader context of how these performances are understood. When interpreting others' self-presentations, we read the explicit content that is conveyed in light of the implicit information that is given off and the context in which everything takes place. The tension between the explicit and implicit signals allows us to obtain much richer information about individuals' attempts to shape how they're perceived. Of course, our reactions to their attempts to impress us enable them to adjust what they give in an attempt to convey what they think is best.

Based on their understanding of the social situation—including the context and the audience—people make decisions about what to share in order to act appropriately for the situation and to be perceived in the best light. When young people are trying to get a sense of the context in which they're operating, they're doing so in order to navigate the social situation in front of them. They may want to be seen as cool among their peers, even if adults would deem their behavior inappropriate.[24] Teens may be trying to determine if someone they're attracted to is interested in them without embarrassing themselves. Or they may wish to be viewed as confident and happy, even when they're facing serious depression or anxiety. Whatever they're trying to convey, they must first get a grasp of the situation and the boundaries of the context. When contexts collapse or when information is taken out of context, teens can fail to make their intended impression.

Self-presentations are never constructed in a void. Goffman writes at length about the role individuals play in shaping their self-presentations, but he also highlights ways in which individuals are part of broader collectives that convey impressions about the whole group. In discussing the importance of "teams" for impression management, he points out that people work together to shape impressions, often relying on shared familiarity to help define any given situation in a mutually agreeable manner. He also argues that, "any member of the team has the power to give the show away or to disrupt it by inappropriate conduct."[25] When teens create profiles online, they're both individuals and part of a collective. Their self-representation is constructed through what they explicitly provide, through what their friends share, and as a product of how other people respond to them. When Alice's friend Bob comments on her profile, he's affecting her self-presentation. Even the photo that Bob chooses as his primary photo affects Alice because it might be shown on Alice's profile when he leaves a comment.[26] Impression management online and off is not just an individual act; it's a social process.

Part of what makes impression management in a networked setting so tricky is that the contexts in which teens are operating are also networked. Contexts don't just collapse accidentally; they collapse because individuals have a different sense of where the boundaries exist and how their decisions affect others. In North Carolina, I briefly chatted with a black high school senior who was gunning for a soccer scholarship at a Division One school. When recruiters and coaches from different schools asked to be his friend on Facebook, he immediately said yes. He had always treated Facebook like a résumé, using the site to position himself as a thoughtful, compassionate, all-American young man. But he was often concerned about what his friends posted on Facebook, and for good reason.

A few days later, I was talking casually with Matthew, one of the soccer player's classmates with whom he was friends on Facebook. Unlike the all-American athlete persona his classmate had crafted, Matthew's profile was filled with crass comments and humor that could easily be misinterpreted. I asked Matthew, a white seventeen-year-old, about his decision to post these items on his profile with a particular eye to how they might get misinterpreted if read by a stranger. Matthew told me that he wasn't friends with anyone who didn't know him and wouldn't understand that he was joking around.

I pointed out that his privacy settings meant that his profile could be viewed by friends-of-friends. When he didn't get my point, I showed him that his classmate had chosen to connect with many coaches and other representatives from schools to which he had applied for admission. Matthew's stunned response was simple: "But why would he do that?" Matthew and his classmate had very different ideas of how to use Facebook and who their imagined audiences might be, but their online presence was interconnected because of the technical affordances of Facebook. They were each affecting the other's attempts at self-presentation, and their sharing and friending norms created unexpected conflicts.

Even when teens have a coherent sense of what they deem to be appropriate in a particular setting, their friends and peers do not necessarily share their sense of decorum and norms. Resolving the networked nature of social contexts is complicated. The "solution" that is most frequently offered is that people should not try to engage in context-dependent impression management. Indeed, Mark Zuckerberg, the founder of Facebook, is quoted as having said, "Having two identities for yourself is an example of a lack of integrity."[27] Teens who try to manage context collapses by segregating information often suffer when that information crosses boundaries. This is particularly true when teens, like the young man from Los Angeles at the beginning of this chapter, are forced to contend with radically different social contexts that are not mutually resolvable. What makes this especially tricky for teens is that people who hold power over them often believe that they have the right to look, judge, and share, even when their interpretations may be constructed wholly out of context.

In 2010, the American Civil Liberties Union received a complaint from a student at a small, rural high school that sheds light on this issue. At a school assembly, in order to set an example, a campus police officer had shown a photo of one of the students holding a beer.[28] The picture was not on that girl's Facebook profile; it was posted by a friend of hers and tagged. The purpose of the assembly was to teach teenagers about privacy, but the students were outraged.

Because of the police officer's attempt to shame students into behaving by adult standards, the student exposed with a beer feared that she would not receive a local scholarship or might face other serious consequences. To complicate matters, she had not chosen to present herself in that light; her friend had done this for her. In choosing to upload and tag this photo, her friend undermined the self-image that the girl wished to present. Some may argue that this girl was at fault for being at a party holding a beer in the first place. She may indeed have been drinking the beer—72 percent of students in high school report having had alcohol at least once—but she may also just have been holding the beer for a friend or simply trying to fit in by appearing to drink.[29] This girl certainly did not think that her decision to attend that party would result in such public shaming, nor is it clear that the punishment fits the crime. In situations like this, teens are blamed for not thinking while adults assert the right to define the context in which young people interact. They take content out of context to interpret it through the lens of adults' values and feel as though they have the right to shame youth because that content was available in the first place. In doing so, they ignore teens' privacy while undermining their struggles to manage their identity.

One might reasonably argue that the girl holding the beer was lucky not to have been arrested, since alcohol consumption by minors is illegal. Yet it is important to note that the same shaming tactics that adults use to pressure teens to conform to adult standards are also used by both teens and adults to ostracize and punish youth whose identities, values, or experiences are not widely accepted. I met plenty of teens who wanted to keep secrets from their parents or teachers, but the teens who struggled the most with the challenges of collapsed contexts were those who were trying to make sense of their sexual identity or who otherwise saw themselves as outcasts in their community. Some, like Hunter—the boy from DC who was trying to navigate his "ghetto" family alongside his educationally minded friends—were simply frustrated and annoyed. Others, like teen girls who are the subject of "slut shaming" were significantly embarrassed and emotionally distraught after photos taken in the context of an intimate relationship were widely shared to shame them by using their sexuality as a weapon. Still others, like the lesbian, gay, bisexual, and transgender (LGBT) teens I met from religious and conservative backgrounds, were outright scared of what would happen if the contexts in which they were trying to operate collapsed.

In Iowa, I ended up casually chatting with a teen girl who was working through her sexuality. She had found a community of other queer girls in a chatroom, and even though she believed that some of them weren't who they said they were, she found their anonymous advice to be helpful. They gave her pointers to useful websites about coming out, offered stories from their own experiences, and gave her the number of an LGBT-oriented hotline if she ran into any difficulty coming out to her conservative parents. Although she relished the support and validation these strangers gave her, she wasn't ready to come out yet, and she was petrified that her parents might come across her online chats. She was also concerned that some of her friends from school might find out and tell her parents. She had learned that her computer recorded her browser history in middle school when her parents had used her digital traces to punish her for visiting inappropriate sites. Thus, she carefully erased her history after each visit to the chatroom. She didn't understand how Facebook seemed to follow her around the web, but she was afraid that somehow the company would find out and post the sites she visited to her Facebook page. In an attempt to deal with this, she used Internet Explorer to visit the chatroom or anything that was LGBT-related while turning to the Chrome browser for maintaining her straight, school-friendly persona. But still, she was afraid that she'd mess up and collapse her different social contexts, accidentally coming out before she was ready. She wanted to maintain discrete contexts but found it extraordinarily difficult to do so. This tension comes up over and over again, particularly with youth who are struggling to make sense of who they are and how they fit into the broader world.[30]

As teens struggle to make sense of different social contexts and present themselves appropriately, one thing becomes clear: the internet has not evolved into an idyllic zone in which people are free from the limitations of the embodied world. Teens are struggling to make sense of who they are and how they fit into society in an environment in which contexts are networked and collapsed, audiences are invisible, and anything they say or do can easily be taken out of context. They are grappling with battles that adults face, but they are doing so while under constant surveillance and without a firm grasp of who they are. In short, they're navigating one heck of a cultural labyrinth.

2 privacy
why do youth share
so publicly?

Many teens feel as though they're in a no-win situation when it comes to sharing information online: damned if they publish their personal thoughts to public spaces, and damned if they create private space that parents can't see. Parent-teen battles about privacy have gone on for decades. Parents complain when teens demand privacy by asking their parents to stay out of their bedroom, to refrain from listening in on their phone conversations, and to let them socialize with their friends without being chaperoned. In the same breath, these same parents express frustration when teens wear ill-fitting clothes or skimpy outfits. They have long seen revealing clothing as an indicator of teens' rejection of privacy. In other words, common and longstanding teen practices have historically been sure signs of teens' unhealthy obsession with, or rejection of, privacy.

Social media has introduced a new dimension to the well-worn fights over private space and personal expression. Teens do not want their parents to view their online profiles or look over their shoulder when they're chatting with friends. Parents are no longer simply worried about what their children wear out of the house but what they photograph themselves wearing in their bedroom to post online. Interactions that were previously invisible to adults suddenly have traces, prompting parents to fret over conversations that adults deem inappropriate or when teens share "TMI" (too much information).

While my childhood included "Keep Out" bedroom signs and battles over leather miniskirts and visible bras, the rise of the internet has turned fights over privacy and exposure into headline news for an entire cohort of youth.

Teens often grow frustrated with adult assumptions that suggest that they are part of a generation that has eschewed privacy in order to participate in social media. In North Carolina, I asked "Waffles" about this issue, and he responded with exasperation. "Every teenager wants privacy. Every single last one of them, whether they tell you or not, wants privacy." Waffles is a geeky white seventeen-year-old teen who spends hours each day interacting with people through video games and engaging deeply in a wide variety of online communities. He balked at the idea that his participation in these networked publics signals that he doesn't care about privacy. "Just because teenagers use internet sites to connect to other people doesn't mean they don't care about their privacy. We don't tell everybody every single thing about our lives. . . . So to go ahead and say that teenagers don't like privacy is pretty ignorant and inconsiderate honestly, I believe, on the adults' part." Waffles articulated a sentiment that I usually saw expressed through an eye roll: teenagers, acutely aware of how many adults dismiss their engagement in social media, have little patience for adults' simplistic assumptions about teen privacy.[1]

Although teens grapple with managing their identity and navigating youth-centric communities while simultaneously maintaining spaces for intimacy, they do so under the spotlight of a media ecosystem designed to publicize every teen fad, moral panic, and new hyped technology. Each week, news stories lament the death of privacy, consistently referring to teen engagement with public social media services as proof of privacy's demise.[2] In her *New York Magazine* article describing people's willingness to express themselves publicly, Emily Nussbaum articulated a concern about youth that is widespread: "Kids today. They have no sense of shame. They have no sense of privacy. They are show-offs, fame whores, pornographic little loons who post their diaries, their phone numbers, their stupid poetry—for

God's sake, their dirty photos!—online."[3] Throughout the United States, I heard this sentiment expressed in less eloquent terms by parents, teachers, and religious officials who were horrified by what teens were willing to share. They often approached me, genuinely worried about their children's future and unable to understand why anyone who cared about themselves and their privacy would be willing to be actively engaged online.

The idea that teens share too much—and therefore don't care about privacy—is now so entrenched in public discourse that research showing that teens do desire privacy and work to get it is often ignored by the media.[4] Regardless of how many young people engage in privacy practices, adults reference teens' public expressions as decisive evidence of contemporary teen immodesty and indecency. Meanwhile, technology executives like Facebook's founder Mark Zuckerberg and Google chairman Eric Schmidt reinforce the notion that today's teens are different, arguing that social norms around privacy have changed in order to justify their own business decisions regarding user privacy. They cite youth's widespread engagement with social media as evidence that the era of privacy is over.[5] Journalists, parents, and technologists seem to believe that a willingness to share in public spaces—and, most certainly, any act of exhibitionism and publicity—is incompatible with a desire for personal privacy.

The teens that I met genuinely care about their privacy, but how they understand and enact it may not immediately resonate or appear logical to adults. When teens—and, for that matter, most adults—seek privacy, they do so in relation to those who hold power over them. Unlike privacy advocates and more politically conscious adults, teens aren't typically concerned with governments and corporations. Instead, they're trying to avoid surveillance from parents, teachers, and other immediate authority figures in their lives. They want the right to be ignored by the people who they see as being "in their business." Teens are not particularly concerned about organizational actors; rather, they wish to avoid paternalistic adults who use safety and protection as an excuse to monitor their everyday sociality.

Teens' desire for privacy does not undermine their eagerness to participate in public. There's a big difference between being *in* public and *being* public. Teens want to gather in public environments to socialize, but they don't necessarily want every vocalized expression to be publicized. Yet, because being in a networked public—unlike gathering with friends in a public park—often makes interactions more visible to adults, mere participation in social media can blur these two dynamics. At first blush, the desire to be in public and have privacy seems like a contradiction. But understanding how teens conceptualize privacy and navigate social media is key to understanding what privacy means in a networked world, a world in which negotiating fuzzy boundaries is par for the course. Instead of signaling the end of privacy as we know it, teens' engagement with social media highlights the complex interplay between privacy and publicity in the networked world we all live in now.[6]

Navigating Conflicting Norms

In 2006, seventeen-year-old Bly Lauritano-Werner wrote a piece for Youth Radio in which she explained what privacy meant to her.[7] She recorded the segment with her mother in order to highlight the generational disconnect that was at the heart of her frustration. The radio piece that aired on National Public Radio reveals a tension between Bly and her mother over the boundaries that underpin privacy. "My mom always uses the excuse about the Internet being 'public' when she defends herself. It's not like I do anything to be ashamed of, but a girl needs her privacy. I do online journals so I can communicate with my friends, not so my mother could catch up on the latest gossip of my life." When Bly interviews her mother during the segment, her mother claims that she has the right to look at what Bly posts. She argues that she should be able to look "because I have a connection with you. I'm your mom, but also I just feel like it would be more interesting to me than it would be to someone who didn't know you. . . . You publish it and it's for general viewing therefore I feel I'm part of the general public, so I can view it." Much to Bly's frustration, her mother believes that she has the right to look precisely because the content is accessible to a broad audience, even though she knows that Bly doesn't want her mother among that audience.

Although many adults believe that they have the right to consume any teen content that is functionally accessible, many teens disagree. For example, when I opened up the issue of teachers looking at students' Facebook profiles with African American fifteen-year-old Chantelle, she responded dismissively: "Why are they on my page? I wouldn't go to my teacher's page and look at their stuff, so why should they go on mine to look at my stuff?" She continued on to make it clear that she had nothing to hide while also reiterating the feeling that snooping teachers violated her sense of privacy. The issue for Chantelle—and many other teens—is more a matter of social norms and etiquette than technical access.

Erving Goffman—the sociologist described in the previous chapter for his analysis of self-presentation—also wrote about the importance of "civil inattention" in enabling people to respectfully negotiate others in public spaces.[8] For example, even when two people happen to be sitting across from each other on the subway, social norms dictate that they should not stare at each other or insert themselves into the other's conversations. Of course, people still do these things, but they also feel a social responsibility to avert their eyes and pretend that they cannot hear the conversation taking place.[9] What's at stake is not whether someone *can* listen in but whether one *should*. Etiquette and politeness operate as a social force that challenges what's functionally possible.

Although Bly and her mother do not find resolution in the three-minute radio segment, Bly accepts that there is nothing she can do to stop her mother from snooping. She concludes instead that journaling sites "are becoming lame" because parents are starting to create their own profiles and use these services to meet strangers, failing to recognize the hypocrisy in their advice about talking to strangers. Made in 2006, Bly's arguments are specific to the journaling site LiveJournal, but I heard these same sentiments repeated over the years in reference to numerous other social media sites, especially Facebook. In 2012, when I asked teens who were early adopters of Twitter, Tumblr, and Instagram why they preferred these services to Facebook, I heard a near-uniform response: "Because my parents don't know about it." The sites of practice change, but many teens get frustrated when adults "invade" teen-centric spaces, and so, in an attempt to achieve privacy, some move on to newer sites and apps to avoid parents and other adults.

Although Bly's desire to seek freedom from her mother's gaze prompted her to leave a service she once enjoyed, the increasing popularity of social media—and the challenges brought on by multiple audiences—are forcing other teens to reconsider how they achieve privacy in networked publics more generally. Some are perennially searching for adult-free zones, but this cat-and-mouse game gets tiresome, especially when parents quickly catch on to the "new" site. Much to many adults' surprise, teens aren't looking to hide; they just want privacy.[10] As a result, many teens are developing innovative solutions to achieve privacy in public. To get there, they must grapple with the tools that are available to them, the norms that shape social practices, and their own agency.

Achieving Privacy by Controlling the Social Situation

Privacy is a complex concept without a clear definition.[11] Supreme Court Justice Louis Brandeis described privacy as "the right to be let alone," while legal scholar Ruth Gavison describes privacy as a measure of the access others have to you through information, attention, and physical proximity.[12] Taking a structuralist tactic, legal scholar Alan Westin argues that privacy is "the claim of individuals, groups, or institutions to determine for themselves when, how, and to what extent information about them is communicated to others."[13] These different—but related—definitions highlight control over access and visibility. Although the failure to reach consensus on a definition of privacy may be frustrating to some, legal scholar Daniel Solove argues that each approach to privacy reveals insight into how we manage privacy in everyday life.[14]

Public discourse around privacy often centers on hiding or opting out of public environments, whereas scholars and engineers often focus more on controlling the flow of information. These can both be helpful ways of thinking about privacy, but as philosopher Helen Nissenbaum astutely notes, privacy is always rooted in context.[15] Much of the scholarly conversation around privacy focuses on whether or not someone has—or has lost—privacy. Yet, for the teens that I interviewed, privacy isn't necessarily something that they have; rather it is something they are actively and continuously trying to achieve in spite of structural or social barriers that make it difficult to do so. Achieving privacy requires more than simply having the levers to control information, access, or visibility. Instead, achieving privacy requires the ability to control the social situation by navigating complex contextual cues, technical affordances, and social dynamics. Achieving privacy is an ongoing process because social situations are never static. Especially in networked publics, the persistent, searchable nature of interactions complicates any temporal boundaries. Comments written weeks ago can easily be fodder for current dramas, and it's often difficult to discern when a conversation starts and ends in an asynchronous texting channel.

Controlling a social situation in an effort to achieve privacy is neither easy nor obvious. Doing so requires power, knowledge, and skills. First, people must have a certain degree of agency or power within a social situation, which means that they must either have social status or take measures to effectively resist those who are more powerful within that situation. Second, people must have a reasonable understanding of the social situation and context in which they are operating. And third, people must have the skills to manage the social situation in order to both understand and affect how information flows and is interpreted. These prerequisites for achieving privacy can be overwhelming. Furthermore, they are often taken for granted by those questioning why youth don't do more to manage their privacy.

When teens try to achieve privacy in networked publics, they often struggle with these foundational elements. In social settings where parents lurk over teens' shoulders under the guise of making sure their children are safe, teens often lack the agency necessary to control the social situation.[16] The dynamics of mediated social situations—including invisible audiences, collapsed contexts, and persistent content—further complicate things, making it incredibly difficult for teens to imagine the boundaries of these mediated social situations. Finally, it's hard to develop the skills to manage how information will flow within a social situation when the underlying affordances change regularly. For example, when sites like Facebook repeatedly alter their privacy settings, developing the necessary skills to manage how visible content should be becomes, if not next to impossible, then incredibly labor-intensive. Given all of this, teens cannot easily control the flow of information on social media. Some teens understand this intuitively; others struggle with this because popular rhetoric focuses so heavily on access and control. The most creative teens often respond to the limitations they face by experimenting with more innovative approaches to achieving privacy in order to control the social situation. This typically involves working around technical affordances, reclaiming agency, and using novel strategies to reconfigure the social situation.

Public by Default, Private Through Effort

The default in most interpersonal conversations, even those that take place in public settings, is that interactions are private by default, public through effort. For example, when two people are chatting in a café, they can assume a certain level of privacy. Parts of the conversation may get recounted later, but unless someone within hearing range was surreptitiously recording the conversation, the conversation most likely remains somewhat private due to social norms around politeness and civil inattention. There are many examples of people violating this norm, including Linda Tripp's decision to record Monica Lewinsky's confession and paparazzi using long-range cameras to capture celebrities from afar.[17] However, these are seen as violations because most people do not assume that their conversation will be publicized if they understand the social situation to be intimate.

In a mediated world, assumptions and norms about the visibility and spread of expressions must be questioned. Many of the most popular genres of social media are designed to encourage participants to spread information. On a site like Facebook, it is far easier to share with all friends than to manipulate the privacy settings to limit the visibility of a particular piece of content to a narrower audience. As a result, many participants make a different calculation than the one they would make in an unmediated situation. Rather than asking themselves if the information to be shared is significant enough to be broadly publicized, they question whether it is intimate enough to require special protection. In other words, when participating in networked publics, many participants embrace a widespread public-by-default, private-through-effort mentality.

Because of this public-by-default framework, most teens won't bother to limit the audience who can see what they consider to be mundane conversations on Facebook. Teens will regularly share things widely on Facebook simply because they see no reason to make the effort to make those pieces of content private. For example, teens will share "Happy Birthday" messages or bored notes where they ask others what they're doing openly because they don't see these particular interactions as having much significance. The sum of interactions that they have online appear to be much more public because teens don't go out of their way to make minutiae private.[18] Adults complain that teens are wasting their time publicizing trivia, whereas teens feel as though their audience can filter out anything that appears to be irrelevant.

This does not mean that teens never restrict the visibility of content. When they think something might be sensitive, they often switch to a different medium, turning to text messages or chat to communicate with smaller audiences directly. Of course, sometimes they also mess up, intentionally or unintentionally. They might post an inappropriate comment that they know will spark a fight because they're trying to get attention or because they're lashing out. They might post a photo that they don't think will be particularly controversial given their imagined audience, only to have that photo cause drama or result in other unexpected trouble. Teens do think through the social cost to what they post, but they don't always get it right.

Teens are aware that technology has shifted sharing norms, but they see this more in terms of what's visible than as an underlying value change. In North Carolina, I met Alicia, a white seventeen-year-old who articulated how she felt technology had shaped information sharing.

> I just think that [technology is] redefining what's acceptable for people to put out about themselves. I've grown up with technology so I don't know how it was before this boom of social networking. But it just seems like instead of spending all of our time talking to other individual people and sharing things that would seem private we just spend all of our time putting it in one module of communication where people can go and access it if they want to. It's just more convenient.

Alicia recognizes that the public-by-default dynamic creates a conflict around privacy, but she thinks that it's a red herring. "When [adults] see [our photo albums] or when they see conversations on Facebook wall to wall, they think that it's this huge breach of privacy. I just think it's different. . . . I think privacy is more just you choosing what you want to keep to yourself." Alicia is not giving up on privacy just because she chooses to share broadly. Instead, she believes that she can achieve privacy by choosing what not to share.

By focusing on what to keep private rather than what to publicize, teens often inadvertently play into another common rhetorical crutch—the notion that privacy is necessary only for those who have something to hide. Indeed, many teens consciously seek out privacy when they're trying to restrict access to a narrower audience either out of respect or out of fear. But as content becomes increasingly persistent, teens are also much more aware of the unintended consequences of having data available that could easily be taken out of context at a later time.

In DC, I met an African American seventeen-year-old named Shamika who found that her peers loved to use old status updates and point to them in a new context in order to "start drama." She found this infuriating because the posts that she wrote a month earlier were never intended as fodder for current arguments. To deal with this, Shamika took radical measures to delete content from the past. Each day, when she logged into Facebook, she'd read comments she received and then delete them. She'd scan through the comments she'd left on friends' updates and photos and delete those. She systematically cleansed her Facebook presence in a practice known as "whitewalling" in which she made certain that the front of her Facebook page—originally called the "wall"—was blank, revealing the background color of white. When I remarked to Shamika that anyone could copy and paste that content and bring it back at a later date, she nodded knowingly before telling me that doing so would be "creepy." In other words, by using technology to signal what was expected, she shifted the burden from being a matter of technological access to being about a violation of social norms.

Although persistence has become de facto on most major social media, new apps have begun to emerge that call this normative affordance into question. For example, in 2013, teens starting using Snapchat, a photo-sharing app in which images purportedly self-destruct after being viewed. Given the assumption that teens use such services only to share inappropriate content, journalists often referred to this application in the same breath as sexting or the sharing of inappropriate sexual images. But in casually asking teens about Snapchat, I found most were using the app to signal that an image wasn't meant for posterity. They shared inside jokes, silly pictures, and images that were funny only in the moment. Rather than viewing photographs as an archival production, they saw the creation and sharing of these digital images as akin to an ephemeral gesture. And they used Snapchat to signal this expectation.

As discussed in the introduction, technical affordances and design defaults do influence how teens understand and use particular social media, but they don't dictate practice. As teens encounter particular technologies, they make decisions based on what they're trying to achieve. More often than not, in a technical ecosystem in which making content private is more difficult than sharing broadly, teens choose to share, even if doing so creates the impression that they have given up on privacy. It's not that every teen is desperate for widespread attention; plenty simply see no reason to take the effort to minimize the visibility of their photos and conversations. As a result, interactions that would be ephemeral in an unmediated space are suddenly persistent, creating the impression that norms have radically changed even though they haven't. Instead of going out of their way to achieve privacy by restricting the visibility of particular pieces of content, teens develop other strategies for achieving privacy in public.

Social Steganography

Children love to experiment with encoding messages. From pig latin to invisible ink pens, children explore hidden messages when they're imagining themselves as spies and messengers. As children grow up, they look for more sophisticated means of passing messages that elude the watchful eyes of adults. In watching teens navigate networked publics, I became enamored of how they were regularly encoding hidden meaning in publicly available messages. They were engaged in a practice that Alice Marwick and I called "social steganography," or hiding messages in plain sight by leveraging shared knowledge and cues embedded in particular social contexts.

The practice of hiding in plain sight is not new. When ancient Greeks wanted to send a message over great distances, they couldn't rely on privacy. Messengers could easily be captured and even encoded messages deciphered. The most secure way to send a private message was to make sure that no one knew that the message existed in the first place. Historical sources describe the extraordinary lengths to which Greeks went, hiding messages within wax tablets or tattooing them on a slave's head and allowing the slave's hair to grow out before sending him or her out to meet the message's recipient.[19] Although these messages could be easily read by anyone who bothered to look, they became visible only if the viewer knew to look for them in the first place. Cryptographers describe this practice of hiding messages in plain sight as *steganography*.

Social steganography uses countless linguistic and cultural tools, including lyrics, in-jokes, and culturally specific references to encode messages that are functionally accessible but simultaneously meaningless. Some teens use pronouns while others refer to events, use nicknames, and employ predetermined code words to share gossip that lurking adults can't interpret. Many teens write in ways that will blend in and be invisible to or misinterpreted by adults. Whole conversations about school gossip, crushes, and annoying teachers go unnoticed as teens host conversations that are rendered meaningless to outside observers.

These practices are not new. Teens have long used whatever tools are around them to try to share information under the noses of their teachers and parents. At school, passing notes and putting notes in lockers are classic examples of how teens use paper, pen, and ingenuity to share information. Graffiti on bathroom walls may appear simply to be an act of vandalism, but these scrawled markings also convey messages. As new technologies have entered into teen life, it's not surprising that teens also use them in similarly cryptic ways to communicate with one another. Texting gossip during class serves much of the same purpose as passing a note, yet it doesn't require having to move a physical object, which reduces the likelihood of getting caught. But encoding messages guarantees only that if all else fails, the meaning will not become accessible, even if control over the information itself is unsuccessful.

When Carmen, a Latina seventeen-year-old living in Boston, broke up with her boyfriend, she "wasn't in the happiest state." She wanted her friends to know how she was feeling. Like many of her peers,

Carmen shared her emotions by using song lyrics. Thus, her first instinct was to post song lyrics from an "emo" or depressing song, but she was worried that her mother might interpret the lyric in the wrong way. This had happened before. Unfortunately, Carmen's mom regularly "overreacted" when Carmen posted something with significant emotional overtones. Thus, she wanted to find a song lyric that conveyed what she felt but didn't trigger her mom to think she was suicidal.

She was also attentive to the way in which her mother's presence on Facebook tended to disrupt the social dynamics among her friends. Carmen and her mom are close and, for the most part, Carmen loves having her mom as one of her friends on Facebook, but her mom's incessant desire to comment on Facebook tends to discourage responses from her friends. As Carmen told me, when her mother comments, "it scares everyone away. Everyone kind of disappears after the mom post." She wanted to make sure to post something that her friends would respond to, even if her mom jumped in to comment.

Carmen settled on posting lyrics from "Always Look on the Bright Side of Life." This song sounds happy but is sung during a scene in the Monty Python movie *Life of Brian* in which the main character is being crucified. Carmen knew that her immigrant Argentinean mother would not understand the British cultural reference, but she also knew her close friends would. Only a few weeks earlier, she and her geeky girlfriends had watched the film together at a sleepover and laughed at the peculiar juxtaposition of song lyric and scene. Her strategy was effective; her mother took the words at face value, immediately commenting on Facebook that it was great to see her so happy. Her friends didn't attempt to correct her mother's misinterpretation. Instead, they picked up their phones and texted Carmen to see if she was OK.

Part of what makes Carmen's message especially effective is that she regularly posts song lyrics to express all sorts of feelings. As a result, this song lyric blended into a collection of other song lyrics, quotes, and comments. She did not try to draw attention to the message itself but knew that her close friends would know how to interpret what they saw. And they did. Her friends had the cultural knowledge about what references were being made to interpret and contextualize the message underneath the song lyric. Thus, she conveyed meaning to some while sharing only a song lyric with many more.

While many teens encode meaning as a strategy for navigating visibility, other teens leverage similar techniques to tease their classmates with secrets. For example, some teens use pronouns and song lyrics in ways that make it very clear to the onlooker that they are not "in the know." In North Carolina, I was browsing Facebook with a white seventeen-year-old named Serena when we stumbled across a status update written by her classmate Kristy. Kristy's update said, "I'm sick and tired of all of this," and was already "Liked" by more than thirty people. I asked Serena what this meant, and she went into a long explanation about the dramas between Kristy and Cathy. Sure enough, over on Cathy's profile was a status update that read, "She's such a bitch," which was also liked by dozens of people. As an outsider, I had no way of knowing that these two posts were related to each other, let alone what was referenced by the pronouns "this" and "she." But Serena could fully interpret the drama that was unfolding; she knew the players, and she knew what the fight was about. She brought all of this knowledge to her interpretation of what she saw on Facebook, yet she also knew that many of her classmates and none of her teachers would know what was happening. Although outsiders were surely seeing these individual messages, few would dare ask.

When teenagers post encoded messages in a visible way, they are aware that people outside of their intended audience will be curious. Some will find the uninterpretable messages to be a frustrating marker of popularity, while others will see them as an enticing opportunity to learn more. Some will investigate, while others will ignore what they can't understand. When I asked Jenna, a white seventeen-year-old from a different North Carolina school, how she felt about seeing encoded messages, she told me that it depended on who was writing the message.

If it's someone that I want to know what they're talking about, then I'll try to investigate it. I'll look at the wall, a conversation or something. But [sometimes] I don't really care what so-and-so is doing. I have friends from when I went to Malaysia. They were all about Facebook. . . . And sometimes I hide them because whatever they're talking about is confusing to me because I don't know what they're talking about or I get stuff from them that I don't really want.

Many teens are happy to publicly perform their social dramas for their classmates and acquaintances, provided that only those in the know will actually understand what's really going on and those who shouldn't be involved are socially isolated from knowing what's unfolding. These teens know that adults might be present, but they also feel that, if asked, they could create a convincing alternate interpretation of what was being discussed. Through such encoded language, teens can exclude people who are not part of the cycle of gossip at school, including parents, teachers, and peers outside their immediate social sphere.[20]

Over the decade that I observed teens' social media practices, I watched encoding content become more common. In 2010–2011, teens started talking about subliminal tweeting, or "subtweeting," to refer to the practice of encoding tweets to render them meaningless to clueless outsiders. More often than not, they employed this term when referencing various teen dramas that occurred between friends and classmates that required insider knowledge to decode. In other words, teens subtweet to talk behind someone else's back. Although this is only one technique for encoding information, the rise of this term highlights how popular the practice has become.[21]

Encoding content, subtweeting, and otherwise engaging in social steganography offers one strategy for reclaiming agency in an effort to achieve privacy in networked publics. In doing so, teens recognize that limiting access to meaning can be a much more powerful tool for achieving privacy than trying to limit access to the content itself.

Although not all teenagers are carefully crafting content to be understood by a limited audience, many are exploring techniques like this to express themselves privately in situations in which they assume that others are watching.

Living with Surveillance

In 2008, the *New York Times* published an article called "Text Generation Gap: U R 2 Old (JK)." The piece begins with an anecdote about a father shuttling around his daughter and her friend. They are talking, and Dad interrupts to give his opinion; the girls roll their eyes. And then there is silence, while the girls start texting. When Dad comments to his daughter that she's being rude for texting on her phone rather than talking to her friend, the daughter replies: "But, Dad, we're texting each other. I don't want you to hear what I'm saying."[22]

Teens have many words for the kinds of everyday surveillance that they have grown accustomed to: lurking, listening in, hovering, and being "in my business." Many of the privacy strategies that teens implement are intended to counter the power dynamic that emerges when parents and other adults feel as though they have the right to watch and listen. They shift tools and encode content, use privacy settings, and demand privacy.[23] Some teens even go to extremes to challenge adults' surveillance.

In Washington, DC, my colleague Alice Marwick interviewed an eighteen-year-old black teen named Mikalah who had grown accustomed to ongoing surveillance by adults. Having been in and out of different foster care settings, she was used to having state agencies and her varying guardians regularly check in on her, online and offline. Frustrated by their attempts to access what she posted on Facebook, she decided to delete her account. When she went to do so, she was shown a message discouraging her from leaving Facebook. Pictures of her friends were portrayed, along with a note about how they would miss her on the site. Facebook also gave her a different option—she could simply deactivate her account. If she took this option, her profile would disappear, but she could login at any time and reactivate her account, making her profile reappear. Doing so would allow her to preserve her account, including her content, friends, comments, and settings.

Presented with this option, Mikalah had an idea. She deactivated her account. The next day, she logged in and reactivated her account, chatted with friends, and caught up on the day's conversations. When she was done, she deactivated her account again. The next night, she repeated this same pattern. By repeatedly deactivating and reactivating her account, she turned Facebook into a real-time tool. Anyone who checked in on her when she was logged in would find her account, but if they searched for her during off hours, she was missing. From Mikalah's perspective, this was a privacy-achieving practice because she only logged in at night, whereas the adults she encountered seemed to log in only during the day. By repurposing the deactivation feature to meet her needs, Mikalah found a way to control the social situation to the best of her ability.

Mikalah's approach is extreme, but it highlights the measures that some teens take to achieve privacy in light of ongoing surveillance. Teens' experiences with surveillance vary tremendously. Those who are marginalized—typically because of their race or socioeconomic status—are much more likely to experience state surveillance than those who are privileged, but even privileged youth must contend with parental surveillance.[24]

Although not all parents and guardians are trying to control their children's every move, many believe that being a "good" parent means being all-knowing. I regularly heard parents say that being a responsible parent required them to violate their children's privacy, especially when the internet is involved. In an online forum, Christina, a mother from New York, explained her reasoning. "I do not believe teenagers 'need' privacy—not when it comes to the Internet. I track everything my kids do online. I search their bedrooms too. I'm the parent—I'm not their friend." When a teen responds to her post by arguing that parents should not look over their children's shoulders, Christina responds critically.

Annoying or not, I do it and will always do it. It's MY computer. I also log in and check their history, and track where they go, who they talk to . . . everything. I'm a mom. It is my responsibility to protect them. I wouldn't let them talk to strangers "irl" so why would I let them do it online without supervising? That's just foolish, imo. If my girls don't like my spying, they're free to not use the computer.

Christina's attitude is not universal, but it does reflect a style of "intensive" parenting that is quite common in the United States.[25] Legal scholars Gaia Bernstein and Zvi Triger have found that the norms around intensive parenting are increasingly part of public discourse and inscribed into law, making parents liable if they don't abide by the cultural logic of intensive parenting.[26] Thus, even when parents don't share Christina's attitudes, there is significant pressure for them to engage in acts of surveillance to be "good" parents. And given the digital traces that teens leave behind as a byproduct of their mediated conversations, many parents feel the need to track, read, and consume every interaction their children have in networked publics, even though doing so in an unmediated world is completely untenable.

Christina may feel that she has the right to track her children's movements as long as they are in her house, but other parents make themselves all-knowing by being always present. In Michigan, Bianca, a white sixteen-year-old, told me that there is no such thing as privacy in her house because of her family dynamics. The problem isn't just that her parents are always around, but they seem to feel as though they have the right to be a part of any interaction that occurs within earshot. Bianca told me that it's impossible to have a conversation with her best friend in her house because "my family butts in to everything." Not only do Bianca's parents listen in on her conversations—whether they occur on the phone, via instant messaging, or in the living room—but they even interrupt to ask for clarifications. Rolling her eyes in agreement, Bianca's best friend explained that it's much better for them to hang out at her house because her mother gives the girls "space."

Parental nosiness is not new. In an era before cell phones, teens prized cordless phones precisely because they could be taken to a private space.[27] Even then, parents—and siblings—often used separate phones to listen in. Today, parental nosiness extends to kids' online encounters. In many households, the computer occupies a shared space—in part because parents are told that kids' safety depends on parental awareness of what their children are doing online.

Although most of the teens I interviewed did not mind the central location of the computer, quite a few complain about their parents' ongoing tendency to hover. In Massachusetts, Kat, a white fifteen-year-old, told me that she found her mother's behavior annoying. "When I'm talking to somebody online, I don't like when they stand over my shoulder, and I'll be like, 'Mom, can you not read over my shoulder?' Not that I'm saying something bad. It just feels weird. I don't like it." Kat isn't ashamed of what she's doing online—and she has even willingly given her mother her Facebook password—but she hates feeling watched. Some teens see privacy as a right, but many more see privacy as a matter of trust. Thus, when their parents choose to snoop or lurk or read their online posts, these teens see it as a signal of distrust. Teens like Kat get upset when their parents never leave them alone when they're online because they read this as a lack of confidence in their actions.

This issue of trust also emerges in relationship to passwords. Many teens are comfortable sharing their passwords with their parents "in case of an emergency" but expect that their parents will not use them to snoop. Christopher, a white fifteen-year-old from Alabama, told me that his parents had all of his passwords but that he expected them not to log in to his accounts unless there was a serious issue. He respected his parents' concern and desire to protect him, but in return, he expected them to trust him. Although he believed nothing in his accounts would upset his parents, he also said he would be angry if they logged in just to see what he was doing. Like many of his peers,

Christopher believes that there is a significant difference between having the ability to violate privacy and making the choice to do so.

Whether privacy is a "right" that children can or cannot have, or a privilege that teens must earn, adult surveillance shapes teens' understanding of—and experience with—privacy. In his book *Discipline and Punish*, philosopher Michel Foucault describes how surveillance operates as a mechanism of control. When inmates believe they are being watched, they conform to what they believe to be the norms of the prison and the expectations of their jailors. Surveillance is a mechanism by which powerful entities assert their power over less powerful individuals. When parents choose to hover, lurk, and track, they implicitly try to regulate teens' practices. Parents often engage in these acts out of love but fail to realize how surveillance is a form of oppression that limits teens' ability to make independent choices. Regardless of how they explicitly choose to respond to it, teens are configured by the surveillance that they experience. It shapes their understanding of the social context and undermines their agency, challenging their ability to control the social situation meaningfully. As a result, what teens do to achieve privacy often looks quite different than what most adults would expect as appropriate tactics. Teens assume that they are being watched, and so they try to find privacy within public settings rather than in opposition to public-ness.

Privacy as Process

Taylor is not one to share, and if she had her druthers, she wouldn't tell her friends much about what's happening in her life. She understands that her friends mean well, but the Boston-based white fifteen-year-old is a reserved person, and she doesn't like it when people are "in [her] business." To combat nagging questions from friends and classmates, she has started creating a "light version" of her life that she'll regularly share on Facebook just so that her friends don't pester her about what's actually happening. Much to her frustration, she finds that sharing at least a little bit affords her more privacy than sharing nothing at all.

She's not alone. Many public figures find that the appearance of unlimited sharing allows them to achieve privacy meaningfully. Heather Armstrong, a well-known blogger referred to by her nickname "Dooce," once remarked: "People I meet tell me, 'It's so weird I know everything about you.' No you don't! Ninety-five percent of my life is not blogged about."[28] Through the act of sharing what appears to be everything, bloggers like Armstrong appear to be vulnerable and open while still carving off a portion of their lives to keep truly private.

In a world in which posting updates is common, purposeful, and performative, sharing often allows teens to control a social situation more than simply opting out. It also guarantees that others can't define the social situation. Sitting in an afterschool program in Los Angeles, I casually asked a teen participant why she shared so many embarrassing photos of herself on her profile. She laughed and told me that it was a lot safer if she shared her photos and put them in context by what she wrote than if she did not because she knew that her friends also had embarrassing photos. They'd be happy to embarrass her if she let them. But by taking preemptive action and mocking herself by writing dismissive messages on photos that could be interpreted problematically, she undermined her friends' ability to define the situation differently. After explaining her logic, she continued on to explain how her apparent exhibitionism left plenty of room for people to not focus in on the things that were deeply intimate in her life.

In most cases where people share to maintain privacy, they do because they do not want someone to have power over them. Performative sharing may or may not be healthy. For example, I've met lesbian, gay, and transgendered teens who extensively share to appear straight so that people don't ask about their sexuality, and I've met abused teens who tell extravagant stories about their lives so that no one asks what's really happening at home. Issues emerge when teens start to deceive in order to keep the truth private. But by and large, when teens share to create a sense of privacy, they are simply asserting agency in a social context in which their power is regularly undermined. The most common way that this unfolds is when teens systematically exclude certain information from what is otherwise a rich story. For example, plenty of teens tell their parents about what happened at school without telling them information that would reveal that they have a crush. On one hand, these teens are hiding, but on the other hand, they're sharing in order to hold onto a space for privacy.

Privacy is not a static construct. It is not an inherent property of any particular information or setting. It is a process by which people seek to have control over a social situation by managing impressions, information flows, and context. Cynics often suggest that only people who have something to hide need privacy. But this argument is a distraction.[29] Privacy is valuable because it is critical for personal development. As teenagers are coming of age, they want to feel as though they matter. Privacy is especially important for those who are marginalized or lack privilege within society. Teenagers have not given up on privacy, even if their attempts to achieve it are often undermined by people who hold power over them. On the contrary, teens are consistently trying out new ways of achieving privacy by drawing on and modernizing strategies that disempowered people have long used.[30] Rather than finding privacy by controlling access to content, many teens are instead controlling access to meaning.

It's easy to think of privacy and publicity as opposing concepts, and a lot of technology is built on the assumption that you have to choose to be private or public. Yet in practice, both privacy and publicity are blurred. Rather than eschewing privacy when they encounter public spaces, many teens are looking for new ways to achieve privacy within networked publics. As such, when teens develop innovative strategies to achieve privacy, they often reclaim power by doing so. Privacy doesn't just depend on agency; being able to achieve privacy is an expression *of* agency.

3 addiction
what makes teens obsessed with social media?

In a 2009 *New York Times* article, "To Deal with Obsession, Some Defriend Facebook," psychologist Kimberly Young, director of the Center for Internet Addiction Recovery, describes dozens of teenagers she's met who tried to quit Facebook. "It's just like any other addiction," Young says. "It's hard to wean yourself."[1]

I also came across several teens who, because of limited time, challenging social dynamics, or a need to disengage, decided to quit different social media sites.[2] Andrew, a white high school senior in Nashville, made a pact with a friend to leave Facebook, or to commit "Facebook suicide," because he felt "addicted" to it. He found that he'd login at night, stay on the site until two o'clock in the morning, and then be frustrated with himself for not getting any sleep. He recounted telling himself, "This is stupid and it's having control of my life and I don't want that with anything." Andrew and his friend deactivated their profiles within minutes of each other, using the same computer.

Andrew's decision had consequences. He said that not having an account cramped his social life. He had more trouble finding out about social activities, and he found negotiating interpersonal relationships more challenging. He explained not being able to look up or "stalk" new friends as one example. To justify his decision, he thought about how older generations managed to get by without Facebook and decided that he was both willing to make and capable of making the sacrifice. "I just kind of remind myself that it's a social networking site," he said, "which is kind of a smart and dumb idea at the same time to me." Then he added, "Not really. It's a smart idea, but . . . I should be more mature and get off Facebook." Thinking of his relationship to Facebook as an addiction allowed him to question what had become normative. By dismissing Facebook as insignificant and his frequent participation as immature, Andrew felt that he gained control over his relationship to the site and all that the relationship signaled.

Although teens often use the word *addiction* in passing reference to their online activities, media coverage of teens' use of social media amplifies the notion that the current generation of youth is uncontrollably hooked on these new technologies and unable to control their lives. Fear mongering stories often point to accounts of internet addiction boot camps in China and South Korea, where the compulsion allegedly rivals alcoholism, drug addiction, and gambling.[3] In the United States, media coverage frequently portrays American youth in dark bedrooms with only the glow of the screen illuminating their faces, implying that there's a generation of zombified social media addicts who are unable to tear themselves away from the streams of content from Facebook, Twitter, and Instagram. This media-driven image of social media addiction looks nothing like the dynamic that Andrew was describing when he used the same term.

There is no doubt that some youth develop an unhealthy relationship with technology. For some, an obsession with gaming or social media can wreak havoc on their lives, affecting school performance and stunting emotional development. However, the language of addiction sensationalizes teens' engagement with technology and suggests that mere participation leads to pathology. This language also suggests that technologies alone will determine social outcomes. The overarching media narrative is that teens lack the capacity to maintain a healthy relationship with social media. It depicts passionate engagement with technology as an illness that society must address. It is easier for adults to blame technology for undesirable outcomes than to consider other social, cultural, and personal factors that may be at play.

When talking about teens' engagement with social media, many adults use the concept of addiction to suggest that teens lack control. Some even cite their own obsession with social media as evidence to support this perspective. Anxieties about teens' engagement with technology aren't new, but few ask why teens embrace each new social technology with such fervor. The pictures of teens' faces illuminated by computer screens mirror earlier images of televisions' entertaining glow luring in teenagers.[4] Parents in previous generations fretted about the hours teens whiled away hanging out or chatting on the phone. Today's teens aren't spending hours on landlines, but they *are* still conversing—updating others on social network sites, posting pictures and videos, and sending text messages to friends. Both entertainment and sociality are key reasons why teens invest so much energy in their online activities.

Although teens complain about how time drags when they must do things that they do not find enjoyable, time seems to slip away when in mediated environments with their peers. This can be disorienting and a source of guilt. It is also the root of anxiety about social media addiction. Consider the following conversation that took place when I was interviewing a pair of white sophomores and best friends in Kansas at the height of MySpace's popularity:

Lilly: It's really awful with MySpace that I'll click on somebody who's sent a comment to me and I'll look at somebody else, 'cause they have a "Top 10 Friends" and I'll click on one of them, and then I'll end up looking at people's MySpaces in Tennessee and I started back with my neighbor.

Melanie: And it's five hours later and you're like, "Oh my God. Where have I been?"

Lilly: Yeah. You just get sucked in. I don't know who the genius was that thought it up because it really sucks you in.

Addiction is one way to understand the dynamic that Lilly and Melanie are describing, but another is what psychologist Mihaly Csikszentmihalyi calls "flow."[5] For Csikszentmihalyi, flow is the state of complete and utter absorption. It's the same sense that's colloquially described it as being "in the zone." Time disappears, attention focuses, and people feel euphorically engaged. This is the ideal state for creativity and artistry; athletes, musicians, and actors try to harness this mindset before they perform. It is critical to leadership, writing, software development, and education. Yet people also experience this state when they gamble and play video games, two activities that society often associates with compulsion or addiction.[6] Deep engagement does not seem to be a problem in and of itself, unless coupled with a practice that is socially unacceptable, physically damaging, or financially costly.

Unlike most compulsions, teens are not less social when they engage deeply with social media. On the contrary, their participation in social media is typically highly social. Listening to teens talk about social media addiction reveals an interest not in features of their computers, smartphones, or even particular social media sites but in each other.[7] Teen "addiction" to social media is a new extension of typical human engagement. Their use of social media as their primary site of sociality is most often a byproduct of cultural dynamics that have nothing to do with technology, including parental restrictions and highly scheduled lives. Teens turn to, and are obsessed with, whichever environment allows them to connect to friends. Most teens aren't addicted to social media; if anything, they're addicted to each other.

The Addiction Narrative

Addiction is a relatively modern concept. Although references to people being "addicted to the bottle" date back centuries, it wasn't until the early twentieth century that both medical professionals and the public consistently used the term *addiction* to refer to substance abuse.[8] Before that, the term referred to a strong interest in or devotion to a particular pursuit such as gardening or reading.[9] As concerns about addiction took hold in the late nineteenth and early twentieth centuries, addiction became a medical concern. Medical practitioners consistently blamed the substance, even while having conflicted feelings about how responsible an individual was for the problem. As the *Journal of the American Medical Association* opined in 1906, "It matters little whether one speaks of the opium habit, the opium disease, or the opium addiction."[10]

As the twentieth century progressed, the public joined medical practitioners in taking addiction seriously, and the term *addiction* gained traction in popular discourse. Alcoholics Anonymous coalesced from a community of compulsive drinkers in 1935 to a national organization, structured to help those struggling to get sober. In 1949, the World Health Organization convened a committee to consider "drugs liable to produce addiction."[11]

Addiction initially referred only to drug and alcohol abuse, but as it entered popular parlance, the term came to mean behavioral compulsions as well, including gambling, overeating, self-injury, and sex. The Diagnostic and Statistical Manual of Mental Disorders, the American Psychiatric Association's classification of mental disorders, differentiates chemical dependence as *substance disorders* and behavioral compulsions as *impulse-control disorders*. Over the past twenty years, excessive use of information and communication technologies has become part of the addiction narrative, often under the umbrella of an impulse-control disorder.

In 1995, psychiatrist Ivan Goldberg coined the term *internet addiction disorder*. He wrote a satirical essay about "people abandoning their family obligations to sit gazing into their computer monitor as they surfed the Internet." Intending to parody society's obsession with pathologizing everyday behaviors, he inadvertently advanced the idea. Goldberg responded critically when academics began discussing internet addiction as a legitimate disorder: "I don't think

Internet addiction disorder exists any more than tennis addictive disorder, bingo addictive disorder, and TV addictive disorder exist. People can overdo anything. To call it a disorder is an error."[12]

Although Goldberg rejects the notion of internet addiction, other practitioners and researchers have called for labeling compulsive internet usage a disorder.[13] Most of the clinical discussion around internet addiction focuses on whether "overuse" or "misuse" of the internet constitutes a disorder—as opposed to an obsession or compulsion. Experts also debate whether problematic engagement is simply a manifestation of depression, anxiety, or other disorders. Although some individuals' unhealthy relationships with the internet seem to impede their ability to lead active lives, it is not clear that the internet is the source of the problem. But addiction is an easy and familiar trope.

Addiction is often represented in the media as a problem with youth culture. In 1938, the film *Reefer Madness* started a mass frenzy, depicting marijuana as a "killer weed" turning vulnerable young people into addicts. Rising heroin use in the late 1950s and 1960s heightened popular concern, amplified by the drug-related deaths of rock idols Janis Joplin and Jim Morrison at the start of the 1970s. Then, in 1971, an anonymously authored book brought the issue of addiction into direct contact with childhood, magnifying already widespread anxiety among parents. *Go Ask Alice*, purportedly the diary of a teenage girl, documents descent into addiction, ending with what the prologue indicates as an eventual overdose. Although some parents and educators want the book banned for describing drug use, others tout the book's stark portrayal of substance abuse as proof of the dangers of drugs.[14] Throughout the 1980s and 1990s, popular media simultaneously valorized and demonized substance abuse, with young addicts taking center stage in movies like *Trainspotting*, *Drugstore Cowboy*, and *The Basketball Diaries*. This practice continues into the twenty-first century with TV shows like *Skins* and *Celebrity Rehab*.

Public discussions of addiction introduce conflicting sentiments. On one hand, American society takes medical and mental health concerns more seriously. On the other, celebrities often celebrate—and are still celebrated for—their out-of-control substance use. When Amy Winehouse, a beloved blues singer with a bad girl reputation, died in 2011, the media broadly discussed her death in terms of addiction. News reports detailed her struggles with alcohol and drugs, often referencing the lyrics of her signature song "Rehab," which focus on her refusal to go to a drug rehabilitation clinic. Meanwhile, upon hearing of her death, many young people used a Twitter hashtag to celebrate her membership in #27club, a collection of famous musicians, including Jimi Hendrix, Janis Joplin, Jim Morrison, and Kurt Cobain, whose drug and alcohol abuse contributed to early deaths at the age of twenty-seven.

The problem with popular discussions about addiction is that it doesn't matter whether people are chemically or psychologically dependent on a substance or behavior. Anyone who engages in a practice in ways that society sees as putting more socially acceptable aspects of their lives in jeopardy are seen as addicted. When teenagers choose to use the internet for social or entertainment purposes instead of doing homework, parents are suspicious. When socializing or play results in less sleep or poorer grades, parents blame the technology. Of course, it is easy to imagine that teens may prefer to socialize with friends or relax instead of doing homework, even if these activities are not societally sanctioned. Instead of acknowledging this, many adults project their priorities onto teens and pathologize their children's interactions with technology.

There are teens who do struggle significantly with impulse control, and we should not ignore the difficulties they face in managing their priorities. But instead of prompting a productive conversation, addiction rhetoric positions new technologies as devilish and teenagers as constitutionally incapable of having agency in response to the temptations that surround them.

Many adults believe that they have a sense of what's "good" for teens—school, homework, focus, attention, and early bedtime—and many teens are acutely aware of how much society values such adult-oriented pursuits. But many adults are unaware of how social their everyday experiences are and how desperate teens are to have access to a social world like that which adults take for granted.

Although a century's worth of research on chemical addiction, compulsion, and flow has offered tremendous insights into human psychology, not everyone is powerless in relation to the world around them. Teenagers may seem like a uniquely vulnerable population, but nothing is gained from framing their social media interactions in terms of a disease. Teens, like adults, are deeply social. But unlike adults, teens often have little freedom to connect with others on their own terms, and they clamor for sociality in ways that may look foreign to adults.

Growing Up with Limited Freedom

Reflecting on her love for Facebook, Tara, a Vietnamese American sixteen-year-old from Michigan, explains that her use of the site "is kinda like an addiction." She laughs as she says this, noting, "It's like everyone says all these bad things about it. It does take up your time. It does, but you can't help it." Tara likes Facebook because it allows her to connect with her friends. Like many of her peers, Tara spends hours each week viewing her friends' photos and updates, writing comments, and reading comments left by others. For Tara, participating on Facebook is a social necessity, a crucial component of her social life. This is not to say that it is the only part of that life, or even her preferred way of being with friends. When I tried to ask Tara why she spent so much time on Facebook instead of connecting offline, she cut me off, explaining that she would much prefer to hang out with her friends face to face but finds it impossible. At that point, her eighteen-year-old sister Lila jumped in to explain, "If you don't have the option [of getting together in person], then you can just go online."

Both girls made very clear that what mattered to them was hanging out with friends, and they were happy to use any means necessary to do so. In using the term *addiction* to describe their extensive use of Facebook, both Tara and Lila acknowledged that their parents didn't approve of the amount of time they spent on the site. But their parents also forbade them from socializing out of the home as often as they would like. They struggled to find a term to express the gap between their perspective towards Facebook and their parents' attitudes, particularly because they felt that it was easier to sneak in time on Facebook than to sneak out of the house. They nonchalantly referred to their extensive time online through the lens of addiction to highlight that they felt as though participation was central to their lives because their friends and peers really mattered to them. For them, Facebook was the only way to stay connected.

To many parents, the amount of time that teens spend on social media is evidence of addiction in a negative sense. These parents often believe that the technologies are in and of themselves the draw for their children. Such parents often go to great lengths to get their children off of social media, particularly when they're concerned about how often or in what ways their children are using these sites. In Boston, a father paid his fourteen-year-old daughter two hundred dollars to deactivate her Facebook account for five months.[15] After a teen girl in North Carolina used Facebook to complain about her father, her father responded by posting an irate video on YouTube in which he reads a letter he wrote to his daughter and then fires a gun at his daughter's laptop.[16] These are admittedly extreme responses—and there is a lot more to question in these cases than teens' supposed addiction to social media—but these parents' drastic measures reveal the frustration parents have with the technological artifacts themselves.

I often heard parents complain that their children preferred computers to "real" people. Meanwhile, the teens I met repeatedly indicated that they would much rather get together with friends in person. A gap in perspective exists because teens and parents have different ideas of what sociality should look like. Whereas parents often highlighted the classroom, after-school activities, and prearranged in-home visits as opportunities for teens to gather with friends, teens were more interested in informal gatherings with broader groups of peers, free from adult surveillance. Many parents felt as though teens had plenty of social opportunities whereas the teens I met felt the opposite.

Today's teenagers have less freedom to wander than any previous generation.[17] Many middle-class teenagers once grew up with the option to "do whatever you please, but be home by dark." While race, socioeconomic class, and urban and suburban localities shaped particular dynamics of childhood, walking or bicycling to school was ordinary, and gathering with friends in public or commercial places—parks, malls, diners, parking lots, and so on—was commonplace. Until fears about "latchkey kids" emerged in the 1980s, it was normal for children, tweens, and teenagers to be alone. It was also common for youth in their preteen and early teenage years to take care of younger siblings and to earn their own money through paper routes, babysitting, and odd jobs before they could find work in more formal settings. Sneaking out of the house at night was not sanctioned, but it wasn't rare either.

Childhood has changed. As a result of attending schools outside their neighborhoods, many teens know few youth their age who live in walking distance. Fear often dictates the edges of mobility. Even in suburban enclaves where crimes are rare, teens are warned of the riskiness of wandering outside. In countless communities I visited, families saw biking around the neighborhood as inherently unsafe. Many of the teens I met believed that danger lurked everywhere. They often echoed concerns presented by their parents. For example, Jordan, a fifteen-year-old living in a suburb in Austin, told me that she is not allowed to be outside without adult supervision. Although her father was born into a white middle-class family in the United States, her foreign mother's fear shaped her childhood. "My mom's from Mexico . . . and she thinks I'll get kidnapped," she said. Jordan felt as though getting kidnapped was unlikely, but she wasn't interested in tempting fate to find out. She too was scared of going to the neighborhood park because strangers lurked there, but she wished her mom would let her rollerblade on the street in front of the house.

In many communities, parenting norms focus on limiting children's access to public places, keeping an eye on their activities, and providing extensive structure. Many parents—especially those from wealthier and less crime-ridden communities—know that they have restricted their children's mobility more than their parents restricted theirs. They argue that these restrictions are necessary in an increasingly dangerous society, even though the data suggest that contemporary youth face fewer dangers than they did twenty years ago.[18]

Parents aren't the only ones limiting teens' mobility. Teens often self-restrict either to appease parents or because they believe that there are significant risks. Teens regularly echoed parental fears, also arguing that today's world is much more unsafe than it previously was. Natalie, a white fifteen-year-old in Seattle, told me that she understands why her parents do not allow her to walk anywhere, but she wishes that the world were not so dangerous. She genuinely believes that the risks that her peers face are unprecedented.

The public and commercial spaces that I grew up with are now often seen as off-limits by both parents and teens.[19] Policymakers have implemented countless curfew and loitering laws to address gangs, delinquency, and teen violence, thereby limiting teens' access to public places.[20] Even when parents don't object and there are no legal restrictions involved, many food, shopping, and entertainment venues limit teens explicitly or implicitly, banning all teens or groups of teens. Some venues have even installed a new sound technology to ward off teens through a high-pitched sound that only children and adolescents can hear.[21] If teens have the freedom and a place to go, they encounter new struggles when they try to get there. Limited access to cars was a regular refrain among teens I interviewed. In towns where public transit is an option, independent travel is often forbidden by parents. Even in cities, many teens never ride public transit alone except to take a school bus to and from school.

A study of how children get to school reveals the stark changes in mobility that have taken place over four decades. In 1969, 48 percent of children in grades kindergarten through eighth grade walked or biked to school compared to 12 percent who were driven by a family member. By 2009, those numbers had reversed; 13 percent walked or bicycled while 45 percent were driven.[22] In a safety-obsessed society, parents continue to drop off and pick up students well into high school. Although studies that focus on the decline of biking and walking usually address the implications for childhood obesity, this shift also has significant social implications. For many youth, walking or biking to school historically provided unstructured time with friends and peers. Even when teens commuted alone, they often arrived early enough to hang out near their lockers before school or stayed late enough to get some time with friends before heading home. This is no longer the case in many of the schools I observed.

On top of fear, restrictions, and limited mobility, the issue of time often arises as a key factor in limiting teens' opportunities to socialize. Many teens have limited free time, due to afterschool activities, jobs, religious services, and family expectations. Nicholas, a white sixteen-year-old from Kansas, told me that he lacked free time because sports took up time after school and on weekends. On the rare occasions when he had downtime, his options for socializing were limited. His parents expected him to attend sports events if he was participating in the sport, but his parents would not take him to other school sports events just to hang out. If he had free time outside of his activities, they told him to focus on schoolwork, community service, or other approved activities. Hanging out with friends was viewed as a waste of time. His parents felt that he had plenty of opportunities to socialize during the group activities he was involved in. Nicholas disagreed.

Many parents believe that keeping their children busy can keep them out of trouble. After I blogged about the restrictions on teenagers' mobility, I received an email from Enrique, a parent in Austin. In it, he explained:

Bottom line is that we live in a society of fear; it is unfortunate but true. As a parent, I will admit that I protect my daughter immensely, and I don't let my daughter go out to areas I can't see her. Much different when I was a kid. Am I being over protective? Maybe. But it is the way it is. Is it depressing? No it is not as we keep her busy very busy w/o.making it depressing :-) .

Rather than enacting physical restrictions, Enrique focused on structuring his daughter's time to limit the likelihood that she would get into trouble, without making her feel overly constrained.

The decision to introduce programmed activities and limit unstructured time is not unwarranted; research has shown a correlation between boredom and deviance.[23] In response to reports of such studies, many parents have gone into overdrive so that their children are never bored. As a result, many teens from middle- and upper-class backgrounds spend most of their days and nights in highly structured activities—sports, clubs, music lessons, and so on. This leaves little downtime for teens to reflect, play, socialize, or relax.

My interview with Myra, a middle-class white fifteen-year-old from Iowa, turned funny and sad when "lack of time" became a verbal tick in response to every question I asked her about connecting with friends. From learning Czech to track, from orchestra to work in a nursery, she told me that her mother organized "98%" of her daily routine. Myra did not like all of these activities, but her mother thought they were important. She was resigned to them. Lack of freedom and control over her schedule was a sore topic for Myra. At one point, she noted with an exasperated tone that weekends were no freer than weekdays: "Usually my mom will have things scheduled for me to do. So I really don't have much choice in what I'm doing Friday nights. . . . I haven't had a free weekend in so long. I cannot even remember the last time I got to choose what I wanted to do over the weekend." Myra noted that her mother meant well, but she was exhausted and felt socially disconnected because she did not have time to connect with friends outside of classes. The activities she participated in were quite formal, leaving little room for casual interactions as she raced from one pursuit to the next. In between, Myra would jump on the computer in the hopes of chatting with a friend. Friendship and sociality—always mediated but still important—filled the interstices of her life.

From wealthy suburbs to small towns, teenagers reported that parental fear, lack of transportation options, and heavily structured lives restricted their ability to meet and hang out with their friends face to face. Even in urban environments, where public transportation presumably affords more freedom, teens talked about how their parents often forbade them from riding subways and buses out of fear. At home, teens grappled with lurking parents. The formal activities teens described were often so highly structured that they allowed little room for casual sociality. And even when parents gave teens some freedom, they found that their friends' mobility was stifled by their parents. While parental restrictions and pressures are often well intended, they obliterate unstructured time and unintentionally position teen sociality as abnormal. This prompts teens to desperately—and, in some cases, sneakily—seek it out. As a result, many teens turn to what they see as the least common denominator: asynchronous social media, texting, and other mediated interactions.

Reclaiming Sociality

Amy, a biracial sixteen-year-old from Seattle, used MySpace to socialize because her mobility was curtailed. Every day, after school she immediately goes home, where she feeds her younger sister, helps her with her homework, and does household chores. Occasionally, her parents allow her to go out on weekends, but when I asked her how often, her friend James responded by saying, "Slim to none." Amy just shrugged in agreement. I asked her what she needed to do for her parents to allow her to go out. She spoke of the need to make sure the house was clean, while James rolled his eyes and said, "Your mom being in a good mood." I asked her how she got permission to come to the interview with me, and she told me that her mom saw it as equivalent to a job because I was offering money for teens' time. Amy told me that she was excited for the opportunity to hang out with her friends at the interview. After we finished, I got the sense that they were intending to tell her parents that the interview ran long just to buy more time.

Amy made it very clear that she didn't prefer hanging out with friends online but felt that technology provided a rare opportunity to connect even when she couldn't leave the house. When I asked her what she'd rather do, she explained, "Just go anywhere. I don't care where, just not home. Somewhere with my friends, just out hanging out." Resigned that this was not feasible, she spent as much time online as possible. As she explained, "My mom doesn't let me out of the house very often, so that's pretty much all I do, is I sit on MySpace and talk to people and text and talk on the phone, 'cause my mom's always got some crazy reason to keep me in the house."

Looking just at her participation on MySpace, an outsider might argue that Amy appears to be addicted to social media. Talking with her, it's clear that she craves time with friends and uses any excuse to go online to do so. She is responding to the structural restrictions that make it difficult for her to achieve an age-old teen goal: get together with friends and hang out. Social media has become a place where teens can hold court. Their desire to connect, gossip, and hang out online makes sense in response to the highly organized and restricted lives that many teens lead.

Social media introduces new opportunities for housebound teens to socialize and people-watch, but it also provides an opportunity to relax. Serious and diligent students like friends Sasha and Bianca, white sixteen-year-olds from Michigan, often emphasized the need for social downtime. Sasha described her daily schedule this way: "I'll study for a couple of hours and then I'll talk to my friends for a couple of hours or whatever, and that just helps refocus my mind and helps me absorb the information more than just constantly studying." Then Bianca chimed in. "My brain has to stop taking in all the information." She needed time to just "relax for a while." Both of these teens were diligent students, and they saw socializing as an important complement to their hard work, a mechanism of rejuvenation.

When I asked what they gained from these online interactions, Bianca defended socializing using adult-oriented language. She highlighted the opportunity to learn "social skills" and clarified by stating, "You learn how to deal with different situations and different people, and just to work with people that you don't like so much. So it just helps you." This language is not how most teens explain their practice, but it is a spot-on assessment. When teens interact with others, they engage in tremendous informal learning, developing a sense of who they are in relation to others while building a holistic understanding of the social world. Teens may clamor to get access to social media simply to hang out, but there they gain access to a rich learning environment.

Being "addicted" to information and people is part of the human condition: it arises from a healthy desire to be aware of surroundings and to connect to society. The more opportunities there are to access information and connect to people, the more people embrace those situations. Whereas the colloquial term *news junkie* refers to people who rabidly consume journalistic coverage, I've never met a parent who worried that their child read the newspaper too often. Parents sometimes tease their children for being "bookworms," but they don't fret about their mental health. But when teens spend hours surfing the web, jumping from website to website, this often prompts concern. Parents lament their own busy schedules and lack of free time but dismiss similar sentiments from their children.

Unfortunately, when teens turn to social media for sociality and information, adults often see something wrong, and they blame the technology for the outcomes. For example, in *The Shallows*, technology critic Nicholas Carr denounces the internet as insidious. He argues that the internet radically reworks our brains, destroying our ability to focus by distracting us with irrelevant information. There is little doubt that teens' brains are being rewired through their mediated interactions. As cognitive scientist Steven Pinker points out, stimuli have *always* reworked, and are continuously reworking, our brains. Challenging Carr, Pinker argues that, "far from making us stupid, these technologies are the only things that will keep us smart."[24] Popular science writer Steven Johnson makes a similar point in *Everything Bad Is Good for You*, pointing out that engaging with the increasingly sophisticated world of media sharpens our brains. The limitation of Carr's argument stems from his assumption that technology alone does cultural work and that resultant outcomes lead to change that is inevitably bad. This logic, rooted in technological determinism, fails to recognize the sociocultural context in which technology is situated.

I have little doubt that socializing online is rewiring teens' brains. Through their engagement with social media, teens are learning to understand a deeply networked and intertwined world. Yet unlike Carr, I do not think that the sky is falling. My views are closer to those of scholar Cathy Davidson, who, in *Now You See It*, argues that children embrace new technologies to learn. This results in changes to learning that often confound adults who relish the environments with which they are familiar and in which they had opportunities to learn. When teens engage with networked media, they're trying to take control of their lives and their relationship to society. In doing so, they begin to understand how people relate to one another and how information flows between people. They learn about the social world, and as Bianca points out, they develop social skills.

What's at stake is not whether teens' brains are changing—they are always changing—but what growing up with mediated sociality means for teens and for society generally. Teenagers may not yet be experts on navigating a world drowning in information and flush with opportunities for social interaction, but there is no reason to believe that they won't develop those skills as they continue to engage with social media. There's also no reason to think that digital celibacy will help them be healthier, happier, and more capable adults.

Coming of Age Without Agency

Around the turn of the twentieth century, at the same time that the conception of addiction was emerging, psychologist G. Stanley Hall embarked on a mission to define adolescence in order to give youth space to come of age without having to take on the full responsibilities of adulthood.[25] He used data about behavioral differences to make an argument about maturation and cognition. Hall argued that children were savages incapable of reasoning and that adolescence marked a developmental stage in which young people began to recognize morality. He believed that it was important to protect youth during this stage and worked with moral reformers to put limitations on child labor, to mandate compulsory education, and to introduce a notion of juvenile justice. His work set in motion a shift that resulted in American society understanding adolescents simultaneously as a vulnerable population that needed protection and as a potentially delinquent population that had not yet matured.

Hall was part of the significant social transformation of the late nineteenth and early twentieth centuries known as the Progressive Era.[26] This period in American history was a source of social activism and political reform affecting a wide array of issues. Alongside emerging concerns about addiction was a rise in interest about the well-being of children that led to the curtailment of child labor and the creation of compulsory high school education.[27] Hall played a central role in helping define what childhood and adolescence should look like, using protectionist rhetoric to insulate children as vulnerable populations that resembled the language being used by political reformers seeking to outlaw alcohol. Although the attitudes and beliefs professed by these moral reformers were not widespread during the Progressive Era, they are now nearly universal in contemporary discourse about childhood.

A century later, the frame of vulnerable children that Hall and his cohort popularized is still pervasive, and child protection has gone far beyond Hall's initial prescriptions. Protecting children from forced labor, providing opportunities for education, and treating youth differently in criminal justice are all beneficial mainstays from Hall's endeavors, but contemporary youth also face state-imposed curfews, experience limitations on where they can gather, and must get parental approval before they engage in a host of activities. By imagining teens as balls of uncontrollable hormones, society has systematically taken agency away from youth over the past century.[28] This hampers their maturation, while the resultant restrictions prompt youth to either submit to or resist adult authority.

Although child protective services is another productive output of this movement, the current state of foster care and mental health infrastructure is so fractured that it often results in children being doubly oppressed. Most adults are well meaning and supportive, but the same system that empowers parents also forces some youth to face abuse. Meanwhile, many teenagers see education no longer as an opportunity but as a requirement; rather than having the space to mature, teens must inhabit a highly structured environment that is supposedly for their own good. For many teens, learning is not relished but despised, even as they engage in accidental learning whenever they interact with others.

As the outcome of Hall's movement unfolded over the twentieth century, the period between childhood and adulthood widened, and twenty-first-century American youth spend an extended period in a liminal stage with restricted opportunities and rights. In buying into adolescence, what we've created is a pressure cooker. Teens are desperate to achieve the full rights of adulthood, even if they don't understand the responsibilities that this may entail. They are stuck in a system in which adults restrict, protect, and pressure them to achieve adult-defined measures of success. It's a testament to the strength of teens that so many have developed strong coping mechanisms to manage the awkwardness of this liminal stage. Social media—far from being the seductive Trojan horse—is a release valve, allowing youth to reclaim meaningful sociality as a tool for managing the pressures and limitations around them.

As they make their way toward adulthood, teens need to learn how to engage in crucial aspects of maturation: self-presentation, managing social relationships, and developing an understanding of the world around them. The structured and restrictive conditions that comprise the lives of many teens provides little room for them to explore these issues, but social media gives them a platform and a space where they can make up for what's lost.

Grappling with Restrictions

As teens seek out new spaces where they have agency, adults invent new blockades to restrict youth power. The rhetoric of addiction is one example, a cultural device used to undermine teens' efforts to reclaim a space. Restrictive adults act on their anxieties as well as their desire to protect youth, but in doing so, they perpetuate myths that produce the fears that prompt adults to place restrictions on teens in the first place. But this cycle doesn't just undermine teens' freedoms; it also pulls at the fabric of society more generally.

After reading a news article about my work, Mike, a father in Illinois, emailed me to explain that he is strict with his children because of what he perceives to be a decline in societal values.

> The reason my children do not hang out as I used to as a teen is not due to predators necessarily, but due to other teens who have been raised on MTV, lack of parental guidance, and are treated as adults by their parents. . . . I believe MySpace further sends the entire dynamic down the rabbit hole. If parents took more responsibility for instilling values, morals and standards in their children (versus relying on the educational system, television, and the media), I feel that we could reclaim some of this lost teen freedom for our children.

Mike's email highlights a wide array of intertwined issues. He blames technology, institutions, and individuals. Rather than focusing on how he can help his children navigate this ecosystem, he blames other families and implies that the best solution for his children is social isolation.

The concern that we've become disconnected as a society has become a common trope over the past two decades, and both scholars and the media have blamed everything from changes in food acquisition to neighborly isolation.[29] Whatever the cause, fear and distrust of others is palpable and pervasive. Driving around the United States, I was shocked by the skepticism many parents held for other parents. For example, Anindita—a seventeen-year-old of Indian and Pakistani descent living in Los Angeles—told me that she wasn't allowed to spend the night at friends' places because her dad was concerned that other fathers or brothers might get drunk and take advantage of her. Although I initially thought that her experience was unique, I was surprised to find other parents who forbade their children from participating in sleepovers, too.

When parents distrust others or the values of families around them, they often respond by trying to isolate their children. In a different community in Los Angeles, I met a fifteen-year-old boy named Mic whose Egyptian parents didn't want him to socialize with American teens, whom they perceived as upholding unhealthy values learned from American parents. As a result, he was forbidden from making friends at school, talking on the phone, and using social media; he was allowed to socialize only with cousins and trusted friends of the family when his family went to the mosque. To manage this, his father dropped him off at school and made him wait in the car until the bell rang; he picked him up again for lunch and then immediately after school. These restrictions weighed on Mic, and he was regularly seeking out opportunities to connect with others in interstitial times at school, often trying to sneak access to the internet between classes to have some form of social outlet.

Mic's father sent him to school because he believed that this was the only way for Mic to get an education. Unfortunately, Mic's father failed to recognize that his restrictions hindered his son's ability to succeed owing to the heavy emphasis that American educational systems place on collaboration, both in and out of the classroom. As the school began demanding extracurricular coordination through information technologies, Mic floundered, which only resulted in more restrictions at home. Mic's father failed to realize that American educational systems take sociality for granted. Rather than seeing socializing as a distraction from learning, schools are increasingly integrating learning with social experiences to prepare youth for collaborative, social work environments.

Although many parents have historically worked to minimize their children's exposure to diverse cultural mores, teens' use of social media often subverts the goals sought by moving to gated communities or limiting exposure to broadcast media. By exploring broad networks of people and diverse types of content, teens can easily get access to values and ideas that differ from what their parents try to instill. This is alluring to curious teens and terrifying to protective parents. As with earlier media genres that parents distrusted, many parents have chosen to demonize technologies that allow youth to escape their control. The rhetoric of addiction positions children as vulnerable to the seductiveness of technology, which in turn provides a concrete justification for restricting access and isolating children.

Most youth aren't turning to social media because they can't resist the lure of technology. They're responding to a social world in which adults watch and curtail their practices and activities, justifying their protectionism as being necessary for safety. Social media has become an outlet for many youth, an opportunity to reclaim some sense of agency and have some semblance of social power. It has provided a window into society and an outlet for hanging out that these teens didn't even know they had lost. But teen sociality is fraught and many adults are uncomfortable with teens having access to unstructured time and unmanaged relationships.

The activities at the core of teens' engagement with social media look quite similar to those that took place in shared settings in previous generations—at sock hops, discos, and football game stands. Teens hang out, gossip, flirt, people watch, joke around, and jockey for status. These dynamics are at the heart of teen life, and because they play out in a mediated world, teens relish any opportunity to log in and engage with their peers and the teen-oriented social world that unfolds through networked publics. But this is not comforting to those adults who want their children to spend less time socializing with peers and more time engaging in adult-approved activities.

Teens' engagement with social media—and the hanging out it often entails—can take up a great deal of time. To many adults, these activities can look obsessive and worthless. Media narratives often propagate the notion that engagement with social media is destructive, even as educational environments increasingly assume that teens are networked. Many adults put pressure on teens to devote more time toward adult-prioritized practices and less time socializing, failing to recognize the important types of learning that take place when teens do connect. When teens orient themselves away from adults and toward their peers, parents often grow anxious and worried about their children's future. The answer to the disconnect between parent goals and teen desires is not rhetoric that pathologizes teen practices, nor is it panicked restrictions on teen sociality. Rather, adults must recognize what teens are trying to achieve and work with them to find balance and to help them think about what they are encountering.

4 danger
are sexual predators lurking everywhere?

Fred and Aaron, white fifteen-year-old friends living in suburban Texas, are avid gamers. When we first met in 2007, their mothers were present. I asked about their participation on social network sites, and they explained that they didn't use those sites but loved sites like Runescape, a fantasy game with customizable avatars. Their mothers nodded, acknowledging their familiarity with Runescape before interrupting their children's narrative to express how unsafe social network sites were. Something about Fred and Aaron's gritted nod in response left me wondering how these teens really felt about MySpace and Facebook—sites that were all the rage with their peer group at the time. Later, almost immediately after I sat with the boys alone to talk with them in-depth, they offered a different story.

Aaron explained that he was active on MySpace but that his mother didn't know. Since many of his friends were using Facebook, he would have liked to create an account there, too, but his mother had an account on Facebook for work and he feared she would accidentally stumble onto his profile. Out of deference to his mother, Fred had yet to create an account on either site, but he was struggling to decide whether to keep abiding by his mother's restrictions going forward. Fred told me that his parents forbade him from Facebook and MySpace after seeing "all the stuff on the news." He said that his parents were afraid that "if I get on it, I'll be assaulted." Aaron chimed in to sarcastically remark, "He'll meet in real life with a lonely forty-year-old man." They both laughed at this idea.

Neither Fred nor Aaron believed that joining MySpace would make them vulnerable to sexual predators, but they were still concerned about upsetting their mothers. Both felt that their mothers' fears were ill founded, but they also acknowledged that this fear was coming from a genuine place of concern. Although their demeanor was lighthearted, their discussion of their mothers' fears was solemn: they worried that their mothers worried.

Although Aaron had violated his mother's restriction by joining MySpace, he was conscientious about his profile there. His profile was private and filled with fake information and a non-identifiable photo, in part to minimize his mother's concerns if she were to find out about the account and in part to minimize the likelihood of her finding out at all. In explaining his actions, Aaron spoke of protecting his mom just as she had told me about her desire to protect him. He wanted to save his mother from fretting about him. This dynamic—children worrying about mothers and mothers worrying about children—was something I saw often.

Like their parents, Aaron and Fred's understanding of MySpace was shaped by the concern that unfolded over sexual predators in the mid-2000s. They understood where their mothers' anxieties came from, even if they found the explanation illogical. Starting in 2005, news media across the United States began to suggest that MySpace was an unsafe place for youth, a place where sexual predators—understood to be older men with malicious intentions—sought out vulnerable children.[1] Although this was not the first time that the issue of online sexual predators emerged in the media, previous discussions had taken place before the internet had become mainstream among teens and before social media had become a media phenomenon.[2] Parents were warned to keep their kids away from MySpace completely, lest they become someone's prey.

This message of danger was heard loud and clear. The teens I interviewed had all heard terrible stories of teenagers being harmed by older male sexual predators they met on MySpace. In particular, girls believed these stories and feared the possibility of being raped, stalked, kidnapped, or assaulted by strangers as a result of their participation online. Their fears were rooted not in personal experience but in media coverage magnified by parental concerns. Teens often referred to the Dateline NBC TV show *To Catch a Predator* as proof that evil men are lurking behind every keyboard, ready to pounce on them. From news stories to school assemblies, teens were surrounded by messages about the dangers of predation. Although some teens rejected such messages as unfounded, others internalized them. Yet all were aware of the issue and were grappling with their feelings regarding the risks of social media.

From the advent of social media, it has been impossible to talk about teens' engagement without addressing the topic of online safety and sexual predators. More than any other issue presented in this book, the topic of online safety generally—and sexual predators specifically— has played a significant role in configuring teens' relation to mediated communication, adults' attitudes toward teens' participation, and policy discussions about social media regulation. Online safety is also a particularly complicated issue, in part because a culture of fear is omnipresent in American society, and no parent wants to take risks when it comes to their children's safety.[3] Statistics showing the improbability of harm fail to reassure those who are concerned. Even when highly publicized stories turn out to be fabrications, parents still imagine that somewhere, somehow, their child might fall victim to a nightmarish fate. They are afraid because terrible things *do* happen to children. And although those violations most commonly take place in known environments—home, school, place of worship, and so on— the internet introduces an unknown space that is harder to comprehend. Nothing feeds fear more than uncertainty.

The Foundation of Our Fears

Since the mid-1990s, alongside utopian rhetoric about the opportunities that the internet would enable, journalists have written salacious stories reviling online communities as sinister worlds where naive teens fall prey to assorted malevolent forces.[4] Some adults have also vilified teens for using the internet to indulge their darkest and wildest impulses—notably, their sexual desires—typically below the radar of parental supervision.[5] Those who portray the internet as a dangerous place for teenagers to inhabit seem to be motivated by several anxieties, but chief among them is a long-standing fear about teens' access to public places.

Examining attitudes toward public spaces in the 1980s, geographer Gill Valentine documents how parental concerns about childhood safety—often discussed through the lens of "stranger danger"—have resulted in children being restricted from public spaces.[6] Public parks and malls were at the center of parental anxieties because they were seen as sites where teens could encounter harmful strangers. Not all of the focus was on dangerous older men; the visible presence of youth gangs was also a concern for many parents. Although unease about delinquents date back decades, 1980s and 1990s parents were especially fearful that manipulative peers would conscript vulnerable youth into gangs.

Beyond broader concerns about childhood safety, fears about sex and sexuality have consistently dominated public debate, with topics like pornography, teenage pregnancy, and sexual predation regularly provoking public angst. Parks and other public spaces are consistently demonized as spaces where unseemly sexual conduct takes place after dark. News media magnifies fears about pedophiles and child rapists. Protecting children from public places—and protecting society from teenagers roaming the streets—has become a cultural imperative. As always happens whenever adults obsess over child safety, restrictions emerge and fearful rhetoric abounds.

As moral panics about child safety take hold, politicians feel that they should take action—or at least capitalize on the appearance of doing so. They regularly campaign over safety issues and implement or expand laws targeted at curtailing the freedoms of minors. In the 1980s and 1990s, this included curfew laws, anti-loitering laws, and truancy laws. To expunge teens from public places, cities and towns limited where, when, and for how long teens could gather or hang out in public places. Many believed that curfew laws would combat crime; a 1997 survey of US mayors found that 88 percent believed that youth curfews reduced crime.[7] It did not. As researchers began to examine the effects of these laws, they found that there was no correlation between curfews and youth crime. After analyzing the data, sociologist Michael Males concluded that authority figures use curfews more as a symbol of social control than an actual crime deterrent.[8] In the late 1990s, when asked to justify teen curfew laws in light of data suggesting that they are ineffective, New Orleans mayor Marc Morial responded on the radio by saying, "It keeps teenagers off the streets. They need it, there's too many teenagers hanging around the streets."[9] Despite no effect on reducing crime, cities continued to implement curfews, and aside from a few laws that have been declared unconstitutional, most laws restricting the mobility of minors remain in force.

The same fears that shaped children's engagement with parks and other gathering places in the latter half of the twentieth century are now configuring networked publics created through social media. Adults worry that youth may be coerced into unseemly practices or connect with adults who will do them harm. For decades, adults have worked to limit teen access to and mobility within public spaces. Simultaneously, teens have worked to circumvent adult authority in order to have freedom and mobility. The internet limits adult control precisely because it makes it harder for parents to isolate youth from material that they deem unacceptable and from people whose values may differ from theirs or who are unfamiliar in other ways. Discomfort with teen sexuality further fuels this general anxiety about teens' access to public spaces. American society despises any situation that requires addressing teen sexuality, let alone platforms that provide a conduit for teens to explore their desires. At a more acute level, fears are especially intense whenever the possibility arises that strangers might exploit teens sexually.

Excluding teens from public places may give parents or politicians a sense of control, but it systematically disenfranchises youth from public life. Though authorities may see scaring teens as a valiant effort to protect vulnerable youth from danger, this approach can have significant consequences. As Valentine argues, "By reproducing a misleading message about the geography of danger, stranger-danger educational campaigns contribute towards producing public space as 'naturally' or 'normally' an adult space where children are at risk from 'deviant' others."[10] As a result, adult society isolates teens, limiting their opportunities to learn how to engage productively with public life.

Each new cultural shift, media development, or emergent technology reinvigorates anxieties about youth safety. When fears escalate out of control, they produce what sociologist Stanley Cohen calls "moral panics" as adults worry about the moral degradation that will be brought on by the shifting social force.[11] A moral panic takes hold when the public comes to believe that a cultural artifact, practice, or population threatens the social order. Moral panics that surround youth typically center on issues of sexuality, delinquency, and reduced competency. New genres of media—and the content that's shared through them— often trigger such anxieties. Eighteenth-century society saw novels as addictive and therefore damaging to young women's potential for finding a husband.[12] Introduced in the 1930s, comic books were seen not only as serving no educational purpose but as encouraging young people to get absorbed in fantasy worlds and to commit acts of violence. In the mid-1950s Elvis Presley's vulgar, gyrating hips prompted great concern that broadcasting him on TV would corrupt teens.[13] These are but a few of the unsubstantiated moral panics surrounding youth's engagement with earlier forms of popular media.[14]

Unsurprisingly, as the internet started gaining traction among youth, the same fears and anxieties that surrounded other publics and media genres reemerged in relation to networked publics and social media.[15] Girls' online social practices, in particular, are often the target of tremendous anxiety.[16] When MySpace launched and grew popular among teenagers—notably, teen girls—a widespread moral panic unfolded.[17] Many of the teens I met referenced *To Catch a Predator*, which fueled the media frenzy. In this television series, which ran from 2004 to 2007, adults would impersonate young teenagers in online chatrooms in order to find men interested in talking with underage minors. After contact was initiated, the show's team would lure the men into meeting the "teen" in person only to be confronted by the TV show's host. The show was controversial, leading to significant legal and ethical questions as well as raising issues about the relevance of such stings on teen behavior.[18]

As the media was amplifying public concern, Congress introduced the Deleting Online Predators Act to restrict minors from interacting with strangers online; this bill would have forbidden young people from participating in online comment threads or posting content to public forums on computers paid for by government money, including those at schools and in libraries.[19] Even though the data suggested that dynamics surrounding sexual crimes against children did not remotely resemble what was depicted on *To Catch a Predator*, the US attorneys general began looking for technical interventions to stop the kinds of sexual predation depicted by the show.[20] Legislators never pursued these flawed approaches, yet their mere proposals reveal how powerful cultural furors over youth safety can be.

Moral panics and the responses to them reconfigure the lives of youth in restrictive ways, more than any piece of legislation could possibly achieve. Legal scholar Larry Lessig argues that four forces regulate social systems: market, law, social norms, and technology or architecture.[21] Fear is often used in service of these forces. Companies sell fear to entice parents to buy products that will help them protect their children. Policymakers respond to fear by regulating children's access to public spaces, even when doing so accomplishes little. The media broadcasts fears, creating and reinforcing fearful social norms. And technologies are built to assuage or reproduce parents' fears. Given the cultural work done in the name of fear, it's astounding that young people have as much freedom as they do.

Moral panics surrounding youth tend to reveal teens' conflicted position within American society. Authority figures simultaneously view teens as nuisances who must be managed and innocent children who must be protected. Teens are both public menaces and vulnerable targets. Society is afraid of them and for them. The tension between these two views shapes adults' relationship with teens and our societal beliefs about what it is that teenagers do. This schism leads to power struggles between teens and adults and shapes teens' activities and opportunities. Parental fear—and teens' response to it—complicates the lives of teens as they're coming of age.

Incorporating Fear into Everyday Life

On a gorgeous spring Saturday in 2007, I drove around a predominantly white upper-middle-class suburb in the middle of Texas trying to find where teenagers might hang out. It was a newly planned community and there were no public parks or other obvious gathering spots. The school's parking lot was empty; no one gathered at the local church; a highway blocked any foot traffic to nearby shops. As I wove in and out of meticulously designed subdivisions, I started to wonder whether the town was deserted. There were plenty of cars in the driveways and many of the automatic sprinklers were busy watering the lawns, but there were very few people. After about a half an hour of driving and scouting, I had seen one father playing in a driveway with two small children and another man walking a dog. I made a mental note to ask the teens I was interviewing about when and where they gathered and met new people.

When I arrived at Sabrina's house at the edge of a picture-perfect cul-de-sac in this idyllic community, I casually remarked how odd it was that no one was outside. She looked at me strangely and asked me where they would go. I knew that, at fourteen, she didn't have a driver's license, so I asked her if she ever biked around the neighborhood. She told me that doing so was futile because all her friends lived at least ten miles away. Because of how the community assigned students to schools, she said, she knew no one who lived in walking or biking distance. She had once walked home from school just to see if she could, but it had taken her over two hours so she didn't try it again. She told me that there was a shopping mall in walking distance but that it required crossing a major road, which was scary.

This prompted a conversation about the dangers of walking around town; she told me that safety was a big topic in her house. I wanted to understand what this meant in her family, given that her parents were both active in the military. I had to imagine that in their various tours of duty, they had been exposed to far riskier environments than I could imagine this pristine suburb to be. What I learned was that their experiences at war did not make them feel any safer at home. When I asked about the source of her parents' concern, Sabrina told me that they were news junkies and were afraid about what might happen to her based on the stories they'd heard on TV. Both Sabrina and her parents felt that it was better to be safe than sorry. From Sabrina's perspective, staying inside was much safer than walking around outside, and therefore, there was no point in trying to go out.

As our conversation continued, it became clear that Sabrina believed that the internet posed even greater risks than her suburban neighborhood. While her online safety concerns were far greater than those of most of her peers, they played a significant role in shaping her mediated interactions. She liked to read messages in online communities, but she did not post messages or talk to anyone in online forums because "any person could be a forty-year-old man waiting to come and rape me or something. I'm really meticulous about that, because I've heard basically my whole life, don't talk to people you don't know online, 'cause they'll come kill you." Sabrina has never personally known any victims of such crimes, but she told me that she had seen episodes of *Law and Order* in which terrible things happened to people who talked to strangers online. For a long time, she was afraid to get on MySpace—the social network site popular with her friends at the time—because she thought stalkers might find her. Her friends convinced her to join by pointing out that she could protect herself through privacy settings. Still, she worried that someone might stalk her, so she was very reticent. "It's still like a possibility," she said, "because I mean anyone can just click on your profile and find out kind of what's going on." Sabrina feared that if she gave any indication of where she lived or where she went to school, some evil man might track her down and abduct her. As she explained her concerns, I could see genuine fear in her eyes.

Pervasive talk of "stranger danger" shaped Sabrina's interactions with social media. Even though she was cautious and limited her online activities, she was terrified that something would go wrong. In telling me about all of the risks that she faced online, she cited stories she'd heard, referring to incidents that had received widespread news attention. Although many teens rolled their eyes when I raised the issue of online safety, these issues were very present and real for Sabrina.[22]

While Sabrina was more reluctant to engage in social media than most teens that I interviewed, the fears she expressed reflect concerns shared by many adults. When my colleagues and I surveyed a national sample of parents, 93 percent of them were concerned that their child might meet a stranger online who would hurt them even though only 1 percent of them indicated that any of their children had ever met a stranger who had been hurtful.[23] Surprisingly to us, parents were no more afraid for their daughters than their sons. Also in the survey, before there was any reference to specific online dangers, parents consistently reported "sexual predators," "child molesters," "pedophiles," and "sex offenders" as their primary concern in an open-ended question about their biggest worries about their children's online participation. For example, one parent explained, "My Biggest fear is that [my child] would become the 'target' of some online predator that intends to either: 1) lure my child away to meet them ALONE! Or 2) Convince my child to reveal personal information that could jeopardize his safety and that of my family while in our home." Via survey and in person, I heard variations of this fear repeated by parent after parent throughout the country.

Although many teens think that parental fears are unwarranted, a sizable number—like Sabrina—share their parents' anxiety about sexual predators and worry for their own safety and for the safety of their siblings. When I asked Sabrina how common she thought online sexual predators were, she referred to *To Catch a Predator* as evidence of their pervasiveness. Although she had never known anyone who had been a victim of an online stalker or rapist, she was determined to be vigilant, both for herself and for her peers.

Parental fear regarding sexual predators is understandable. No parent wants to imagine her or his child being harmed, and the potential cost of such a violation is unfathomable, regardless of how statistically improbable such an event might be. Combine this with the media's magnification of the cultural mythos of the online sexual predator and it's no wonder that countless parents become hyperprotective without considering the costs of their actions.[24] But this distorted fear obscures the very real and costly risks that some youth do face. Untangling these issues requires stepping back and rethinking what we think we know regarding sexual predation.

The Online Sexual Predator Myth

Abduction, molestation, and rape reasonably top the charts of parental fears. From the Catholic Church predatory priest scandals to the 1993 Polly Klaas murder, society struggles to comprehend how adults can harm children.[25] Each new horrific story raises the blood pressure of parents and motivates policymakers to try and enact new restrictions that might prevent future abuse.[26] The approach that politicians take is rarely applied evenly. Although lawmakers are happy to propose interventions that limit youth's rights to access online spaces, they have not proposed laws to outlaw children's access to religious institutions, schools, or homes, even though these are statistically more common sites of victimization.

A central challenge in addressing the sexual victimization of children is that the public is not comfortable facing the harrowing reality that strangers are unlikely perpetrators. Most acts of sexual violence against children occur in their own homes by people that those children trust.[27] Sexual predation did not begin with the internet, nor does it appear as though the internet has created a predatory epidemic.[28]

Internet-initiated sexual assaults are rare. The overall number of sex crimes against minors has been steadily declining since 1992, which also suggests that the internet is not creating a new plague.[29] At the same time, fear-based advertising campaigns continue to propagate the belief that the internet has introduced a new flood of predators into the living rooms of families across the United States.

Consider a widely distributed poster produced by the Ad Council that ran from 2004 to 2007, which reads, "To the list of places you might find sexual predators add this one." These words appear above a grid of twelve images, eleven of which are public places like parks and streets; the twelfth, the image behind the words "this one," is a child's bedroom with a computer monitor. The message is clear: predators are lurking behind the computer and will enter your home through it. The television version of this campaign is even more nerve-racking. Alongside this message is a statistic: one in five children is sexually solicited online.

This campaign, along with the many salacious news stories designed to use fear to convince the public about the imminent threat of sexual predation, is extraordinarily misleading. First, the picture of the bedroom with a computer monitor on its desk is intended to suggest that the computer is what puts children at risk. Many children are actually victimized in their bedrooms, but not because of the computer.[30] Second, the statistic, commonly used by the National Center for Missing and Exploited Children and other safety groups, isn't what it might seem. It is a misappropriation of scholarly research intended to trigger anxiety by capitalizing on the public's assumption that sexual solicitations occur when sketchy older guys solicit prepubescent children.

The one-in-five statistic comes from a 2000 report by the Crimes Against Children Research Center (CCRC), a highly respected institution dedicated to understanding youth victimization.[31] In its study, CCRC surveyed youth to understand all internet-initiated sexual contact, including that which minors desired. It asked youth about "sexual solicitation," which was defined as including everything from flirtation to sexual harassment. The survey also asked youth about the age of the initiator. The study found that only 4 percent of solicitations came from people known to be over twenty-five, whereas 76 percent came from other minors and the rest came from adults aged eighteen to twenty-four. In 75 percent of the incidents reported, youth indicated that they were not upset or afraid as a result of the solicitation. Furthermore, in spite of parents' worries about the potential of offline harm, 69 percent of solicitations involved no attempt at offline contact. In other words, although any sexual solicitation that a youth receives might be problematic, this statistic does not signal inherently dangerous encounters.

With the rise of social media, many safety advocates presumed that sexual solicitations would spike. Repeating their study in 2006 with an identical definition to allow for comparisons, CCRC found that one in seven minors had been sexually solicited online, a 5 percent decline from 2000.[32] Other scholars also found that youth were far more likely to be problematically solicited in online environments that were previously popular but were no longer considered cool.[33] In other words, the teens who were getting into trouble were not those who were hanging out with friends in the online venues most popular with their peers but those who were socializing with strangers elsewhere online. During the years in which MySpace was the most popular online environment, the teens who were engaging in risky encounters online were chatting in obscure chatrooms filled with people looking for trouble.

Although sexual solicitation as it is colloquially understood is rare, it's important to understand the smaller number of incidents in which youth are violated or harassed, coerced or manipulated. These incidents are unacceptable, and it is important to take steps to prevent any child from ever being victimized. But doing so requires understanding the youth most at risk. In examining cases in which unwanted sexual solicitations have occurred, it's clear that these cases are not random. Teens who are especially at risk are often engaged in a host of risky sexual encounters online. There's a strong correlation between risky online practices and psychosocial problems, family issues, drug and alcohol abuse, and trouble in school. In other words, teens who are struggling in everyday life also engage in problematic encounters online. Rather than putting all youth at risk, social media creates a new site where risky behaviors are made visible and troubled youth engage in new types of problematic activity.[34]

Sexual solicitations are disturbing, but most parents are more concerned about the potential for their child to be physically sexually abused. Typically, the vision that parents conjure involves an innocent girl being lured into conversation by an older man who deceives her about his age and then psychologically manipulates her to trust him and distrust others. The discussion of sexual predation often includes the notions of psychological manipulation (also known as "grooming") and deception, abduction and rape. But by examining police records and interviewing youth, CCRC found that when adults employ the internet in order to commit a sex crime involving a minor, it rarely takes that form.

Not all cases involving the internet involved a stranger. Looking specifically at the small number of arrests for internet-facilitated sexual crimes, CCRC found that approximately one in five (18 percent) involved victims' family members or offline acquaintances such as family friends or neighbors.[35] Even in cases in which the perpetrator was not someone that the victim initially knew, the perpetrator rarely deceived the teen. More often than not, the abused teens were aware of the offender's age when they chatted online. Surprisingly, many teens were more deceptive about their age, intentionally portraying themselves as older. In criminal cases that prompted an arrest, the teens involved were typically in high school and the men they were encountering were most commonly in their twenties or early thirties. Their online conversations were sexual in nature, and the teens knew that sex was in the cards before meeting the offender in person. These abused teens believed that they were in love and often had sex with the offender on multiple occasions. As CCRC explained, these encounters often took the legal form of statutory rape.

Statutory rape is a criminal offense to prevent adults from using their status, experience, and authority to manipulate youth into engaging in sexual acts. At the same time, there is a significant difference between an abduction rape scenario and a statutory rape scenario. In the latter, youth often believe that they should have the right to consent to such an encounter, even if the law and their parents disagree.[36] This difference matters because it affects what kinds of interventions are needed. What motivates teens to engage in these power-laden sexual encounters is often a desire for attention and validation in light of problems at home, mental health issues, or a history of abuse. Although the dynamics surrounding individual cases are often complex—and there are both legal and social issues at play—the teenagers who are victimized are at risk in different ways than is typically imagined by mainstream media. Helping combat this form of sexual exploitation requires a different model than the one presented by *To Catch a Predator*.

In order to intervene successfully, it is essential to understand the dynamics that surround the sexual victimization of children. What's needed to combat grooming, deception, and abduction rape is very different than what's needed to address the underlying issues that motivate a young person to engage in risky sexual encounters or to deliberately put themselves in vulnerable situations. Language that positions youth as passive victims diverts the public's attention from the marginalized youth who are the most common victims of sexual abuse. By focusing media attention on potential sex crimes committed by evil, older men, the mythical construction of the online sexual predator can obscure the unhealthy sexual encounters that youth are more likely to experience.

Unhealthy Sexual Encounters

In 2011, *Rolling Stone* published an exposé of a young woman named Kirsten "Kiki" Ostrenga that depicted what can happen when teen sexuality, attention, social media, and mental health issues crash headlong into one another.[37] After her family moved from Illinois to

Florida, Kirsten struggled to make friends. When classmates started teasing her for being an outsider, she stopped trying to fit in, preferring to wear what she described as "scene queen" clothing. In order to find a community of like-minded souls, she turned to the internet, where she developed a digital persona whom she called Kiki Kannibal. Online, she sold jewelry and shared modeling photos, collected followers and posted fashion advice.

When she was thirteen, Kiki met a young man by the name of Danny Cespedes on MySpace. Kiki was desperate for attention and validation when she met Danny, a teen boy who told her that he was seventeen even though he had recently turned eighteen. Kiki and Danny chatted online for a while. As Kiki's fourteenth birthday arrived, Danny asked her mom for permission to meet Kiki. They met at a local mall on her birthday, with Kiki's mom in attendance. Kiki's mom was impressed by Danny's politeness and supported the relationship. The two started dating, and Danny regularly spent hours at Kiki's house.

One night, Danny was acting drunk, so Kiki's parents allowed him to spend the night at their house. After everyone had gone to bed, he forced himself onto Kiki. Although she was uncomfortable with the encounter, their relationship continued. As time went on, Danny started acting more and more bizarre. Kiki's parents began to worry, and eventually, Kiki tried to break up with Danny. He attempted suicide. Their relationship became rocky, and, through a series of conversations online, Kiki learned that Danny had dated a series of girls aged thirteen to fifteen, many of whom had had similar forced sexual encounters with him. She eventually told her parents what happened, and they called the police. After collecting extensive evidence, the police attempted to arrest Danny on seven felony counts of statutory rape. When they cornered him, he threw himself over a nearby railing. He died on impact. As *Rolling Stone* reported, "Kiki's rapist and first love was dead."

The article clearly portrays Danny Cespedes as a disturbed individual, but the article also highlights how Kiki believed that she was madly in love with the boy who raped her. This dynamic, far from being rare, is often the reality in cases of statutory rape. By all accounts, Danny manipulated and hurt a series of young girls, preying on their vulnerability and then abusing them. But Danny was also the product of abuse. He came from a chaotic household in which prison, violence, and threats were common threads. His father had been deported after being convicted of a sexual crime against a minor. Kiki's parents had felt bad for Danny, not realizing that he was continuing the cycle of abuse.

The internet played multiple roles in this story. It was through the internet that Kiki found Danny, but it was also through the internet that the other girls found each other and learned that they were not alone. All the girls that Danny abused had willingly connected with him online and had believed themselves to be in love. Because of their feelings toward Danny, they suppressed their feelings about his sexual violations until they learned that it was a pattern.

Although Danny sexually assaulted Kiki when he forced himself on her, the police chose to address this as statutory rape, because the age difference alone meant that he was violating the law, making it much easier to prove. For many teens, statutory rape laws can be complicated and controversial. Although they are designed to protect young people from predatory acts—such as Danny's—age differences alone do not necessarily imply abuse.

In 2009, I interviewed a black fifteen-year-old named Sydnia who lived in Nashville. Unlike many of her peers, she used MySpace to meet new people, notably other lesbians. One day, while downtown, she approached a woman whom she recognized from MySpace. They had been talking and flirting online but had never met, nor had Sydnia intended to meet her. During that chance encounter, Sydnia got the woman's number and they started texting. Over time, they became lovers, and when I met Sydnia the two had been dating for over a month. Although Sydnia obscured her girlfriend's age when discussing their relationship with me, she made a passing reference to the fact that her girlfriend could go to bars even though she could not, making her girlfriend at least twenty-one. As we talked about their relationship, I learned that Sydnia had introduced her girlfriend to her mother and that her mother approved, enough even to tease her about the relationship; teasing was a central component of their mother-daughter bond. Yet Sydnia clearly recognized that her relationship was taboo. When I asked about her girlfriend's age, she balked and indicated that my question was off-limits. Sydnia was aware that the age difference mattered, if not to her, then at least to an outsider. At a different point in our conversation, we talked about online safety, and Sydnia told me that she had heard about online sexual predators but had never known anyone who was attacked by them. I didn't have the heart to tell Sydnia that, taken from another perspective, her girl-friend could be viewed as an online predator.

Unlike Kiki and Sydnia, most of the teens I interviewed met their older boyfriends or girlfriends through friends, family, religious activities, or in other face-to-face encounters. Although parents in more privileged communities broadly condemned teens' relationships with older individuals, attitudes regarding age and teen sexuality are not universal. In many lower-income and immigrant communities I visited, it was widely acceptable for a teen girl to date an older man. Some of the parents that I met even encouraged such relationships, indicating that an older man would be more mature and responsible than a teenage boy and that he might take care of her. Even though those in the more privileged communities I visited often ridiculed such a perspective, I couldn't help but find it ironic that the most popular young adult fiction book in those same communities at that time was *Twilight*, a love story focused on a teen girl and a 104-year-old vampire in which their age difference is a central plot point.

In some communities, an age difference is seen as inherently suspicious, but it does not always result in harmful relationships. Nor are same-age relationships inherently healthy. No parent wants his or her child to be exploited or abused, but age is not necessarily a defining factor in problematic relationships. Some teenagers develop unhealthy relationships with older people, but some also develop deeply problematic if not abusive relationships with their peers. Unfortunately, teen dating violence is not uncommon, and it typically involves teens in relationships with same-age peers.[38]

Age differences may be taboo, but teens' interest in adults is not new. Furthermore, the taboo of a marked age difference often fuels teens' interest in older people.[39] Fiction often romanticizes star-crossed lovers of different ages, and countless vampire tales recount older men being enamored of teen girls. Teens have long fantasized about older celebrities, and even teachers and countless teen films reproduce these frames. Teens have also consistently engaged in risky activities in an effort to get attention and validation from older people. My age cohort trafficked in fake college IDs so that we could attend local frat parties. Getting attention from older people can often be a source of status for teens. None of this is to say that there aren't unhealthy relationships between people of different ages, but focusing on age can obscure as much as it reveals.

A Parent's Worst Nightmare

The internet may make it easier for adults and teens to engage in inappropriate conversations, but a conversation with a stranger does not inherently put youth at risk. For all the ways that the internet allows people to connect, there is still a physical gap between interlocutors. Unlike teens' encounters with predatory adults in face-to-face settings, it is not easy for an online conversation to move offline without a teen's knowledge. Abduction by strangers is rare: when children are abducted, it is usually by a noncustodial parent. Yet the prospect of abduction by a stranger sends chills down the spine of any parent and sends communities into overdrive to get the word out because the first twenty-four hours matter tremendously in recovering a missing child. When a child disappears, people drum up media attention in the hopes of finding the child before anything worse happens. The American public often hears about abductions in this crucial window of time, but not all reported cases turn out to be what they may at first seem.

In February 2006, thirteen-year-old Alexandra Nicole Dimarco and fifteen-year-old Alexis Anne Beyer disappeared in the middle of the night from the same condominium complex in Los Angeles. All signs seemed to point to abduction: the girls left behind their wallets and prescription medication, and they had not packed anything of sentimental value. The girls' parents contacted the media, informing a journalist that the girls had been talking with strangers on MySpace. A headline in a Los Angeles paper read "Mothers Think Girls Were Lured Away by MySpace.com Suitors."[40] Media coverage was swift, and the girls' pictures appeared on local television and across the town.

Meanwhile, the police began their investigation in the hopes of finding the girls as quickly as possible. Given the parents' reports of trouble involving MySpace, the police contacted the company. The company began working with local law enforcement to help. Although the parents had publicly pegged MySpace as the conduit, both girls had stopped logging onto the social network site a week before they disappeared. Alexis's mother told the media that she had banned her daughter from using the site after Alexis had allegedly met men on MySpace who had been calling the house looking for her before she disappeared.

As more information emerged, the initial portrait of abducted friends grew murky. In talking with MySpace representatives, I learned that the girls logged into their accounts two hours after they'd disappeared—from a computer in another part of Los Angeles. Using this information, police officers were able to identify the location of the girls, and they sent out a rescue team. At that point, the public still believed that the girls had been abducted, but what investigators found through MySpace suggested otherwise. The content and intensity of messages between the two girls suggested that they were lovers, that their parents disapproved of their relationship, and that they had been forbidden from seeing each other or communicating online.

When the police arrived at the girls' suspected location, they found that the girls were safe, that they had chosen to run away, and that one in particular was not interested in going home. No scary, older male sexual predator had lured them away. They'd run away together to get away from their parents.

Relying on information from the girls' parents and wanting to help, the media was quick to accept the conclusion that the girls had been abducted but did little to correct the original breathless story. News organizations reported that the police had found the girls but did not provide details about what had actually happened. In talking with families in the Los Angeles region, I found that many had heard that the girls had been abducted because of MySpace, but no one I met had learned that they had actually run away.

It's not clear whether the girls' parents knew that they had run away when they told the police that the girls had been abducted, nor is it clear whether they referenced MySpace to increase the likelihood that journalists would cover the story, but the combination prompted immediate action by both law enforcement and the company while also triggering a media circus. In capitalizing on people's fear of new technologies and abduction, stories like this may prompt action, but they also help to reproduce the culture of fear. They leave the public with an even more exaggerated conception of the risks that youth face while failing to address the dynamics that prompt teens to engage in risky behaviors in the first place.

Society often blames technology for putting youth at risk, but the traces that youth leave behind can be valuable in making certain that they are safe. When Alexandra and Alexis ran away, technology's traces and MySpace's willingness to collaborate with law enforcement enabled the police to track down the two girls extraordinarily quickly. The public never saw this side of the story.

Blaming the Technology

In February 2007, a girl in Colorado named Tess killed her mother with the help of her boyfriend, Bryan. When the news was reported on TV, the takeaway was, "A girl with MySpace kills her mother." The implication was that Tess had become deviant because of her use of MySpace and that this had prompted her to murder her mother.

This was not the first time that the public blamed communication or entertainment media for inciting a teen to kill. In 1999, video games and the band Marilyn Manson supposedly prompted two boys to shoot their classmates at Columbine High School in Littleton, Colorado.[41] After two young women in New Jersey died by suicide during a wave of teenage deaths in 1987, the community blamed Metallica because one of the girls left behind a letter referencing the song "Fade to Black," which directly addresses emptiness and pain and makes implicit overtures to suicide.[42] Even though the technological platform provided by MySpace is different than the content produced by popular musicians, it is not uncommon for people to try to make sense of teens' violent acts by turning to the media that they embrace.

Curious to learn more about Tess, I decided to see whether her MySpace page was publicly accessible; it was. What I saw was heartbreaking. For months, she had documented her mother's alcoholic rages through public postings. She left detailed accounts of how her mother physically abused her and psychologically tormented her. Her comments and messages were flush with emotional outpourings, frustration and rage, depression and confusion. In one post, she explained:

Everyone knows the story of me and my mom . . . and everyone knows how much I've tried to fix it my whole life. And everyone knows how it never works. I tried to get her help. I tried moving to California. I tried moving back to Colorado. I tried moving in with CJ, Hassan, Jermy and Bryan, then Burt and Bryan. Then moving back home with Bryan. And its just never enough. I could write a book about how confusing it is trying to please that woman . . . and trying to do whatever I can to get her to stop drinking. Like honestly, I'd do anything. But nothing really ever works. And the shit that goes on at home, frays out and effects every part of my life.

Tess documented her experiences and emotional confusion extensively. On MySpace, she described her struggles with being bipolar, her decision to start abusing alcohol, and her own confusion about how to make her life work. Her friends had left comments, offering emotional support and asking after her. But it was clear that they were in above their heads. In scouring the comments, I found no indication that an adult had been present in any of those conversations.

After Tess's arrest, her profile turned into a public discussion board. Acquaintances and friends alike were leaving all sorts of comments—hateful, supportive, and concerned. Reading through them, I found that one girl, who appeared to be a close friend of Tess's, was regularly defending Tess to detractors. This friend's page was also public, filled with heart-wrenching confusion, hurt, and uncertainty. Unable to ignore this girl's pain, I reached out to her to make sure she had support behind her. We exchanged a few messages as I offered Colorado-based resources for her to get help. She told me about how all of Tess's friends knew that Tess's mom beat her, but no one knew what to do. No adult was willing to listen. This young woman went on to tell me that some of Tess's friends had reported the MySpace posts to teachers but that, because the school blocked MySpace, teachers said that they were unable to look into the matter. Lost, and distrustful of adults in their community, her friends didn't know where else to go.

As the story unfolded, I learned that social workers had been informed of potential abuse from teachers but that nothing was done. Apparently, there wasn't enough physical evidence to make this case a priority. Social services had not looked at her MySpace page or talked with her friends.

Even in the aftermath, the teens in Tess's life felt powerless, unable even to get support in their community. I counseled Tess's friend into seeking support from a trained adult, unable to be a proper counselor for her from afar. I gave her the names of hotlines and counselors who might be able to help. I offered her information she could give to her friends. She clearly had no adult to whom she could turn. Instead, she was lashing out at those who attacked her online as her sole way of coping.

When teens are struggling like Tess's friend was, they often turn to social media. Some engage in risky behavior, but many more make visible the challenges they are facing: crying out for help through their posts and behavior online. All too often, their pleas go unseen or are ignored. Sometimes, this is because those posts are anonymous, which make them impossible to track down. But in other cases, no one bothers to look or ask questions.

In September 2012, Canadian fifteen-year-old Amanda Todd posted a nine-minute video on YouTube entitled "My Story: Struggling, Bullying, Suicide, Self Harm," in which she used note cards to describe how she was sexually harassed and blackmailed by an anonymous individual online and tormented by classmates at school.[43] She described being tricked into sexual acts, being beaten by girls at school, and attempting suicide. She accounted for her insecurity and anxiety as well as her attempts to get help. Although the description that she provided for this video states, "I'm struggling to stay in this world, because everything just touches me so deeply. I'm not doing this for attention. I'm doing this to be an inspiration and to show that I can be strong," the final two cards she displayed read, "I have nobody . . . I need someone :(" and "My name is Amanda Todd. . . ." A month later, Amanda died by suicide at her home in British Columbia. Afterward, her video spread widely.

The internet is not just a place where people engage in unhealthy interactions. It's also a place where people share their pain. Although not all youth who are struggling cry out for help online, many do. And when they do, someone should be there to recognize those signs and react constructively. Increasingly, there are tremendous opportunities to leverage online traces to intervene meaningfully in teens' lives. But it requires creating a society in which adults are willing to open their eyes and pay attention to youth other than their own children.

Eyes on the Digital Street

The risks that youth face online are not evenly distributed. Teens who are most at risk online are often struggling everywhere. And although many parents are deeply involved in their own children's lives, not all teens are lucky enough to have engaged or stable parents.

During my research, I met teens who looked after addicted parents, homeless teens struggling to survive, and teens whose parents were too focused on their work to notice them. All too often, teens who engage in risky behaviors do so in reaction to what's happening at home or in the hopes that their parents might notice.

In 2008, researchers Melissa Wells and Kimberly Mitchell surveyed youth about potentially risky online behaviors. They found that 15 percent of a nationally representative sample of American youth with online access reported experiencing sexual or physical abuse or high parental conflict in the preceding year.[44] These young people were labeled as "high risk" and were disproportionately likely to be older, African American, and/or not living with their biological parents. They also showed significantly more problematic online behavior than the rest of the sample. Youth reporting online victimization or experiences with sexual solicitation show similar risk factors as those who are vulnerable in offline contexts: they might experience sexual or physical abuse, parental conflict, substance use, low caregiver bonding, depression, sexual aggression, and other negative issues. Regular development of close relationships via the internet is also correlated with problems offline, including a poor home environment in which there is conflict or a poor caregiver-child relationship, depression, previous sexual abuse, and delinquency. The presence of unhealthy offline relationships may thus increase the risk of internet-based sexual victimization.

It can become a vicious cycle. Engaging in risky online behaviors—including speaking with strangers about sex—is intrinsically problematic as well as a signal of broader problems. Youth who are struggling are more likely to use less widely known services and to seek more attention from people they meet online, while those who have experienced negative offline encounters were 2.5 times more likely to receive unwanted sexual solicitation than other youth.[45] When teens are crashing, they engage in activities that are more likely to magnify their troubles. And when we see teens whose online activities look problematic, they're often using technology to make visible a broader array of problems that they're facing in every part of their lives.

Although most teens are doing okay, those who aren't *really* aren't. While, as discussed in the chapter on privacy, many teens encode what's happening in their lives so that it's not visible, others are quite open about the troubles they face. In these situations, the digital environment becomes a platform for displaying their pain to the world. When we see these teens' outbursts, it's easy to blame the technology because, for most of us, truly at-risk youth are otherwise invisible. Offline, those from abusive homes or facing mental health crises are often struggling in isolation or in an environment where no adult is paying attention. Online, they can be visible. And what they share in plain sight is often frightening for people who imagine that childhood is always a precious experience to be cherished. Although the internet may not be an inherently dangerous place, it's certainly a place where we can see kids who are in danger, if we are willing to look.

In protecting their own children, many parents turn a blind eye to the struggles others are facing; they go out of their way to keep their children from encountering those who are struggling. Moving to the suburbs or into a gated community are just two examples of how wealthier parents have historically tried to isolate their children from the rawness of less privileged environments. And when mental health issues seep through, many people try to ignore what's happening. One of the reasons that the parents I met fear the internet is because they believe it makes it harder for them to set boundaries and isolate themselves and their teens from communities in which the values are different or teens are not doing well. This results in fewer adults being willing to help those who are seriously struggling. And when the message that teens get is one of isolation, few teens know what to do, where to go, or how to cope when things do go wrong.

Parents and society as a whole often use fear to keep youth from engaging in practices that adults see as dangerous. This can backfire, undermining trust and resulting in lost opportunities. I grew up with Nancy Reagan's "Just Say No" messages alongside images like cracked eggs in a frying pan with the caption, "This is your brain on drugs."

Like many of my peers, I was taught to fear drugs. In rebellion, some of my classmates began experimenting with marijuana in early high school. Once they realized that pot didn't destroy their brains any more than alcohol did, many became vocal critics of the war on drugs, convinced that adults were trying to dupe them. Unfortunately, the all-encompassing "drugs are bad" message left no room for nuance, and I watched as some of my classmates began exploring cocaine and then crystal methamphetamine with the logic that these drugs must be equivalent to marijuana, since they had been lumped together in the war on drugs. I watched numerous classmates struggle with addiction for years. Looking back, I'm frustrated by how the fear-driven abstinence-only message regarding drugs left no room for meaningful conversation, let alone a framework for understanding abuse or addiction. When adults jump to fear and isolationism as their solution to managing risk, they often undermine their credibility and erode teens' trust in the information that adults offer.

Many teens turn to networked publics to explore a wider world, and that often includes a world that their parents want to protect them from. When parents create cocoons to protect their children from potential harms, their decision to separate themselves and their children from what's happening outside their household can have serious consequences for other youth, especially those who lack strong support systems. Communities aren't safe when everyone turns inward; they are only safe when people work collectively to help one another and those around them. In *The Death and Life of Great American Cities*, urban theorist Jane Jacobs argues that society benefits when everyone is willing to contribute their attention to the dynamics of the street. The more eyes there are on the street, the safer a community is.

Jacobs is arguing not for a form of surveillance in which powerful entities regulate social behavior through an unwanted gaze but for one in which people collectively look out for vulnerable populations and intervene when needed. People may appear to ignore a child biking down the street, but in a healthy community, if the child falls off the bike, concerned individuals will come out to help because they are all paying attention. Young people need the freedom to explore and express themselves, but we all benefit from living in an environment in which there's a social safety net where people come together to make sure that everyone's doing okay. Far from being an abuse of power, Jacob's notion of shared eyes on the street provides a necessary form of structural support in an individualistic society.

Through social media, teenagers have created digital streets that help define the networked publics in which they gather. In an effort to address online safety concerns, most adults respond by trying to quarantine youth from adults, limit teens' engagement online, or track teens' every move. Rhetoric surrounding online predation is used to drum up fear and justify isolation. But neither restrictions nor either adult or institutional surveillance will help those who are seriously struggling. Instead of trying to distance ourselves from teens in this new media, we have a unique opportunity to leverage visibility and face the stark and complex dynamics that shape teens' lives head on. If we want to make the world a safer place, we need people to pay attention to what's happening in their communities, not just in their households. We need concerned adults and young people to open their eyes on the digital street and reach out to those who are struggling. And we need to address the underlying issues that are at the crux of risky behaviors rather than propagate distracting myths. Fear is not the solution; empathy is.

5 bullying
is social media amplifying meanness and cruelty?

When I met white seventeen-year-old Abigail at a Starbucks in North Carolina, I was struck by her poise. A competitive swimmer, she was applying to highly respected colleges like Georgetown and Brown. She really liked Brown, but it didn't have a swim team as strong as those at less academically oriented schools actively recruiting her. In explaining her decision-making process, she showed the elegance and confidence of a typical upper-middle-class white teen trying to impress an adult. As our conversation continued and veered into more personal subjects, I started to notice self-doubt, particularly when issues of friendship and interpersonal conflict emerged.

While I was talking to Abigail, my collaborator, Alice Marwick, was interviewing her fourteen-year-old sister across the room, out of earshot. When I would glance over at their conversation, I couldn't help but reflect on how different the sisters' demeanor was. Unlike Abigail, Ashley appeared uninterested in composing herself for adult approval. Her cross-armed slouch and nonconformist fashion suggested a more rebellious spirit. I began to wonder how the sisters got along.[1]

At one point, as I was asking Abigail about her relationship with her parents on Facebook, she brought up her sister. Almost as a side note, Abigail mentioned that her mother treated her differently than Ashley. I asked her to explain. Her expression changed and she sighed in a way that suggested a long-standing household issue. Abigail told me that she is the darling of the house and that her mother doesn't trust Ashley. Immediately after saying that, Abigail quickly and nervously attempted to justify her mother's differential treatment by highlighting how Ashley always managed to get into trouble.

Abigail explained that when Ashley and her friends were in fourth grade, they used an instant messenger to say mean things about another girl at school.

And then the other girl found out about it and it became a bullying thing and my mom was like that's not acceptable, so [Ashley] was like banned from IM. Then when she was old enough so she could get a Facebook—and she wanted to get a Facebook because her friends were getting Facebooks—[Mom] got one too just so she could monitor [Ashley].

Abigail recounted stories of her sister getting into trouble at school and how Ashley would threaten to put embarrassing information on Facebook to humiliate Abigail in front of her friends. While explaining all of this, Abigail fidgeted uncomfortably, so I tried not to push the issue too far. Later, after I turned the recorder off and while we were waiting for Alice and Ashley to finish talking, I casually asked about Ashley again. More comfortable now, Abigail told me that she saw her sister as a bully. She didn't trust her sister, but at the same time, she felt sorry for her. From Abigail's perspective, Ashley didn't seem to understand that she hurt people whenever she lashed out. Abigail had tried—and, from her perspective, failed—to help Ashley see the consequences of her attitude and behavior, but she had since given up on helping her. Her mother and those in her school focused more on restricting and punishing Ashley. This made Ashley more frustrated and less cooperative.

While I was talking with Abigail, Ashley told Alice that there was very little outright bullying in her community; the meanness and cruelty she saw at school often took the form of what she called "indirect bullying"—gossip and rumors—or "drama." Ashley told Alice about various incidents that took place at school and among classmates, such as when boys mocked cheerleaders for their eating habits. Gossip about who might be pregnant, who was hooking up with whom, and who did what while drunk appeared to be standard fare. Ashley also described the cliques at school, the normalized fashion statements meant to show who was in and who was out, the dynamics of good and bad attention, and the politics of "frenemies"—friends who are sometimes enemies when faced with competition, jealousy, and mistrust.

As Alice and I shared notes about our interviews, Alice realized that Ashley used gossip and aggression to enforce her own social mores while simultaneously rejecting the idea that she was initiating any social conflict. Ashley's joyous recounting of school gossip paralleled her stated love of watching TV characters engage in drama and her general appreciation for knowing what's happening in people's lives. She liked being in the middle of what was happening. At the same time, Ashley told Alice that she thought her mother and sister were overreacting to the fights she got into and that her actions were justifiable, given how others treated her. When conflict emerged, Ashley saw other people as the ones causing problems while she was just left to react; although she didn't mind reacting, she couldn't see why people got upset by how she reacted.

Ashley's behaviors—and Ashley and Abigail's divergent perceptions of those behaviors—reveal some of the tensions at the heart of how both teens and adults experience and perceive conflict. The language of bullying and drama often emerges, but the practices involved range wildly. Both bullying and drama have imprecise definitions, and technologically mediated meanness and cruelty is interwoven with school conflict.

In communities like Ashley and Abigail's, the rise of social media has prompted tremendous concern about "cyberbullying." Although the data suggests otherwise, the assumption among many parents and journalists is that social media radically increases bullying.[2] In light of highly publicized—but often inaccurately portrayed—cases of teen suicide seemingly driven by peer cruelty, combating bullying has become a national obsession.[3] Lawmakers have begun to implement anti-bullying laws, and as of 2012, forty-eight states and the federal government have implemented statutes to address bullying, many of which include provisions specifically addressing online interactions.[4]

Nuance often gets lost in the panic. News reports do not explain, for example, why teens like Abigail and Ashley use different language to describe interpersonal conflict or why the dynamics that they describe are so common. Journalists latch onto and publicize data that suggest that the majority of youth are bullied, with little methodological or analytical consideration for what this implies. And few people consider how broader cultural practices and attitudes help shape teens' logic. Untangling these dynamics is essential for understanding what is at stake and for developing intervention strategies.

Defining Bullying in a Digital Era

Although scholars have examined different aspects of youth-related meanness and cruelty over the past four decades, there is no universal definition of bullying. Researchers continue to disagree about how to define and address bullying, but the most commonly accepted definition comes from Swedish psychologist Dan Olweus. In an attempt to differentiate bullying from other forms of youth aggression in the 1970s, Olweus narrowed in on three components that he saw as central to bullying in particular: aggression, repetition, and imbalance in power.[5] He argued that youth aggression was bullying when the situation involved all three components. Those who subscribe to Olweus's definition view bullying as a practice in which someone of differential physical or social power subjects another person to repeated psychological, physical, or social aggression. This matches the stereotypical case of bullying involving a big kid repeatedly physically tormenting a little kid or a popular teen repeatedly spreading nasty rumors about an outcast.

Accepting Olweus's definition means recognizing that individual acts of harassment or one-off fights are not bullying. Nor are reciprocal acts of relational aggression, such as when former best friends begin spreading rumors about each other in response to a recent fight. This does not mean that these practices aren't hurtful—they certainly are—but that repetition and differential power are central to Olweus's definition. As such, these are hurtful acts of peer aggression, but they are not bullying.

The public does not necessarily embrace scholarly definitions of bullying. More often, adults use bullying as an umbrella term. During my fieldwork, I met parents who saw every act of teasing as bullying, even when their children did not. At the other extreme, news media has taken to describing serious criminal acts of aggression by teens as bullying rather than using terms like stalking, harassment, or abuse. Ironically, teens often use the term bullying to refer to the kinds of incidents that Olweus described while adults and news media use this term far more loosely.

When Amanda Todd—the fifteen-year-old Canadian girl discussed in the previous chapter—died by suicide after posting a video about her situation to YouTube, the media widely reported her death as being a result of bullying. Although bullying played a role in Todd's story, the video she shared describes ongoing stalking, sexual harassment, and blackmail by a stranger, followed by a whirlwind of public shaming, harassment, and physical torment. She described trying to escape the pain through self-injury and a change of schools before reaching the point of social isolation and anomie. Parts of what Todd described, particularly her encounters with her classmates, can fit into the rubric of bullying, but to describe her situation as bullying obscures the significant criminal harassment that was at the crux of her pain. When both teasing and horrific acts of aggression become "bullying," it becomes difficult for the public to fully understand the significance of any particular bullying claim.

Networked technologies complicate how people understand bullying. Some people believe that cyberbullying is a whole new phenomenon. Others argue that technology simply offers a new site for bullying, just as the phone did before the internet. Often, what's at stake has to do with disagreements over how to make sense of the role of social media in amplifying the visibility of bullying. There is little doubt that networked technologies can increase the potential audience size of witnesses, but it's not clear that the contours of bullying—or the impact it has on those involved—radically change.

The persistence and visibility of bullying in networked publics adds a new dimension to how bullying is constructed and understood. On one hand, cruel interactions between teens leave traces that enable others to see what's happening. When this results in enabling others to amplify the attacks, heightened visibility can significantly increase the emotional duress of a bullying incident. This prompts people to assume that technology must inherently make bullying more hurtful and damaging, even though teens consistently report that they experience greater stress when they are bullied at school.[6] When cases reach the level of harassment that Amanda Todd received, it's clear that technology enabled people to engage in more sustained harm. Yet most people who experience bullying do not face the level of distributed and continuous cruelty that Todd encountered. Generalizing from cases like Todd's creates distorted pictures of bullying.

The visibility and persistence of networked publics may enable larger audiences to witness acts of bullying. These same affordances create novel opportunities for people to intervene. When children come home with black eyes, their parents know that they got into a fight. When children come home sullen, there are countless explanations for their mood. Parents have little insight into the dynamics that take place at school unless their child or the school offers them. Teens may never share many interpersonal reactions with their parents or teachers, even when they are exceptionally uplifting or hurtful. Through social media, everyday interactions leave traces.

Tumblr is flush with animated GIFs depicting teens' interests and tastes. On Instagram, teens share photographs of everything, including food eaten and friendships cemented. And Facebook is replete with interpersonal interactions from the mundane to the startling. All of this data can create new opportunities for parents and concerned onlookers to start conversations with teens about what's happening in their lives. At the same time, it's essential that concerned outsiders do not take what they see on social media and make assessments without trying to understand the context.

When parents believe that surveillance is the best way to ensure that their children are safe, they often follow their children online or simply look over their shoulders to see what they share. As discussed in the chapter on privacy, teens often respond to parental surveillance by trying to encode their content and obfuscate the meaning. Through surveillance, parents often witness various forms of meanness and cruelty, but may not be able to differentiate between a snide comment posted online as a joke and an intentionally cruel jab. Rather than using the visibility and persistence of online traces to understand their children better, many adults use online traces to jump to conclusions. More often than not, when they see online cruelty, they see others victimizing their children while failing to see how their children may be engaging with or hurting others. Rather than serving as a valuable tool for creating conversations between children and their parents, visibility often further complicates how parents and other adults understand bullying.

Who's at Fault?

When Taylor first moved to her new school in Boston at age fourteen, she felt like an outsider. Her hairstyle and clothes were typical for her old school on the west coast, but her new classmates saw her as an artsy, white "emo" girl. Awkward and shy, she found making friends daunting. The exception was Chris, whom she quickly befriended. He was also pegged as an artistic outsider by their peers. Through Chris, Taylor met Cory, Chris's neighbor and oldest friend. The three started hanging out and quickly became inseparable. Three years later, Taylor and Cory's friendship evolved into something more, and they started dating. Chris became quite jealous, and although Cory assumed that Chris was jealous of him for dating Taylor, Taylor knew something that Cory did not: Chris was gay, more interested in Cory than Taylor, and having a really difficult time coming out.

At first, their relationship was awkward. Chris began fighting with his parents and lashing out at Cory and Taylor. He started spreading rumors about Taylor at school and online, encouraging people not to talk to her. Though Taylor was hurt, she didn't respond and simply kept her distance. Angered by her silence, Chris retaliated by vandalizing her locker, destroying her schoolbooks, and spray painting "slut" on her locker.

Like many schools, Taylor's school had a "zero tolerance" for bullying policy. By destroying school property, Chris was immediately in trouble, and the school swung into action to punish him under their zero tolerance protocols. From the school's perspective, Chris was bullying Taylor, even though Taylor didn't see it that way. She knew that Chris was struggling with his sexuality and was angry with her for what he perceived as her stealing Cory from him. She knew that Chris was afraid to tell his religious parents that he was gay and was engaging in self-destructive, aggressive behavior. Although his ongoing cruelty was making her miserable, she was distraught about Chris. She wanted to help him but also wanted to respect his request for confidentiality. She wanted him to stop, but she didn't want his parents or the school to punish him because she knew that this wouldn't help the situation. Most of all, Taylor was afraid that if everyone turned against Chris, he would do something rash like hurt himself. Taylor decided not to out Chris and the school punished him, prompting his parents to get involved. Chris continued lashing out at Taylor. The more the school did, the more the situation escalated. Taylor found relief only when the school year ended.

Bullying has serious consequences, both for the recipient and for the bully.[7] Bullies are not evil people who decide to torment for fun; those are sociopaths. Most bullies react aggressively because they're struggling with serious issues of their own. Like Chris, many teens lash out when they are trying to negotiate serious identity or mental health issues. Others are reacting to abuse at home. It's easy to empathize with those who are on the receiving end of meanness and cruelty. It's much harder—and yet perhaps more important—to offer empathy to those who are doing the attacking.

Approaching bullying from a punishment-oriented perspective, as many schools do—and are increasingly legally required to do—rarely helps with bullying situations.[8] Often, as was the case for Taylor, school and parental involvement worsens the situation because the adults involved do not understand the details. If young people believe that adults will overreact or won't understand the complexities of the interpersonal dynamics, they aren't particularly interested in conveying the challenges they're facing. In this situation, Taylor was able to turn to her mother and explain the full situation; the support she received at home allowed her to manage unproductive school decisions. Many teens are not that lucky.

The language of bullying often presumes that there's a perpetrator and a victim. By focusing on blaming the perpetrator and protecting the victim, well-intended adults often fail to recognize the complexity of most conflicts. When punishment is the focus, there's often little incentive for understanding how punitive measures enable the cycle of violence to continue. Not only are zero tolerance approaches often unjust and ineffective; they also create additional harm that increases unhealthy interpersonal interactions. In other words, these policies help create the bullies that they're intended to stop.

When adults reframe every interpersonal conflict in terms of bullying or focus on determining who's at fault and punishing that person, they also lose a valuable opportunity to help teens navigate the complicated interpersonal dynamics and social challenges that they face. Bullying is an important issue to address, but figuring out how to address the wide swath of meanness and cruelty that adults identify as bullying requires looking at the language teens use and the cultural norms that surround them.

Teenage Drama

While many adults use bullying to mean every form of youth meanness and cruelty, teenagers use the term more conservatively. Many are quick to say that bullying is not a significant issue in their peer group, and when they give concrete examples of bullying, they describe incidents in which someone is repeatedly tormented for being different. This does not mean that they are oblivious to other forms of meanness and cruelty; they just talk about these issues using different language. In Atlanta, I interviewed two white fifteen-year-olds—Chloe and Vicki—about some of the dynamics they saw in their peer group. I asked if bullying was a problem at their school, and Chloe told me that it was not a major issue because she went to a Christian school. When I followed up to ask about rumors that the girls were referencing, Chloe and Vicki launched into a discussion about different types of gossip that they saw spread online and at school. They saw gossip and rumors as quite distinct from bullying, in part because when gossip and rumors spread, those who were the initial targets immediately responded by launching their own attacks. In other words, because Chloe and Vicki do not see a power differential between those engaged in interpersonal conflict, they do not use the term bullying.

Repeatedly, my collaborator Alice and I interviewed teenagers who told us that bullying was not nearly as significant an issue as adults thought. These teens confidently told us that bullying was "so middle school" and that teenagers "grow out of it." They positioned bullying as "immature," and as Caleb, a black seventeen-year-old from North Carolina, told Alice, "Once you get to high school is when the bullying really just like stops." After telling us that bullying doesn't happen in their school, teens would continue to describe a host of different practices that might easily be identified as bullying by adults using different language—gossip and rumors, pranking and punking, and, above all, drama.

In trying to understand teens' perspective on conflict, Alice and I became increasingly interested in the pervasive use of the term *drama*. Teens regularly used that word to describe various forms of interpersonal conflict that ranged from insignificant joking around to serious jealousy-driven relational aggression. Whereas adults might have labeled many of these practices as bullying, teens saw them as drama. Drawing on what we learned from interviewing teens, Alice and I defined drama as "performative, interpersonal conflict that takes place in front of an active, engaged audience, often on social media."[9]

Drama is not simply a substitute for bullying. Unlike bullying, which presumes a victim and a perpetrator, referring to conflict as drama allows teens to distance themselves from any emotional costs associated with what is happening. Drama does not automatically position anyone as either a target or an abuser. Those involved in drama do not have to see themselves as aggressive or weak but simply as part of a broader—and, often, normative—social process. Even when someone is central to the drama, they have an opportunity to respond, which allows them to feel a sense of power, even when they're hurting. As Carmen, a seventeen-year-old Latina from Boston, told us: "Drama is more there's two sides fighting back. I guess the second you fight back, it's—you're not allowed to call it bullying because you're defending yourself, I guess." This reinforces Olweus's notion that bullying is fundamentally about a difference in power and creates a word to talk about conflict in which power is not central. It also explains why Ashley saw the conflict around her as being about drama rather than bullying.

Most teenagers we met were able to articulate examples of drama that they experienced or witnessed. Many also saw social media as a key factor in the escalation of drama. For some, inciting drama was a source of entertainment and a practice to relieve boredom. For example, when I asked Samantha, a white seventeen-year-old from Seattle, about gossip, she told me that she liked to "start drama" online when she's bored; she found the reactions people have to gossip to be a relief from the tedium of homework. For others, drama is a way of testing out friendships and understanding the dynamics of popularity and status. Drama can be a way of achieving attention, working out sexual interests, and redirecting anger or frustration. Although we heard about drama from boys and girls, the term is typically employed in a gendered fashion, with teens describing the ways in which drama is a distinctly female practice. A white eighteen-year-old from Iowa named Wolf shared the following story with me:

My sister and her friends, when they get angry at each other, they'll try to post the most provocative pictures they can, the ones that will make their friends the most angry. And that's what they do back and forth, and when it gets bad, they'll comment to each other. . . . And by the end of the day, they're ready to tear each other to bits.

Wolf sees the use of social media to escalate conflict as girls' work.

Although the boys we interviewed rarely described their own practices through the language of drama, they referred to similar acts as either punking or pranking.

In North Carolina, Alice and I met Trevor and Matthew, white seventeen-year-old seniors and best friends. They loved to initiate pranks that would cause embarrassment; they saw creating such incidents to be a source of entertainment, even when someone got hurt in the process. When possible, they wanted their pranks to take place online so that their peers could all bear witness. One day, Matthew left his computer unattended without logging off of Facebook. Trevor, recognizing the opportunity, went to Matthew's Facebook account and posted a status update without Matthew's knowledge. His goal was to make others laugh by making Matthew look dumb.

Later that day, still having not seen or heard about what Trevor had written on his profile, Matthew went to his after-school job as a parking attendant. There, a concerned coworker approached him to ask about his school suspension. Matthew was initially confused but quickly realized that his colleague had read something on Facebook. He logged in to find that his last status update stated that he had received an in-school suspension for knocking a girl's books off her desk with his erection. The post also included a complaint, presumably by him, that it wasn't his fault that he couldn't control himself and that teachers should feel sympathy for him.[10] His classmates had flooded this update with their own comments, some taking the post literally and others recognizing it as a joke. Matthew was embarrassed by Trevor's prank, but he didn't let it get to him. Instead, he started plotting ways to get Trevor back even as his classmates continued to tease him for the post.

Trevor and Matthew may have relished the drama that ensued around their efforts to punk each other, but not all punking and pranking is well intentioned. Ana-Garcia, a fifteen-year-old of mixed Indian and Guatemalan heritage living in Los Angeles, recounted stories of her brother impersonating her on various social media. Although her brother often told her he did it because it was funny to upset her, she believed that his actions were spiteful because their parents treated her better. She was frustrated that her friends often didn't realize that it was her brother pretending to be her. On more than one occasion, her brother's posts caused a rift between her and her friends. Although Ana-Garcia was angry with her brother for wreaking havoc on her friendships, she also shrugged it off to me as being little brother behavior.

What makes an act cruel is not only about the act itself but how it is intended, perceived, and experienced. In communities that value having a thick skin, some teens feel the need to accept cruelty from friends, even when it hurts. Teens may not accept the mantle of bullying because they don't want to position themselves as victims, but that does not mean that they don't feel attacked. They smile and laugh off the pain in public because they feel this is what their community expects. They try to ignore any negative emotional response to drama because they don't want their peers to see them as weak.

Alongside the interpersonal conflict that occurs, teens grapple with how others perceive them. Technology can amplify existing dramas, but it can also create new mechanisms for meanness and cruelty to unfold. In 2010, Formspring, a question-and-answer service designed for professionals, became popular among American high school students. Quickly, the site became controversial as incidents of bullying unfolded in the questions and answers. Those with a Facebook account could post a profile on Formspring, which was automatically linked to Facebook. Then anyone could write questions anonymously. The questions and answers both appeared on a person's profile. While some of the questions asked were harmless ("What's your favorite color?"), others were excruciatingly mean ("Why are you such a f*cking slut?"). This outraged parents, educators, and journalists alike. Many argued that Formspring should be banned because it was a source of anonymous cruelty.

As news media debated the costs of anonymity on the site, I found myself puzzled by the interpretation of what was happening on Formspring. What most people who didn't use the site failed to realize was that questions never appeared on Formspring *unless* the recipient chose to answer them. Dumbfounded as to why teens would choose to respond to and post cruel questions, I contacted the company to help me understand what was happening. After investigating some of the most insidious cases, Formspring representatives noticed a pattern. Many of the "anonymous" questions were written by users at the same IP address as the account that responded to them. Furthermore, the questions were answered immediately after they were posted. Although there was a slim possibility that these hurtful messages could have come from siblings in the same house, some teens appeared to be anonymously asking cruel questions to themselves and then responding to them. In other words, some teens were engaging in acts of digital self-harm to attract attention, support, and validation.

To my surprise, digital self-harm turned out to happen more than I realized. Psychologist Elizabeth Englander found that 9 percent of youth she surveyed reported using the internet to bully themselves.[11] About a third of them felt that they achieved what they wanted and felt better as a result. This practice, while neither universal nor even the majority, certainly complicates the boundaries between seeking attention and engaging in bullying.

Acts of meanness and cruelty, pranking and punking, gossip and bullying, and digital self-harm are all wrapped up in other personal, interpersonal, and social dynamics. Teens are struggling with their own sense of self, how they relate to others, and what it means to fit into the broader world. They face pressures to conform and they struggle to understand what's acceptable and normative while listening to the messages that surround them. For better or worse, much of what they're trying to do is figure out where they stand.

Seeking Social Status

In *Freaks, Geeks, and Cool Kids*, sociologist Murray Milner Jr. analyzes American teen social status systems, documenting practices ranging from clique formation to conspicuous consumption, a practice of purchasing clothing and other material objects to show off. In addressing the question, "Why do they behave like that?" Milner explains that even though teens have more autonomy than children, they lack agency in many aspects of their lives. They are regularly reminded of their limited economic or political power when presented with culturally pervasive messages that distinguish adults from children, including age-based restrictions on a range of practices, including consuming alcohol, viewing movies, attending clubs, driving, voting, and simply hanging out at night. As Milner explains, "In one realm, however, their power is supreme; they control their evaluations of one another. That is, the kind of power they do have is status power: the power to create their own status systems based on their own criteria."[12]

Because of how American society constructs and restricts childhood, youth learn to value social information as part of developing a sense for social relations. Social dramas that unfold as youth begin brokering gossip and marking social status shape tween and teen years. In school, gossip and rumors operate as a type of social currency that allows the development and maintenance of social categories and cliques.[13] Teens use gossip to separate themselves from others, often in an effort to be seen as popular by dissing someone else.

In Michigan, I met Summer, a quiet, white fifteen-year-old girl, who told me how her best friend became her worst enemy. Catie and Summer were close throughout elementary school, but as middle school approached, a rift emerged. Catie started sharing intimate stories that Summer had told her, seeding rumors that evolved as they spread. Summer was devastated and didn't know how to respond.

She tried ignoring what was happening, but she couldn't. The foundations of the rumors were true but had been private. Summer had trusted Catie not to share these stories. The situation escalated as new rumors began and spread throughout her school. Summer didn't know exactly how the rumors spread, but she suspected by every communication channel available to her cohort—including word of mouth, telephone, and instant messenger. She tried to fight back, but that only made things worse. Summer found herself alone among her peers, without anyone to support her. Eventually, the pain consumed her, and with the support of her parents, she chose to switch schools. This was a good move for Summer, as she was much happier and more comfortable at her new school.

Summer and Catie were once close friends. They had shared everything. And Summer said she trusted Catie. But as they grew older, Catie began developing friendships with the popular kids in their school. Looking back, the fifteen-year-old version of Summer believes that Catie rejected her eleven-year-old self because she wasn't popular enough. Although it saddened her, Summer believed that Catie's popularity did indeed rise by attacking Summer.

Unfortunately, it's quite common for former friends to turn on each other in a quest for popularity and status, out of spite or jealousy, or in response to perceived wrongs. Some embark on psychological warfare, tormenting those they once adored. Others simply create a wall of silence, suddenly refusing to engage with former friends in the hopes that they can walk away from an aspect of themselves that they believe no longer serves them. Sometimes, these splits are quiet and subtle, but often, they are highly visible and fueled by rumors and drama.

Social media services can play a role in teens' struggles for popularity and status because they enable the easy spread of information and allow teens to keep up with ever-changing school dynamics. These technologies also allow people to maintain social ties more easily, providing infrastructure for the dissemination of social information. Tools like Facebook make it easier for teens to keep up with their classmates' birthdays, breakups and makeups, and adventures to follow social protocols, engage one another in conversation, and provide support. At the same time, what is shared and easily accessible is not always beneficial. Because social media makes it easy to share information broadly, people can also easily spread hurtful gossip in an effort to assert status, get attention, or relieve boredom. These dynamics are often intertwined.

Cachi, a Puerto Rican eighteen-year-old living in Iowa, told me that the flow of information on Facebook's "news feed" is useful because it enables her to "[keep] track of who's talking to who." Through Facebook, she can follow the ebbs and flows of friendships and romantic relationships. Cachi believes that being informed about interpersonal interactions is important because it allows her to avoid embarrassing herself in front of others. She wants to know the status of people's relationships with their significant others so that she can ask about them appropriately without making a faux pas. She explained that being out of the loop can be awkward. Cachi likes the way Facebook allows her to stay on top of what is happening among her peers. She relishes the gossip because it gives her the ability to step in at the right time and act, either to maintain her social standing or to negotiate others' popularity. She is fully aware that social media makes it easier to spin small issues out of proportion to create conflict, but she still wants to be attuned to the drama as it is happening. The same tools that are used to spread the conflict allow her to track it.

Although the impact of gossip can be deeply problematic and many might view spreading gossip with disdain, not all gossip is hurtful. In fact, as the anthropologist Robin Dunbar has shown, gossip plays a central role in helping humans build connections.[14] Like Cachi, many people gossip in order to position themselves in a social group and to maintain social ties. People reveal aspects of themselves to others as a bonding ritual, building trust through reciprocity. They dissect their lives and the lives of others. They maintain connections by keeping each other up-to-date about social happenings and relationships.

Though gossip can be put to good uses, much of the gossip that teens exchange is neither innocent nor benign. What's shared may be untrue, private, or circulated for malicious reasons—such as to hurt a rival, build one friendship at the expense of another, or destroy someone's reputation. The same mechanisms that help people bond also create social fault lines. Having access to information about someone and the ability to use it as a weapon is a form of power in social situations. Gossip, good and bad, helps people broker social status. The higher status an individual is, the more valuable it is to know the intimate details of that person's life. And when they use gossip to reinforce power structures, this can often take on the form of bullying. Individuals are especially advantaged if they know intimate information about someone without having to share anything in return. This motivates people to seek information about others and to exchange information that they have: the practice of gossip in the most widely used and least positive sense of the word.

Gossip can seem to take on a life of its own through social media. When people choose to share or spread content about others, they can use social media to easily transmit the message to a wide and connected audience. A rumor shared on Facebook has the potential to spread farther and faster and persist longer than any school rumor could have in the past. This does not mean that Facebook creates gossip. Rather, someone seeking to spread a message can easily leverage the affordances of networked publics to do so.

People spread the content they find fascinating, fueling the attention that it receives. Although people can and do share helpful or entertaining content, what they share widely is often that which is most embarrassing or humiliating, grotesque or sexual, mean-spirited or shocking. Because sharing is a form of currency and experiencing a cultural artifact together enables bonding, teens look for content that they think those around them will find interesting. Unfortunately, some of the best-known videos online—so-called viral videos—stem from teens choosing to spread content that shame their peers.

The "Star Wars Kid" video is a classic example of a widely viewed video that was shared online to embarrass a teen. In 2002, a fourteen-year-old heavyset boy created a home video of himself swinging a golf ball retriever as though it was a light saber from *Star Wars*. A year later, a classmate of his found this home video, digitized it, and put it up online. Others edited the video, setting the action to music and dubbing in sound effects, graphics, and other special effects. The resultant "Star Wars Kid" video spread rapidly and received extensive media attention.[15] It became the source of new memes and mocking video spin-offs. Even comedians like Weird Al Yankovic and Stephen Colbert produced their own renditions. Although people gained attention for spreading the video or creating their own versions, the cost of this mass attention was devastating to the teenager in the video. His family sued his classmates for emotional duress because of the ongoing harassment he faced.

The "Star Wars Kid" video exemplifies how mass public shaming is a byproduct of widespread internet attention and networked distribution. Teenagers commonly face a lesser version of this when they receive unexpected and unwanted attention, when they become the target of a rumor, or when others share their content beyond its intended audience. Social media complicates the dynamics of social sharing and gossip because it provides a platform for information to spread far and wide, and people are often motivated to spread embarrassing content because others find it interesting. Spreadable media can be used to drum up productive attention, but it can also be used to shame.[16]

People choose what to spread online, but the technologies that they use to do so are created to increase the visibility of content that will attract the most attention. Many social media tools are designed to encourage people to consume streams or feeds of updates. A steady flow of photographs, updates, and comments from friends on Twitter, Instagram, Tumblr, and other services flood teens' screens. Keeping up with everything can be difficult and overwhelming. Facebook tries to address this issue by limiting what users see when they view their feed so that the most algorithmically determined interesting content appears at the top. The algorithms filter most of what people say such that viewers only see a fraction of the updates from their contacts. What bubbles up is inevitably that which has already received tremendous attention through views, comments, and likes. To maximize attention, Facebook designs algorithms to perfect the gossip machine.

Social media is situated within an attention economy in which technologies are built to capture and sustain the interest of users. Many corporate monetization plans are driven by advertising, which measures success through pageviews and other types of engagement like user-generated content. Technical features that show "most watched" or "trending" content amplify what is already gaining traction. Marketers try to find ways to manipulate technology to capture others' attention, but they are not alone. Teens also try to use the same technologies to garner attention from their peers by sharing things that may interest them, whether that content is enlightening or hurtful. In this ecosystem, capturing attention is important for financial and personal gain.

The dynamics of drama and attention don't unfold because of social media, even if teens can use technology for these purposes. They are also not innate properties of being a teenager. Teenagers learn to engage in acts of drama just as they learn different tactics for acquiring attention from others. One of the ways that they develop these sensibilities is through celebrity culture and the dramas between public figures that they watch unfold as part of contemporary entertainment.

The Celebritization of Everyday Life

As a currency, attention has tremendous social and cultural value. Teens learn the value of attention, the cost of gossip, and the power of drama by observing what takes place around them. Reality TV, tabloid magazines, and celebrity news all provide a media-driven template for understanding how attention operates and helps fuel drama for entertainment. The advertising culture that teens witness reveals a market-driven valuation of attention. In school, teens observe how students broker attention with respect to classmates and teachers and start drama to negotiate power and status. Meanwhile, at home, teens often hear their parents gossip about work, neighbors, and family. While society derides attention, gossip, and drama, teens also receive clear cultural signals that these behaviors are normal. Teens may mock peers for being "attention whores," but they also recognize that attention can be—and is often seen as—valuable. They may lament drama in their schools while relishing TV shows that depict so-called reality drama. Teens see gossip, drama, and attention games all around them, and not surprisingly, they mirror what they see.

The norms of celebrity culture, including the politics of attention and drama, seep into everyday life.[17] Teens watch nobodies become famous, and they bear witness to everyday dramas enacted by "reality" stars, online attention seekers, and traditional celebrities alike. They may try to seek the attention of stars that they appreciate, or mock those who are caught up in fandom, but they're broadly aware of how attention circulates around famous individuals and how attention affects celebrities' status. The same practices that they watch celebrities engage in—and themselves participate in as fans—also influence their understanding of how to navigate attention and status.

Social media also allows people to enact celebrity practices.[18] Teens can and do use social media to drum up attention for themselves and shower attention on others. Attention through social media can be both delightful and devastating. Sometimes, it's used to celebrate people's accomplishments. Other times, it's used to challenge people's stature. More than anything, how other teens and celebrities use technologies to negotiate attention sets the stage for what teens understand as normal.

What constitutes good attention versus bad attention often gets blurry, just as the line between drama as entertainment and drama as hurtful activity can be hard to identify. The same aspects of technology that increase the visibility of drama are those that help increase attention more generally. One way of seeing the dynamics that emerge is through the lens of teen celebrity culture, as some teens become celebrities in their own right. Teen celebrity culture is created by and is a byproduct of attention seeking and visibility that can be both healthy and unhealthy.

Media makers have long capitalized on teens' passion for celebrities by producing boy bands and teen starlets, from the 1950s Mouseketeers to the 1990s Backstreet Boys. In doing so, they help sell celebrity culture to the public. Social media has changed various aspects of this dynamic. Most notably, it provides a pathway for teenagers to become famous, as in the case of Canadian teen idol Justin Bieber, who was first identified through YouTube. This creates the illusion that social media makes fame more readily accessible. Social media also allows famous teens to communicate directly with their fans, as Disney-produced starlets Miley Cyrus and Demi Lovato do. Being able to interact directly with stars through social media appears to eliminate the distance between fans and celebrities.[19]

Long before the internet, people produced and consumed gossip about high-status public people, including members of the aristocracy, celebrities, and politicians. Gossip columns and tabloids have large audiences because people want access to the intimate lives of the rich and famous. The same is true with online fan pages and celebrity Twitter accounts. Some people like to live vicariously through the comings and goings of the successful; others prefer to vent their jealousy. Teens, oblivious to the pressure that comes with fame, have long looked to celebrities with awe, imagining their lives to be full of freedom and flexibility and absent of homework or chores. But celebrity can often be stifling.

When people become famous, they are often objectified, discussed, and ridiculed with little consideration for who they are as people. Fans and critics feel as though they have the right to comment on everything celebrities do with little regard to the costs that those in the crosshairs of attention will bear. The cost that celebrities pay for the supposed benefits of being rich and famous is ongoing scrutiny and a lack of privacy. Most people do not understand or appreciate the pressure that results from fame, even though public meltdowns—such as the night that Britney Spears shaved her head in front of numerous photographers—are highly publicized. The public's obsession with obtaining information about the famous puts serious pressure on those people's lives, as the paparazzi's role in Princess Diana's death so brutally reminds us.[20] Few people have sympathy for the kinds of stress that gossip places on public figures who have high status and wealth. At a distance, famous people seem invulnerable.

Social media alters the spectacle around teen stars' activities, but it doesn't lessen the pressure. Fans relish watching high-profile drama—such as fights between Miley Cyrus and Demi Lovato playing out over Twitter or Justin Bieber appearing to have a meltdown on Instagram. They take sides, offer support, and swear loyalty to stars they love, but they have little appreciation for how their attention and infatuation creates pressure and fuels the drama in the first place.

As teens enter into the spotlight, they become objectified in ways that parallel what celebrities face. This is a process that media scholar Terri Senft calls "microcelebrity."[21] Teens who are famous among niche crowds get to face both the costs and the benefits of being on the receiving end of tremendous attention, but without the structural support that celebrities have—including the handlers, managers, and financial resources to cope with the onslaught of attention. This can create a heady situation, with teens simultaneously relishing that positive feedback and being deeply affected by the cruelty and pressure that often comes with it.

In 2011, thirteen-year-old California-based Rebecca Black wanted to make a music video. Her mother paid a vanity music label and production company to work with her daughter and her daughter's friends to record a highly Auto-Tuned song called "Friday." The associated video appeared on YouTube and quickly generated attention, mostly by people who harshly criticized what they saw as poor songwriting and Black's inability to sing. On Twitter, a comedian described the song as the "worst video ever made."[22] As word of the video spread, Black became a target of incessant meanness and cruelty by strangers, classmates, and the media. She was attacked online and at school.[23] But her meteoric rise to global fame also meant that she gained tremendous positive attention, too. In recognition of the phenomenon, the popular musical TV show *Glee* decided to do a rendition of her song, and the pop celebrity Katy Perry paid homage to Black in "Last Friday Night (T.G.I.F.)" by having Black perform alongside Perry in the music video. Black loved the recognition and validation, but she wasn't prepared for the cruelty that came with it. The dynamic that Black faced is a product of celebrity.

When teens achieve overwhelming attention and visibility online, positive feedback and negative attacks often go hand in hand. Sometimes, as with the case of Rebecca Black, the positive attention appears to outweigh the negative feedback. In other situations, like the attention received by "Star Wars Kid," the very act of people seeing and sharing a video feels hurtful. As teens encounter and participate in celebrity culture, either to seek attention themselves or to engage with people who are famous, they regularly experience meanness and cruelty. The scale of negativity that these young celebrities and microcelebrities receive is unprecedented, but so is the level of positive attention that they receive. Far from being justifiable, the meanness and cruelty that these teens receive as a byproduct of becoming famous highlights how society seeks to temper individual success and visibility by challenging people's status and stature. For better or worse, celebrity culture has normalized drama as a de facto aspect of everyday public life.

Addressing a Culture of Meanness and Cruelty

As teens engage with networked publics, they must negotiate a social ecosystem in which their peers are not only hanging out but also jockeying for social status. In these settings, interpersonal conflicts emerge and teens participate in battles over reputation, status, and popularity. Attention becomes a commodity, and at times, teens participate in drama or pranks that can be intentionally or accidently hurtful to others. Not all drama or gossip is problematic, but some of what teens experience is quite painful.

While we cannot protect youth from all forms of meanness and cruelty or stop teens from getting hurt when they negotiate social relations, we can certainly make a concerted effort to empower youth, to strengthen their resilience, and to help recognize when they are hurting.[24] When teens have the strength to cope with stressful situations, they are less likely to either try to escalate the situation or be emotionally shaken by a negative encounter. When teens understand how their actions affect others—including those who appear invulnerable—they are more attentive to the consequences of what they say and do. Many programs exist to help youth develop resilience and empathy, but they are often overlooked once conflict is under way.[25]

Although new forms of drama find a home through social media, teens' behaviors have not significantly changed. Social media has not radically altered the dynamics of bullying, but it has made these dynamics more visible to more people. We must use this visibility, not to justify increased punishment, but to help youth who are actually crying out for attention. Blaming technology or assuming that conflict will disappear if technology usage is minimized is naive. Recognizing where teens are at and why they engage in particular acts of meanness and cruelty is important to creating interventions that work.

6 inequality
can social media resolve social divisions?

In a school classroom in Los Angeles, Keke sat down, crossed her arms defensively, and looked at me with suspicion. After an hour of short, emotionless responses to my questions about her daily life and online activities, I hit a nerve when I asked the black sixteen-year-old to explain how race operated in her community. I saw her fill with rage as she described how gang culture shaped her life. "We can't have a party without somebody being a Blood or somebody being a Crip and then they get into it and then there's shooting. Then we can't go to my friend's house because it's on the wrong side of [the street]. You know what I'm saying? It's the Mexican side." Los Angeles gang culture forces her to think about where she goes, who she spends time with, and what she wears.

> We can't go places because of gangs. . . . We can't go to the mall, can't be a whole bunch of black people together. . . . I hate not being able to go places. I hate having to be careful what color shoes I'm wearing or what color is in my pants or what color's in my hair. . . . I just hate that. It's just not right.

When each color represents a different gang, the choice to wear red or blue goes beyond taste and fashion.

Although Keke understood the dynamics of gang culture in her community and was respected by the gang to which members of her family belonged, she despised the gangs' power. She hated the violence. And she had good reason to be angry. Only a few weeks before we met, Keke's brother had been shot and killed after crossing into the turf of a Latino gang. Keke was still in mourning.

Though almost sixty years had passed since the US Supreme Court ruled that segregation of public high schools is unconstitutional, most American high schools that I encountered organized themselves around race and class through a variety of social, cultural, economic, and political forces. The borders of school districts often produce segregated schools as a byproduct of de facto neighborhood segregation. Students find themselves in particular classrooms—or on academic tracks—based on test scores, and these results often correlate with socioeconomic status. Friend groups are often racially and economically homogenous, which translates into segregated lunchrooms and segregated online communities.

The most explicit manifestation of racial segregation was visible to me in schools like Keke's, where gangs play a central role in shaping social life. Her experiences with race and turf are common in her community. The resulting dynamics organize her neighborhood and infiltrate her school. When I first visited Keke's school, I was initially delighted by how diverse and integrated the school appeared to be. The majority of students were immigrants, and there was no dominant race or nationality. More than other schools I visited, classrooms looked like they were from a Benetton ad or a United Nations gathering, with students from numerous racial backgrounds sitting side by side. Yet during lunch or between classes, the school's diversity dissolved as peers clustered along racial and ethnic lines. As Keke explained,

This school is so segregated. It's crazy. We got Disneyland full of all the white people. . . . The hallways is full of the Indians, and the people of Middle Eastern descent. . . . The Latinos, they all lined up on this side. The blacks is by the cafeteria and the quad. Then the outcasts, like the uncool Latinos or uncool Indians. The uncool whites, they scattered.

Every teen I spoke with at Keke's school used similar labels to describe the different shared spaces where teens cluster. "Disneyland" was the section in the courtyard where white students gathered, while "Six Flags" described the part occupied by black students. When I tried to understand where these terms came from, one of Keke's classmates—a fifteen-year-old Latina named Lolo—explained, "It's just been here for, I think, generations. (Laughs) I'm sure if you're a ninth grader, you might not know until somebody tells you. But I did know 'cause my brother told me." Those same identifiers bled into nearby schools and were used when public spaces outside of school were identified. No one knew who created these labels, but they did know that these were the right terms to use. Each cohort had to learn the racial organization of the school, just as they had to learn the racial logic of their neighborhoods. They understood that flouting these implicit rules by crossing lines could have serious social and physical consequences.

Although Keke's experience of losing a family member to gang violence is uncommon, death is not that exceptional in a community where gun violence is pervasive. Gang members may know one another at school, but the tense civility they maintain in the hallways does not carry over to the streets. Teens of different races may converse politely in the classroom, but that doesn't mean they are friends on social media. Although many teens connect to everyone they know on sites like Facebook, this doesn't mean that they cross unspoken cultural boundaries. Communities where race is fraught maintain the same systems of segregation online and off.

What struck me as I talked with teens about how race and class operated in their communities was their acceptance of norms they understood to be deeply problematic. In a nearby Los Angeles school, Traviesa, a Hispanic fifteen-year-old, explained, "If it comes down to it, we have to supposedly stick with our own races. . . . That's just the unwritten code of high school nowadays." Traviesa didn't want to behave this way, but the idea of fighting expectations was simply too exhausting and costly to consider. In losing her brother, Keke knew those costs all too well, and they made her deeply angry. "We all humans," she said. "Skin shouldn't separate nobody. But that's what happens." Although part of Keke wanted to fight back against the racial dynamics that had killed her brother, she felt powerless.

As I watched teens struggle to make sense of the bigotry and racism that surrounded them in the mid- to late 2000s, the American media started discussing how the election of Barack Obama as the president of the United States marked the beginning of a "postracial" era. And because social media supposedly played a role in electing the first black US president, some in the press argued that technology would bring people together, eradicate social divisions in the United States, and allow democracy to flourish around the world.[1] This utopian discourse did not reflect the very real social divisions that I watched emerge and persist in teens' lives.[2]

The Biases in Technology

Society has often heralded technology as a tool to end social divisions. In 1858, when the Atlantic Telegraph Company installed the first transatlantic cable, many imagined that this new communication device would help address incivility. As authors Charles Briggs and Augustus Maverick said of the telegraph: "This binds together by a vital cord all the nations of the earth. It is impossible that old prejudices and hostilities should longer exist, while such an instrument has been created for an exchange of thought between all the nations of the earth."[3] New communication media often inspire the hope that they can and will be used to bridge cultural divides. This hope gets projected onto new technologies in ways that suggest that the technology itself does the work of addressing cultural divisions.

As I describe throughout this book, the mere existence of new technology neither creates nor magically solves cultural problems. In fact, their construction typically reinforces existing social divisions. This sometimes occurs when designers intentionally build tools in prejudicial ways. More often it happens inadvertently when creators fail to realize how their biases inform their design decisions or when the broader structural ecosystem in which a designer innovates has restrictions that produce bias as a byproduct.

In 1980, technology studies scholar Langdon Winner published a controversial essay entitled, "Do Artifacts Have Politics?" In it, he points to the case of urban planner Robert Moses as an example of how biases appear in design. In the mid-twentieth century, Moses was influential in designing roads, bridges, and public housing projects in New York City and neighboring counties. In planning parkways on Long Island, Moses designed bridges and overpasses that were too low for buses and trucks to pass under. Buses, for example, could not use the parkway to get to Jones Beach, a major summer destination. Winner argues that these design decisions excluded those who relied on public transportation—the poor, blacks, and other minorities and disadvantaged citizens—from getting to key venues on Long Island. He suggests that Moses incorporated his prejudices into the design of major urban infrastructures.

This parable is contested. Responding to Winner's essay, technology scholar Bernward Joerges argues in "Do Politics Have Artefacts?" that Moses's decisions had nothing to do with prejudice but rather resulted from existing regulatory restrictions limiting the height of bridges and the use of parkways by buses, trucks, and commercial vehicles. Joerges suggests that Winner used haphazard information to advance his argument. Alternatively, one could read the information that Joerges puts forward as reinforcing Winner's broader conceptual claim. Perhaps Robert Moses did not intentionally design the roadways to segregate Long Island racially and socioeconomically, but his decision to build low overpasses resulted in segregation nonetheless. In other words, the combination of regulation and design produced a biased outcome regardless of the urban planner's intention.

Companies often design, implement, and test new technologies in limited settings. Only when these products appear in the marketplace do people realize that aspects of the technology or its design result in biases that disproportionately affect certain users. For example, many image-capture technologies have historically had difficulty capturing darker-skinned people because they rely on light, which reflects better off of lighter objects. As a result, photography and film better capture white skin while transforming black skin in unexpected ways.[4] This same issue has reemerged in digital technologies like Microsoft's Kinect, an interactive gaming platform that relies on face recognition. Much to the frustration of many early adopters, the system often fails to recognize dark-skinned users.[5] In choosing to use image capture to do face recognition, the Kinect engineers built a system that is technically—and thus socially—biased in implementation. In other technologies, biases may emerge as a byproduct of the testing process. Apple's voice recognition software, Siri, has difficulty with some accents, including Scottish, Southern US, and Indian.[6] Siri was designed to recognize language iteratively. Because the creators tested the system primarily in-house, the system was better at recognizing those American English accents most commonly represented at Apple.

The internet was supposed to be different from previous technologies. Technology pundits and early adopters believed that the internet would be a great equalizer—where race and class wouldn't matter—because of the lack of visual cues available.[7] But it turns out that the techno-utopians were wrong. The same biases that configure unmediated aspects of everyday life also shape the mediated experiences people have on the internet. Introducing their book *Race in Cyberspace*, scholars Beth Kolko, Lisa Nakamura, and Gilbert Rodman explain that "race matters in cyberspace precisely because all of us who spend time online are already shaped by the ways in which race matters offline and we can't help but bring our own knowledge, experiences, and values with us when we log on."[8]

Cultural prejudice permeates social media. Explicit prejudice bubbles up through the digital inscription of hateful epithets in comments sections and hatemongering websites, while the social networks people form online replicate existing social divisions. Some youth recognize the ways their experiences are constructed by and organized around cultural differences; many more unwittingly calcify existing structural categories.

How American teens use social media reflects existing problems in society and reinforces deep-seated beliefs. This may seem like a letdown to those who hoped that technology could serve as a cultural panacea. But the implications of this unfulfilled potential extend beyond disappointment. Because prominent figures in society—including journalists, educators, and politicians—consider social media to be a source of information and opportunity, our cultural naïveté regarding the ways social and cultural divisions are sewn into our mediated social fabric may have more damaging costs in the future. In order to address emerging inequities, we must consider the uneven aspects of the social platforms upon which we are building.

Social media—and the possibility of connecting people across the globe through communication and information platforms—may seem like a tool for tolerance because technology enables people to see and participate in worlds beyond their own. We often identify teens, in particular, as the great beneficiaries of this new cosmopolitanism.[9] However, when we look at how social media is adopted by teens, it becomes clear that the internet doesn't level inequality in any practical or widespread way. The patterns are all too familiar: prejudice, racism, and intolerance are pervasive. Many of the social divisions that exist in the offline world have been replicated, and in some cases amplified, online. Those old divisions shape how teens experience social media and the information that they encounter. This is because while technology does allow people to connect in new ways, it also reinforces existing connections. It does enable new types of access to information, but people's experiences of that access are uneven at best.

Optimists often point out that all who get online benefit by increased access to information and expanded connections, while pessimists often point to the potential for increased levels of inequality.[10] Both arguments have merit, but it's also important to understand how inequalities and prejudices shape youth's networked lives. Existing social divisions—including racial divisions in the United States—are not disappearing simply because people have access to technology. Tools that enable communication do not sweep away distrust, hatred, and prejudice. Racism, in particular, takes on new forms in a networked setting. Far from being a panacea, the internet simply sheds new light on the divisive social dynamics that plague contemporary society.

The internet may not have the power to reverse long-standing societal ills, but it does have the potential to make them visible in new and perhaps productive ways. When teens are online, they bring their experiences with them. They make visible their values and attitudes, hopes and prejudices. Through their experiences living in a mediated world in which social divisions remain salient, we can see and deal realistically with their more harmful assumptions and prejudices.

Racism in a Networked Age

In 1993, the *New Yorker* published a now infamous cartoon showing a big dog talking to a smaller dog in front of a computer monitor.[11] The caption reads, "On the Internet, no one knows you're a dog." Over the years, countless writers commenting on social issues have used this cartoon to illustrate how privacy and identity operate positively and negatively online. One interpretation of this cartoon is that embodied and experienced social factors—race, gender, class, ethnicity—do not necessarily transfer into the mediated world. As discussed earlier in the chapter on identity, many people hoped that, by going online, they could free themselves of the cultural shackles of their embodied reality.

When teens go online, they bring their friends, identities, and network with them. They also bring their attitudes toward others, their values, and their desire to position themselves in relation to others. It is rare for anyone to be truly anonymous, let alone as disconnected from embodied reality as the *New Yorker* cartoon suggests.[12] Not only do other people know who you are online; increasingly, software engineers are designing and building algorithms to observe people's practices and interests in order to model who they are within a broader system. Programmers implement systems that reveal similarity or difference, common practices or esoteric ones. What becomes visible—either through people or through algorithms—can affect how people understand social media and the world around them. How people respond to that information varies.

During the 2009 Black Entertainment Television (BET) Awards, thousands of those watching from home turned to Twitter to discuss the various celebrities at the ceremony. The volume of their commentary caused icons of the black community to appear in Twitter's "Trending Topics," a list of popular terms representing topics users are discussing on the service at any given moment. Beyoncé, Ne-Yo, Jamie Foxx, and other black celebrities all trended, along with the BET Awards themselves. The visibility of these names on the Trending Topics prompted a response from people who were not watching the award ceremony. In seeing the black names, one white teenage girl posted, "So many black people!" while a tweet from a young-looking white woman stated: "Why are all these black people on trending topics? Neyo? Beyonce? Tyra? Jamie Foxx? Is it black history month again? LOL." A white boy posted, "Wow!! too many negros in the trending topics for me. I may be done with this whole twitter thing." Teens were not the only ones making prejudicial remarks. A white woman tweeted, "Did anyone see the new trending topics? I dont think this is a very good neighborhood. Lock the car doors kids." These comments—and many more—provoked outrage, prompting the creation of a blog called "omgblackpeople" and a series of articles on race in Twitter.[13]

Unfortunately, what happened on the night of the BET Awards is not an isolated incident. In 2012, two athletes were expelled from the London Olympics after making racist comments on Twitter.[14] Racism is also not just an issue only on Twitter, where black internet users are overrepresented compared with their online participation on other sites.[15] The now defunct site notaracistbut.com collected hundreds of comments from Facebook that began with "I'm not a racist, but . . ." and ended with a racist comment. For example, one Facebook status update from a teen girl that was posted to the site said, "Not to be a racist, but I'm starting to see that niggers don't possess a single ounce of intellect." While creators of sites like notaracistbut.com intend to publicly shame racists, racism remains pervasive online.

In countless online communities, from YouTube to Twitter to World of Warcraft, racism and hate speech run rampant.[16] Messages of hate get spread both by those who agree with the sentiment and also by those who critique it. After the critically acclaimed movie *The Hunger Games* came out, countless fans turned to Twitter to comment on the casting of Rue, a small girl described in the book as having "dark brown skin and eyes." Tweets like "Call me a racist but when I found out rue was black her death wasn't as sad" and "Why does rue have to be black not gonna lie kinda ruined the movie" sparked outrage among antiracists who forwarded the messages to call attention to them, thereby increasing the visibility of this hostility.[17] On one hand, calling attention to these messages shames those who contributed them. On the other, it incites a new type of hate, which continues to reinforce structural divides.

Annoyed with what she perceived to be a lack of manners among Asian and Asian American students at her school, Alexandra Wallace posted a racist tirade on YouTube mocking students of Asian descent at UCLA in March 2011. The video depicts Wallace, a white blond-haired girl, criticizing Asian students for not being considerate of others. The central message of the video focuses on her complaint that Asian students are rude because they talk on their cell phones in the library. To emphasize her point, she pretends to speak in a speech pattern that she believes sounds Asian, saying, "Ching chong ling long ting tong," in a mocking tone.

The video—"Asians in the Library"—quickly attracted attention and spread widely, prompting an outpouring of angry comments, reaction videos, and parodies. For example, comedic singer-songwriter Jimmy Wong produced a video in which he sang a mock love song called "Ching Chong!" in response to Wallace's video. Hundreds of videos—with millions of views—were designed to publicly shame her and others with similar racist attitudes. A college lifestyle blog dug up bikini pictures of Wallace and posted them under the title "Alexandra

Wallace: Racist UCLA Student's Bikini Photos Revealed."[18] Meanwhile, Wallace—and her family—began receiving death threats, prompting her to drop out of UCLA and seek police protection. As one of her professors explained to the UCLA newspaper, "What Wallace did was hurtful and inexcusable, but the response has been far more egregious. She made a big mistake and she knows it, but they responded with greater levels of intolerance."[19]

Social media magnifies many aspects of daily life, including racism and bigotry. Some people use social media to express insensitive and hateful views, but others use the same technologies to publicly shame, and in some cases threaten, people who they feel are violating social decorum.[20] By increasing the visibility of individuals and their actions, social media doesn't simply shine a spotlight on the problematic action; it enables people to identify and harass others in a very public way. This, in turn, reinforces social divisions that plague American society.

Segregation in Everyday Life

In the United States, racism is pervasive, if not always visible. Class politics intertwine with race, adding another dimension to existing social divisions. Teens are acutely aware of the power of race and class in shaping their lives, even if they don't always have nuanced language to talk about it; furthermore, just because teens live in a culture in which racism is ever present doesn't mean that they understand how to deal with its complexities or recognize its more subtle effects. Some don't realize how a history of racism shapes what they observe. Heather, a white sixteen-year-old from Iowa, told me,

> I don't want to sound racist, but it is the black kids a lot of times that have the attitudes and are always talking back to the teachers, getting in fights around the school, starting fights around the school. I mean yeah, white kids of course get into their fights, but the black kids make theirs more public and so it's seen more often that oh, the black kids are such troublemakers.

In examining high school dynamics in the 1980s, linguist Penelope Eckert argued that schools are organized by social categories that appear on the surface to be about activities but in practice are actually about race and class.[21] I noticed this as I went through the rosters of various sports teams at a school in North Carolina. At first, when I asked students about why different sports seemed to attract students of one race exclusively, they told me that it was just what people were into. Later, one white boy sheepishly explained that he liked basketball but that, at his school, basketball was a black sport and thus not an activity that he felt comfortable doing. As a result of norms and existing networks, the sports teams in many schools I visited had become implicitly coded and culturally divided by race. Many teens are reticent to challenge the status quo.

Even in schools at which teens prided themselves on being open-minded, I found that they often ignorantly reproduced racial divisions. For example, in stereotypical fashion, teens from more privileged backgrounds would point to having friends of different races as "proof" of their openness.[22] When I asked about racial divisions in more privileged schools or in schools situated in progressive communities, I regularly heard the postracial society mantra, with teens initially telling me that race did not matter in friend groups at their school. And then we'd log in to their Facebook or MySpace page and I would find clues that their schools were quite segregated. For example, I'd find that friend networks within diverse schools would be divided by race. When I'd ask teens to explain this, they'd tell me that the divisions I was seeing were because of who was in what classes or who played what sport, not realizing that racial segregation played a role in those aspects of school life, too.

While on a work trip in Colorado, I met a group of privileged teens who were in town because their parents were at the meeting I was attending. Bored with the adult conversations, I turned to the teens in a casual manner. I started talking with Kath, a white seventeen-year-old who attended an east coast private school renowned for its elite student body and its phenomenal diversity program. Our casual conversation turned to race dynamics in schools; she was a passionate, progressive teen who took the issue of race seriously. Curious to see how this played out in her community, I asked her if we could visit her Facebook page together. I offered her my computer, and she gleefully logged into her account. Given the small size of her school, I wasn't surprised that she was friends with nearly everyone from her grade and many students from other grades. I asked her to show me her photos so that we could look at the comments on them. Although her school had recruited students from diverse racial and ethnic backgrounds, most of those who had left comments on her profile were white. I pointed this out to her and asked her to bring up profiles of other students in her grade from different racial and ethnic backgrounds. In each case, the commenters were predominantly of the same broad racial or ethnic background as the profile owner. Kath was stunned and a bit embarrassed. In her head, race didn't matter at her school. But on Facebook people were spending their time interacting with people from similar racial backgrounds.

When I analyzed friending patterns on social network sites with youth, I consistently found that race mattered. In large and diverse high schools where teens didn't befriend everyone in their school, their connections alone revealed racial preference. In smaller diverse schools, the racial dynamics were more visible by seeing who commented on each other's posts or who appeared tagged together in photographs. Only when I visited schools with low levels of diversity did race not seem to matter in terms of online connections. For example, in Nebraska, I met a young Muslim woman of Middle Eastern descent in a mostly white school. She had plenty of friends online and off, and not surprisingly, all were white. Of course, this did not mean that she was living in a world where ethnic differences didn't matter. Her classmates posted many comments about Middle Eastern Muslim terrorists on Facebook with caveats about how she was different.

Birds of a feather flock together, and personal social networks tend to be homogeneous, as people are more likely to befriend others like them.[23] Sociologists refer to the practice of connecting with like-minded individuals as *homophily*. Studies have accounted for homophily in sex and gender, age, religion, education level, occupation, and social class. But nowhere is homophily more strongly visible in the United States than in the divides along racial and ethnic lines. The reasons behind the practice of homophily and the resultant social divisions are complex, rooted in a history of inequality, bigotry, oppression, and structural constraints in American life.[24]

It's easy to lament self-segregation in contemporary youth culture, but teens' choice to connect to people like them isn't necessarily born out of their personal racist beliefs. In many cases, teens reinforce homophily in order to cope with the racist society in which they live. In *Why Are All the Black Kids Sitting Together in the Cafeteria?* psychologist Beverly Tatum argues that self-segregation is a logical response to the systematized costs of racism. For teens who are facing cultural oppression and inequality, connecting along lines of race and ethnicity can help teens feel a sense of belonging, enhance identity development, and help them navigate systematic racism. Homophily isn't simply the product of hatred or prejudice. It is also a mechanism of safety. Seong, a seventeen-year-old from Los Angeles, echoed this sentiment when she told me, "In a way we connect more 'cause we see each other and we're like, oh." Familiarity mattered to Seong because, as a Korean immigrant, she feels isolated and confused by American norms that seem very foreign to her. She doesn't want to reject her non-Korean peers, but at times, she just wants to be surrounded by people who understand where she comes from. Still, teens' willingness to accept—and thus *expect*—self-segregation has problematic roots and likely contributes to ongoing racial inequality.[25]

Race-based dynamics are a fundamental part of many teens' lives—urban and suburban, rich and poor. When they go online, these fraught dynamics do not disappear. Instead, teens reproduce them. Although the technology makes it possible *in principle* to socialize with anyone online, in practice, teens connect to the people that they know and with whom they have the most in common.

MySpace vs. Facebook

In a historic small town outside Boston, I was sitting in the library of a newly formed charter school in the spring of 2007. One of the school's administrators had arranged for me to meet different students to get a sense of the school dynamics. Given what I knew about the school, I expected to meet with a diverse group of teens, but I found myself in a series of conversations with predominantly white, highly poised, academically motivated teens who were reluctant to talk about the dynamics of inequality and race at their school.

After I met a few of her peers, Kat, a white fourteen-year-old from a comfortable background, came into the library, and we started talking about the social media practices of her classmates. She made a passing remark about her friends moving from MySpace to Facebook, and I asked to discuss the reasons. Kat grew noticeably uncomfortable. She began simply, noting that "MySpace is just old now and it's boring." But then she paused, looked down at the table, and continued. "It's not really racist, but I guess you could say that. I'm not really into racism, but I think that MySpace now is more like ghetto or whatever." Her honesty startled me so I pressed to learn more. I asked her if people at her school were still using MySpace and she hesitantly said yes before stumbling over her next sentence. "The people who use MySpace—again, not in a racist way—but are usually more like ghetto and hip-hop rap lovers group." Probing a little deeper, Kat continued to stare at and fiddle with her hands as she told me that everyone who was still using MySpace was black, whereas all of her white peers had switched to Facebook.[26]

During the 2006–2007 school year, when MySpace was at its peak in popularity with American high school students, Facebook started to gain traction. Some teens who had never joined MySpace created accounts on Facebook. Others switched from MySpace to Facebook. Still others eschewed Facebook and adamantly stated that they preferred MySpace. The presence of two competing services would not be particularly interesting if it weren't for the makeup of the participants on each site. During that school year, as teens chose between MySpace and Facebook, race and class were salient factors in describing which teens used which service. The driving force was obvious: teens focused their attention on the site where their friends were socializing.[27] In doing so, their choices reified the race and class divisions that existed within their schools. As Anastasia, a white seventeen-year-old from New York, explained in a comment she left on my blog:

> My school is divided into the "honors kids," (I think that is self-explanatory), the "good not-so-honors kids," "wangstas," (they pretend to be tough and black but when you live in a suburb in Westchester you can't claim much hood), the "latinos/hispanics," (they tend to band together even though they could fit into any other groups) and the "emo kids" (whose lives are alllllways filled with woe). We were all in MySpace with our own little social networks but when Facebook opened its doors to high schoolers, guess who moved and guess who stayed behind. . . . The first two groups were the first to go and then the "wangstas" split with half of them on Facebook and the rest on MySpace. . . . I shifted with the rest of my school to Facebook and it became the place where the "honors kids" got together and discussed how they were procrastinating over their next AP English essay.

When I followed up with Anastasia, I learned that she felt as though it was taboo to talk about these dynamics. She stood by her comment but also told me that her sister said that she sounded racist. Although the underlying segregation of friendship networks defined who chose what site, most teens didn't use the language of race and class to describe their social network site preference. Some may have recognized that this was what was happening, but most described the division to me in terms of personal preference.

My interviews with teens included numerous descriptive taste-based judgments about each site and those who preferred them. Those who relished MySpace gushed about their ability to "pimp out" their profiles with "glitter," whereas Facebook users viewed the resultant profiles as "gaudy," "tacky," and "cluttered." Facebook fans relished the site's aesthetic minimalism, while MySpace devotees described Facebook profiles as "boring," "lame," "sterile," and "elitist." Catalina, a white fifteen-year-old from Austin, told me that Facebook is better because "Facebook just seems more clean to me." What Catalina saw as cleanliness, Indian-Pakistani seventeen-year-old Anindita from Los Angeles labeled "simple." She recognized the value of simplicity, but she preferred the "bling" of MySpace because it allowed her to express herself.

In differentiating Facebook and MySpace through taste, teens inadvertently embraced and reinforced a host of cultural factors that are rooted in the history of race and class. Taste is not simply a matter of personal preference; it is the product of cultural dynamics and social structure. In *Distinction*, philosopher Pierre Bourdieu describes how one's education and class position shape perceptions of taste and how distinctions around aesthetics and tastes are used to reinforce class in everyday life. The linguistic markers that teens use to describe Facebook and MySpace—and the values embedded in those markers—implicitly mark class and race whether teens realize it or not.

Just as most teens believe themselves to be friends with diverse groups of people, most teens give little thought to the ways in which race and class connect to taste. They judge others' tastes with little regard to how these tastes are socially constructed. Consider how Craig, a white seventeen-year-old from California, differentiated MySpace and Facebook users through a combination of social and cultural distinctions:

> The higher castes of high school moved to Facebook. It was more cultured, and less cheesy. The lower class usually were content to stick to MySpace. Any high school student who has a Facebook will tell you that MySpace users are more likely to be barely educated and obnoxious. Like Peet's is more cultured than Starbucks, and Jazz is more cultured than bubblegum pop, and like Macs are more cultured than PC's, Facebook is of a cooler caliber than MySpace.

In this 2008 blog post entitled "Myface; Spacebook," Craig distinguished between what he saw as highbrow and lowbrow cultural tastes, using consumption patterns to differentiate classes of people and describe them in terms of a hierarchy. By employing the term "caste," Craig used a multicultural metaphor with ethnic and racial connotations that runs counter to the American ideal of social mobility. In doing so, he located his peers in immutable categories defined by taste.

Not all teens are as articulate as Craig with regard to the issue of taste and class, but most recognized the cultural distinction between MySpace and Facebook and marked users according to stereotypes that they had about these sites. When Facebook became more broadly popular, teens who were early adopters of Facebook started lamenting the presence of "the MySpace people." Again, Craig described this dynamic:

> Facebook has become the exact thing it tried to destroy. Like Anikin Skywalker, who loved justice so much, and he decided to play God as Darth Vader, Facebook has lost its identity and mission. It once was the cool, cultured thing to do, to have a Facebook, but now its the same. Girls have quizzes on their Facebooks: "Would you like to hook up with me? Yes, No" without a shred of dignity or subtlety. Again, I must scroll for 5 minutes to find the comment box on one's Facebook. The vexation of bulletins of MySpace are now replaced by those of applications. It alienated its "cultured" crowd by the addition of these trinkets.

From Craig's perspective, as Facebook became popular and mainstream, it, too, became lowbrow. The cultural distinction that existed during the 2006–2007 school year had faded, and now both sites felt "uncivilized" to Craig. He ended his post with a "desperate" plea to Google to build something "cultured."

In differentiating MySpace and Facebook as distinct cultural spaces and associating different types of people with each site, teens used technology to reinforce cultural distinctions during the time in which both sites were extraordinarily popular. These distinctions, far from being neutral, are wedded to everyday cultural markers. In constituting an "us" in opposition to "them," teens reinforce social divisions through their use of and attitudes toward social media. Even as teens espouse their tolerance toward others with respect to embodied characteristics, they judge their peers' values, choices, and tastes along axes that are rooted in those very characteristics.

The racial divide that these teens experienced as they watched their classmates choose between MySpace and Facebook during the 2006–2007 school year is one that happens time and again in technology adoption. In some cases, white teens use different technologies than teens of color. For example, Black and Latino urban youth embraced early smartphones like the Sidekick, but the device had limited traction among Asian, white, and suburban youth. In other cases, diverse populations adopt a particular tool, but practices within the service are divided along race and class lines. Such was the case in 2013 on both Facebook and Twitter, where teens' linguistic and visual conventions—as well as their choice of apps—were correlated with their race.[28]

People influence the technology practices of those around them. Because of this, the diffusion of technology often has structural features that reflect existing social networks. As teens turn to social media to connect with their friends, they consistently reproduce networks that reflect both the segregated realities of everyday life and the social and economic inequalities that exist within their broader peer networks. Teens go online to hang out with their friends, and given the segregation of American society, their friends are quite likely to be of the same race, class, and cultural background.

Networks Matter

The fact that social media reproduces—and makes visible—existing social divisions within American society should not be surprising, but it does challenge a persistent fantasy that the internet will dissolve and dismantle inequalities and create new opportunities to bring people together across race and class lines. In 2010, Secretary of State Hillary Rodham Clinton espoused such idealism in a speech at the Newseum in which she argued: "The internet can serve as a great equalizer. By providing people with access to knowledge and potential markets, networks can create opportunity where none exists. . . . Information networks have become a great leveler, and we should use them to help lift people out of poverty."[29] This rhetoric assumes that, because the internet makes information more readily available to more people than ever before, access to the internet will address historical informational and social inequities. Yet just because people have access to the internet does not mean that they have equal access to information. Information literacy is not simply about the structural means of access but also about the experience to know where to look, the skills to interpret what's available, and the knowledge to put new pieces of information into context. In a world where information is easily available, strong personal networks and access to helpful people often matter more than access to the information itself.[30]

In a technological era defined by social media, where information flows through networks and where people curate information for their peers, who you know shapes what you know. When social divisions get reinforced online, information inequities also get reproduced. When increased access to information produces information overload, sifting through the mounds of available information to make meaning requires time and skills. Those whose networks are vetting information and providing context are more privileged in this information landscape than those whose friends and family have little experience doing such information work.[31]

For many information needs, people turn to people around them. Sociologists have shown that social networks affect people's job prospects, health, and happiness.[32] Opportunities for social and economic support depend heavily on personal connections. Teens turn to their networks to learn about college opportunities. They also develop a sense of what's normative by watching those who surround them. When it comes to information and opportunity, who youth know matters. Just because teens can get access to a technology that can connect them to anyone anywhere does not mean that they have equal access to knowledge and opportunity.[33]

In his famous trilogy *The Information Age*, sociologist Manuel Castells argued that the industrial era is ending and that an information age has begun. His first volume—*The Rise of the Network Society*—makes the case for the power of networks as the organizational infrastructure of an economy based on information. Technology plays a central role in the network society that Castells recognizes is unfolding, and he documents the technological divide that put certain cities in better or worse positions to leverage the economic changes taking place. Although critics have accused Castells of technological determinism, Castells's analysis is more fruitfully understood as a critical accounting of what economic and cultural shifts are possible because of technology and why not everyone will benefit equally from these shifts.[34] In short, not everyone will benefit equally because networks—both social and technical—are neither evenly distributed nor meritocratic.

Social media does not radically rework teens' social networks. As a result, technology does not radically reconfigure inequality. The transformative potential of the internet to restructure social networks in order to reduce structural inequality rests heavily on people's ability to leverage it to make new connections. This is not how youth use social media.

Not only are today's teens reproducing social dynamics online, but they are also heavily discouraged from building new connections that would diversify their worldviews. The "stranger danger" rhetoric discussed in the chapter on danger doesn't just affect teens' interactions with adults; many teens are actively discouraged from developing relationships with other teens online for fear that those teens may turn out to be adults intending to harm them. Not all teens buy into this moral panic, but when teens do make connections online, they focus on engaging with people who share their interests, tastes, and cultural background. For these teens, turning to people who seem familiar allows them to feel safe, confident, and secure. They reinforce the homophilous social networks they inhabit instead of using technology to connect across lines of difference. Access to a wide range of people does not guarantee a reconfiguration of social connections.

The limited scope of teens' engagement with people from diverse backgrounds—and the pressure that they receive to not engage with strangers—is particularly costly for less privileged youth. Although everyone benefits from developing a heterogeneous social network, privileged youth are more likely to have connections to people with more privilege and greater access to various resources, opportunities, and types of information. When information opportunities are tethered to social networks, how social relations are constructed matters for every aspect of social equality. When social divisions are reinforced—and inequities across social networks reproduced—there are material, social, and cultural consequences.

The issue of inequality gets realized when information is structured to flow only to certain groups of people. During the 2006–2007 school year—the period when teens were segmenting themselves into Facebook and MySpace—many college admissions officers also started using social media for college recruitment. They created online profiles, produced spreadable videos, and invited high school students to talk with them and student representatives. Although millions of teenagers were active exclusively on MySpace, most of the colleges tailored their recruitment efforts to Facebook. When I asked admissions officers about their decision to focus on Facebook, they invariably highlighted a lack of resources and a need to prioritize. Universally, when I pointed out that black and Latino youth were more likely to be on MySpace and that their decision was effectively targeting primarily white and Asian students, they were stunned. They had never considered the cultural consequences of their choices.

At the time of this book's writing, it's quite common for companies to turn to LinkedIn, a professional social network site, to recruit college interns and new graduates. Recruiters typically prioritize candidates who already have contacts to the company as performed through social media. Some even explicitly ask applicants to list everyone they know who already works at the company. Those who don't know anyone at the company are disadvantaged as candidates. This tends to reinforce same-ness because people's social networks are rarely diverse. This also provides an additional obstacle for under-represented minorities, those who come from less advantaged communities, and people who generally lack social capital.

We don't live in a postracial society, and social media is not the cultural remedy that some people hoped it would become. Today's youth live in a world with real and pervasive social divisions. Those dynamics are reproduced online and have significant implications for how teens make sense of public life. People help define what's normative for their friends and contacts. And everyone's opportunities are dependent on whom they know. Having access to the information available through the internet is not enough to address existing structural inequities and social divisions. The internet will not inherently make the world more equal, nor will it automatically usher today's youth into a tolerant world. Instead, it lays bare existing and entrenched social divisions.

7 literacy
are today's youth digital natives?

Because teens grew up in a world in which the internet has always existed, many adults assume that youth automatically understand new technologies. From this perspective, teens are "digital natives," and adults, supposedly less knowledgeable about technology and less capable of developing these skills, are "digital immigrants." Two Massachusetts state government officials echoed this notion in 2010: "The children who attend school today are digital natives who think nothing of learning through the use of technology. As adults, we are digital immigrants who remember lessons delivered through film strips and overhead projectors. In a state where digital pioneers flourished, the educational system should catch up to the students."[1] Many of today's teens are indeed deeply engaged with social media and are active participants in networked publics, but this does not mean that they inherently have the knowledge or skills to make the most of their online experiences. The rhetoric of "digital natives," far from being useful, is often a distraction to understanding the challenges that youth face in a networked world.

In my fieldwork, I often found that teens must fend for themselves to make sense of how technologies work and how information spreads. Curiosity may lead many teens to develop meaningful knowledge about social media, but there is huge variation in knowledge and experience. I interviewed teens who used programming scripts to build complex websites. I also talked with teens who didn't know the difference between a web browser and the internet. I encountered teens who had nuanced understandings of different kinds of web content and helped create and spread internet culture via popular memes. I also met teens who couldn't recognize spam.

Teens may make their own media or share content online, but this does not mean that they inherently have the knowledge or perspective to critically examine what they consume. Being exposed to information or imagery through the internet and engaging with social media do not make someone a savvy interpreter of the meaning behind these artifacts. Technology is constantly reworking social and information systems, but teens will not become critical contributors to this ecosystem simply because they were born in an age when these technologies were pervasive.

It is dangerous to assume that youth are automatically informed. It is also naive to assume that so-called digital immigrants have nothing to offer.[2] Even those who are afraid of technology can offer valuable critical perspective. Neither teens nor adults are monolithic, and there is no magical relation between skills and age. Whether in school or in informal settings, youth need opportunities to develop the skills and knowledge to engage with contemporary technology effectively and meaningfully. Becoming literate in a networked age requires hard work, regardless of age.

The Emergence of the Digital Native

The notion of digital natives has political roots, mostly born out of American techno-idealism. In an effort to force the global elite to recognize the significance of an emergent mediated society, John Perry Barlow, a renowned poet and cyberlibertarian, leveraged this concept to divide the world into "us" and "them." Barlow, best known as the former lyricist for The Grateful Dead, was quite comfortable using provocative words to express political views. As mentioned in the Introduction, he penned "A Declaration of the Independence of Cyberspace" for the World Economic Forum in Davos in 1996. His manifesto was an explicit challenge to the "Governments of the Industrial World."

In positioning those who "come from Cyberspace" in opposition to the old world order, he juxtaposed the "native" against the "immigrant":

> You are terrified of your own children, since they are natives in a world where you will always be immigrants. Because you fear them, you entrust your bureaucracies with the parental responsibilities you are too cowardly to confront yourselves. In our world, all the sentiments and expressions of humanity, from the debasing to the angelic, are parts of a seamless whole, the global conversation of bits. We cannot separate the air that chokes from the air upon which wings beat.[3]

Barlow was probably not the first to suggest that the young are native to the emergent digital landscape, but his poetic framing highlights the implicit fear that stems from the generational gap that has emerged around technology.[4] He intended his proclamation to provoke reaction, and it did. But many people took this metaphor literally. It has become popular in public discourse to promote the idea that "natives" have singular technical powers and skills. The suggestion that many take from Barlow's proclamation is that adults should fear children's supposedly natural-born knowledge.

Following a similar line of thinking, Douglas Rushkoff argues in his 1996 book *Playing the Future* that children should be recognized for their ingenuity. He metaphorically describes the differences in linguistic development between older immigrants and children who grow up in a society whose dominant language is different than their parents' native tongue. He uses the concepts of immigrants and natives to celebrate children's development in the digital age.

In describing youth as natives, both Barlow and Rushkoff frame young people as powerful actors positioned to challenge the status quo. Yet many who use the rhetoric of digital natives position young people either as passive recipients of technological knowledge or as learners who easily pick up the language of technology the way they pick up a linguistic tongue. These notions draw on the frames that Barlow and Rushkoff put forward but twist them in ways that are far from their intention.

In 2001, educational consultant Marc Prensky penned an article entitled "Digital Natives, Digital Immigrants." In that article, he claims that "today's students think and process information fundamentally differently from their predecessors."[5] He argues that they should be called "digital natives" because "our students today are all 'native speakers' of the digital language of computers, video games and the Internet." Like Barlow and Rushkoff, Prensky also positions older people as immigrants, noting, "Those of us who were not born into the digital world but have, at some later point in our lives, become fascinated by and adopted many or most aspects of the new technology are, and always will be compared to them, Digital Immigrants." Although Prensky claims to have coined the term *digital native* independently of either Rushkoff or Barlow, many people cite Prensky as the originator because he popularized the notion.[6] Like Barlow and Rushkoff, Prensky did so in order to celebrate young people's purported fluency with technology.

As the term took off and began to permeate popular discourse, scholars began critiquing the underlying implications. From an ethnic studies perspective, the language of "natives" and "immigrants" is particularly fraught. At a private event I attended, anthropologist Genevieve Bell invited everyone in the room to interrogate the underlying implications of these terms. She reminded the room that, throughout history, powerful immigrants have betrayed native populations while destroying their spiritual spaces and asserting power over them. Although this is not the story of all immigrants, this reminder raises serious questions about what is recognized in discussions of digital natives. Is the goal to celebrate youth savvy or to destroy their practices? Do people intend to recognize native knowledge as valuable or as something that should be restricted and controlled?

The notion of the digital native, whether constructed positively or negatively, has serious unintended consequences. Not only is it fraught, but it obscures the uneven distribution of technological skills and media literacy across the youth population, presenting an inaccurate portrait of young people as uniformly prepared for the digital era and ignoring the assumed level of privilege required to be "native." Worse, by not doing the work necessary to help youth develop broad digital competency, educators and the public end up reproducing digital inequality because more privileged youth often have more opportunities to develop these skills outside the classroom. Rather than focusing on coarse generational categories, it makes more sense to focus on the skills and knowledge that are necessary to make sense of a mediated world. Both youth *and* adults have a lot to learn.

We live in a technologically mediated world. Being comfortable using technology is increasingly important for everyday activities: obtaining a well-paying job, managing medical care, engaging with government. Rather than assuming that youth have innate technical skills, parents, educators, and policymakers must collectively work to support those who come from different backgrounds and have different experiences. Educators have an important role to play in helping youth navigate networked publics and the information-rich environments that the internet supports. Familiarity with the latest gadgets or services is often less important than possessing the critical knowledge to engage productively with networked situations, including the ability to control how personal information flows and how to look for and interpret accessible information.

Most formal educational settings do not prioritize digital competency, in part because of the assumption that teens natively understand anything connected to technology and in part because existing educational assessments do not require this prioritization. Although youth are always learning as they navigate these systems, adults—including parents, educators, and librarians—can support them further by helping turn their experience into knowledge.[7]

Youth Need New Literacies

Many of the technologies that youth encounter, from Google to Wikipedia, require users to engage critically with the information they're seeing. When we assume that youth will just absorb all things digital through exposure, we absolve ourselves of our responsibility to help teenagers develop necessary skills. Too often, we focus on limiting youth from accessing inaccurate or problematic information. This is a laudable goal, but alone it does teens a fundamental disservice.

Youth must become media literate.[8] When they engage with media—either as consumers or producers—they need to have the skills to ask questions about the construction and dissemination of particular media artifacts. What biases are embedded in the artifact? How did the creator intend for an audience to interpret that artifact, and what are the consequences of that interpretation?

The notion of media literacy predates the internet. In the United Kingdom, media literacy efforts date back to the 1930s, when educators argued that the public needed the skills to critically think about propaganda.[9] At that time, posters had emerged as key war propaganda. Media literacy education didn't get started in the United States until the 1960s, after advertising practices were well under way.[10] Educators argued that informed citizens needed to be able to critically evaluate the messages that surround them. As new genres of media proliferated, many were concerned that audiences could be manipulated into believing a particular narrative. Although fact-checking can often serve to combat certain aspects of manipulative messaging, people must also learn to question the biases and assumptions underpinning the content they see.

Even though media literacy programs have been discussed and haphazardly implemented for decades, most people have little training in being critical of the content that they consume. Long before the internet, critical media literacy has never been considered essential in schools or communities. Instead, schools have relied on trustworthy publishers, information curators, and other reputable sources. In a networked world, in which fewer intermediaries control the flow of information and more information is flowing, the ability to critically question information or media narratives is increasingly important. Censorship of inaccurate or problematic content does not provide youth the skills they will one day need to evaluate information independently. They need to know how to grapple with the plethora of information that is easily accessible and rarely vetted.

And given the uneven digital literacy skills of youth, we cannot abandon them to learn these lessons on their own.[11]

But what must they learn? Certainly, they need the critical skills that media literacy advocates have promoted for decades. For example, they need to be able to understand the biases in advertising, whether the ads are disseminated online or through more traditional media. But in a digitally saturated society, media literacy is only the first step. Technical skills are increasingly important. Few teens have a basic understanding of how the computer systems they use every day work. Some are curious enough to develop this knowledge, but it takes time and effort as well as opportunities, networks, and training to become active participants and contributors.

Although developing technical skills is not widespread, doing so can become a part of meaningful participation. In the early days of MySpace's popularity, a few teens learned that they could modify the look and feel of their profiles by inserting code in the form of HTML, CSS, or JavaScript. This was the result of a bug in MySpace's development code. After watching teens explore self-expression through code, the company decided not to patch the bug in order to see how users would personalize their pages. Excited by the ability to create "layouts" and "backgrounds," teens started learning enough code to modify their profiles. Some teens became quite sophisticated technically as they sought to build extensive, creative profiles. Others simply copied and pasted code that they found online. But this technical glitch—combined with teens' passion for personalizing their MySpace profiles—ended up creating an opportunity for teens to develop some technical competency.[12] MySpace eventually began blocking the inserted code due to security issues and, instead, created an interface for users to modify their profiles. This simplified the process and resulted in fewer technical problems, but it also closed the unique learning opportunity that MySpace had accidentally created.

In order to attract wide audiences, many technologies are designed to be extraordinarily simple. This was not always true. I spent countless hours as a teen pouring through manuals, debugging network hardware, and learning technical syntax in order to socialize online.

When technologies are designed to make everyday use as easy as possible, it is not necessary for users to learn the technical skills that early internet adoption required. Although it is not necessary to be technically literate to participate, those with limited technical literacy aren't necessarily equipped to be powerful citizens of the digital world. As new technologies emerge to enable people to access information, the issues brought forth by media literacy and technological familiarity intersect to create new challenges. Empowering youth requires much more than calling them native participants.

The Politics of Algorithms

Corinne, a white thirteen-year-old from Massachusetts, proudly exclaimed in a group setting that she didn't use Wikipedia. When asked why, she explained, "I've heard that it's not true, and usually if I'm looking for something that I want, and it's true, I usually go on Google." Corinne's teachers had encouraged her to use Google to search for information. They told her that Wikipedia was full of inaccuracies because anyone could edit it. Like many of her peers, Corinne had interpreted this to mean that anything that appeared at the top of the Google result page must be true. If not, why would it appear at the top? And why would her teachers recommend it? She trusted the content on Google because adults had told her that it was a trustworthy site. She saw Google as having a similar reputation as that of the textbooks that her teacher assigned. Wikipedia, on the other hand, was not to be trusted because her teacher said so.

Wikipedia and Google are fundamentally different sites. Wikipedia is a crowdsourced encyclopedia built using technologies that allow for easy editing. An active community of volunteer moderators shapes the content, regulating it through a set of collectively determined social and technical protocols that provide a framework for appropriate user edits. Users regularly contest and debate content, as moderators and other passionate volunteers work diligently to resolve disagreements and assert their own beliefs about what is legitimate, notable, and of high quality.

Google, by contrast, is both a for-profit company and a search engine that is monetized through advertising.[13] Google is not in the business of verifying content or assessing content's quality. Nor does it have editors whose job it is to verify sources of content. Rather, proprietary algorithms written by the company's engineers produce the results. The algorithms that underpin this powerful search engine rely on links, text, and other data signals to ascertain which pages should appear at the top for any query. Because Google is the source of so much traffic, countless people, corporations, and organizations engage in a practice known as *search engine optimization* in which they manipulate information in order to maximize the likelihood that a particular page will get a high ranking. In response, Google continuously alters its algorithms to minimize the efficacy of those trying to manipulate the results.[14]

Although the pages that Google offers are highly likely to be topically relevant with regard to the query, the company's employees do not try to assess the quality of a given page. There are countless sites dedicated to conspiracy theories and celebrity gossip that have a high ranking, and Google is happy to provide this content if that's what a searcher wishes to find. Google aims to provide links to pages that are relevant to the given search. This is not the same as vouching for the accuracy of those pages. Many teens I met assumed that someone verifies every link that Google shares. This is both naive and inaccurate.

Everywhere I went, I heard parents, teachers, and teens express reverence toward Google. They saw Google as a source of trusted information in a digital ecosystem filled with content of dubious quality. More important, many of the people I met believed that Google was neutral, unlike traditional news sources such as *Fox News* or the *New York Times*. Most people take for granted that someone, typically the editor in chief, chooses what stories appear on the front page of a newspaper or which are covered in a TV segment. Conversely, people naively assume that algorithms, procedural sets of instructions for calculating an output, such as the ones produced by Google, must not have nearly the same biases as an editor.

The notion of an algorithm is foreign to most people, including most youth. But algorithms are fundamental to how many computational systems, including Google, work. Most people who use search engines do not understand that they are made up of complex machine learning algorithms. Even those who do don't necessarily understand how those algorithms work. The specifics of corporate algorithms, like Google's, are considered trade secrets. To complicate matters more, those who build machine learning algorithms for companies like Google cannot account for all of the decisions that the algorithms will make as they evolve based on input.

Although understanding the particulars of the technology is not necessary, it is important to recognize that algorithms are not neutral. When engineers are building machine learning algorithms, they typically use training data and, in some cases, classifications provided by the engineer to help the algorithm analyze the data. These systems are often designed to cluster data in order to provide results. Engineers then test those results with queries that they believe should have a "right" answer, or at least a sensible one. People—and their biases—are involved at each stage. They choose what data to train a system on, what classifications matter, and which examples to test. They make very human decisions about how to adjust the algorithms to provide results that they believe are of high quality. As communication scholar Tarleton Gillespie has argued, there are politics to algorithms.[15]

The results that a search engine produces may reveal biases in the underlying data, or they may highlight how the weights chosen by engineers prioritize certain content over others. Although engineers diligently work to clean the data and minimize biases, they are unable to eliminate their own biases. And because of the complicated nature of the algorithms and the massive quantities of underlying data that algorithms must analyze, engineers cannot easily predict what query will produce what output.[16]

Increasingly, the results people get from search engines like Google are highly personalized and dependent on what Google knows about the person doing the query, including demographic information, search query history, and data obtained through social media. This process results in differential information retrieval, with different people receiving dissimilar results. Some tout such approaches as helpful for users, but others are more cynical about such personalization. In his 2011 book, *The Filter Bubble*, political activist and technology creator Eli Pariser argues that personalization algorithms produce social divisions that undermine any ability to create an informed public. For example, users with a long history of clicking on conservative or liberal news sources might only be shown results that align with their political views, thereby reinforcing an existing political gulf.

As scholars at Harvard's Berkman Center have shown, search engines like Google shape the quality of information that youth experience.[17] Teens view Google as the center of the digital information universe, even though they have little understanding of how the search results are produced, let alone any awareness of how personalization affects what they see. They uncritically trust Google, just as most adults do. In Iowa, white eighteen-year-old Wolf explained, "If you can't Google it, it doesn't exist." His white seventeen-year-old friend Red agreed, adding, "Google knows all."

Given the lack of formal gatekeepers and the diversity of content and authors, it's often hard to determine credibility online. Because youth do not learn to critically assess the quality of information they access, they simply look for new intermediaries who can help them determine what's valuable. For better or worse, they take Google's results for granted while also dismissing high-quality content from other sites that they have been taught to distrust. Like their parents, they assume that Google is neutral and that sites like Wikipedia have dubious information.

Wikipedia as a Site of Knowledge Production

Wikipedia has a bad rap in American K-12 education. The de facto view among many educators is that a free encyclopedia that anyone can edit must be filled with inaccuracies and misleading information. Students' tendency to use the service as their first and last source for information only reinforces their doubts. Ignoring the educational potential of Wikipedia, teachers consistently tell students to stay clear of Wikipedia at all costs. I heard this sentiment echoed throughout the United States.

In Massachusetts, white fifteen-year-old Kat told me that "Wikipedia is a really bad thing to use because they don't always cite their sources. . . . You don't know who's writing it." Brooke, a white fifteen-year-old from Nebraska explained that "[teachers] tell us not to [use Wikipedia] because a lot of—some of the information is inaccurate." These comments are nearly identical to the sentiments I typically hear from parents and teachers. Although it is not clear whether students are reproducing their teachers' beliefs or have come to the same conclusion independently, students are well aware that most teachers consider Wikipedia to have limited accuracy.

When people dismiss Wikipedia, they almost always cite limited trust and credibility, even though analyses have shown that Wikipedia's content is just as credible as, if not more reliable than, more traditional resources like *Encyclopedia Britannica*.[18] Teachers continue to prefer familiar, formally recognized sources. Educators encourage students to go to the library. When they do recommend digital sources, they view some as better than others without explaining why.[19] As Aaron, a white fifteen-year-old from Texas explained, "A lot of teachers don't want you to use [Wikipedia] as a source in a bibliography because it's not technically accredited. And they'd rather you use a university professor's website or something." Although Aaron didn't know what it meant for a source to be accredited, he had a mental model of which sources his teachers viewed as legitimate and which they eschewed. Similarly, Heather, a white sixteen-year-old from Iowa, explained, "Our school says not to use Wikipedia as our main source. You can use it as like a second or third source but not as a main source. They say MSN Encarta. . . . They say to use that because it's more reliable." When I asked students why they should prefer sites like Encarta and professors' webpages, they referenced trust and credibility, even though students couldn't explain what made those particular services trustworthy.

Although nearly every teenager I met told me stories about teachers who had forbidden them from using Wikipedia for schoolwork, nearly all of them used the site anyhow. Some used the site solely as a starting point for research, going then to Google to find sources they could cite that their teachers considered more respectable. Others knowingly violated their teachers' rules and worked to hide their reliance on Wikipedia. In Boston, I met a teen boy who told me that his teachers never actually checked the sources, so he used Wikipedia to get information he needed. When he went to list citations, he said they came from more credible sources like Encarta, knowing that his teachers would never check to see whether a particular claim *actually* came from Encarta. In other words, he faked his sources because he believed his teachers wouldn't check. Although he had found a way of working around his teachers' rules, he had failed to learn why they wanted citations in the first place. All he had learned was that his teachers' restrictions on using Wikipedia were "stupid."

Because many adults assume that youth are digitally savvy—and because they themselves do not understand many online sources— they often end up giving teens misleading or inaccurate information about what they see online. A conflict emerges as teens turn to Wikipedia with uncritical eyes while teachers deride the site without providing a critical lens with which to look at the information available.

Wikipedia can be a phenomenal educational tool, but few educators I met knew how to use it constructively. Unlike other sources of information, including encyclopedias and books by credible authors, the entire history of how users construct a Wikipedia entry is visible. By looking at the "history" of a page, a viewer can see when someone made edits, who did the editing, and what that user edited. By looking at the discussion, it's possible to read the debates that surround the edits. Wikipedia isn't simply a product of knowledge; it's also a record of the process by which people share and demonstrate knowledge.

In most educational institutions, publishers and experts vet much of the content that teens encounter and there is no discussion about why something is accurate or not. Some teachers deem certain publications trustworthy and students treat that content as fact. Reading old history books and encyclopedias can be humorous—or depressing, depending on the content and your point of view—because of what the writers assumed to be accurate at one point in time or in one cultural context. Just like today, past students who were given those materials were also taught that all of the information they were receiving was factual.

Although many students view textbooks as authoritative material, the content is neither neutral nor necessarily accurate. Textbooks often grow outdated more quickly than schools can replace them. The teens I interviewed loved finding inaccuracies in their own textbooks, such as lists of planets that included Pluto. Of course, not all inaccuracies are the product of mistakes or outdated facts. Some writers insert biases into texts because they reinforce certain social or political beliefs. In the United States, Texas is notorious for playing a significant role in shaping the content of textbooks in all states.[20] So when educators in Texas insist on asserting that America's "founding fathers" were all Christian, it creates unease among historians who do not believe this to be accurate. What goes into a textbook is highly political.

History, in particular, differs depending on perspective. I grew up hearing examples of this in my own family. Born to a British father and a Canadian mother, my mother moved to New York as a young girl. She recalls her confusion when my grandfather complained about her American history lessons and threatened to destroy her textbook. Compared to the British narratives my patriotic British veteran grandfather had learned, the American origin story was outright offensive.

American and British high schools teach events like the American Revolutionary War very differently—and rarely do schools in either country consider such things as the role of women or the perspectives of slaves or Native Americans. This is a topic of deep interest to historians and the driving force behind books like Howard Zinn's *A People's History of the United States*, which tells American history through the perspective of those who "lost." Although many people believe that the winner gets to control the narrative, accounts also diverge when conflicting stories don't need to be resolved. When countries like the United States and the United Kingdom produce their own textbooks, they don't need to arrive at mutually agreeable narratives. However, when people like my mother cross the ocean and must face conflicting perspectives, there's often little room for debating these perspectives. In my mother's childhood household, there was a right history and a wrong history. According to my grandfather, my mother's textbook was telling the wrong history.

Wikipedia often, but not always, forces resolution of conflicting accounts. Critics may deride Wikipedia as a crowdsourced, user-generated collection of information of dubious origin and accuracy, but the service also provides a platform for seeing how knowledge evolves and is contested. The Wikipedia entry on the American Revolution is a clear product of conflicting ideas of history, with information that stems from British and American textbooks interwoven and combined with information on the role of other actors that have been historically marginalized in standard textbooks.

What makes the American Revolution Wikipedia entry interesting is not simply the output in the form of a comprehensive article but the extensive discussion pages and edit history. On the history pages, those who edit Wikipedia entries describe why they made a change. On discussion pages, participants debate how to resolve conflicts between editors. There's an entire section on the American Revolution discussion page dedicated to whether colonists should be described as "patriots"—the American term—or "insurgents"—the British term. In the discussion, one user suggests a third term: "revolutionaries." Throughout the

Wikipedia entry, the editors collectively go to great lengths to talk about "American patriots" or use terms like "revolutionaries" or simply describe the colonists as "Americans." The American Revolution discussion page on Wikipedia is itself a lesson about history. Through archived debate, the editors make visible just how contested simple issues are, forcing the reader to think about why writers present information in certain ways. I learned more about the different viewpoints surrounding the American Revolution by reading the Wikipedia discussion page than I learned in my AP American history class.

Although most teens that I met who used the internet knew of Wikipedia and most of those who had visited the site knew it was editable, virtually none knew about the discussion page or the history of edits. No one taught them to think of Wikipedia as an evolving document that reveals how people produce knowledge. Instead they determined whether an article was "good" or "bad" based on whether they thought that their teachers could be trusted when they criticized Wikipedia. This is a lost opportunity. Wikipedia provides an ideal context for engaging youth to interrogate their sources and understand how information is produced.

Wikipedia is, by both its nature and its commitments, a work in progress. The content changes over time as users introduce new knowledge and raise new issues. The site has its share of inaccuracies, but the community surrounding Wikipedia also has a systematic approach to addressing them. At times, people actively and intentionally introduce false information, either as a hoax or for personal gain. Wikipedia acknowledges these problems and maintains a record for observers. Wikipedia even maintains a list of hoaxes that significantly affected the site.[21]

Many digital technologies undermine or destabilize institutions of authority and expertise, revealing alternative ways of generating and curating content.[22] Crowdsourced content—such as what is provided to Wikipedia—is not necessarily better, more accurate, or more comprehensive than expert-vetted content, but it can, and often does, play a valuable role in making information accessible and providing a site for reflection on the production of knowledge. The value of Wikipedia would be minimal if it weren't for sources that people could use in creating entries. Many of Wikipedia's history articles, for example, rely heavily on content written by historians. What Wikipedia does well is combine and present information from many sources in a free, publicly accessible, understandable way while also revealing biases and discussions that went into the production of that content. Even with their limitations and weaknesses, projects like Wikipedia are important for educational efforts because they make the production of knowledge more visible. They also highlight a valuable way of using technology to create opportunities for increased digital literacy.

Digital Inequality

The challenges brought forth by media literacy stem from and reinforce the broader issue of digital inequality, which is often elided by the frame of digital natives. As media theorist Henry Jenkins eloquently explains:

> Talk of "digital natives" helps us to recognize and respect the new kinds of learning and cultural expression which have emerged from a generation that has come of age alongside the personal and networked computer. Yet, talk of "digital natives" may also mask the different degrees of access to and comfort with emerging technologies experienced by different youth. Talk of digital natives may make it harder for us to pay attention to the digital divide in terms of who has access to different technical platforms and the participation gap in terms of who has access to certain skills and competencies or for that matter, certain cultural experiences and social identities. Talking about youth as digital natives implies that there is a world which these young people all share and a body of knowledge they have all mastered, rather than seeing the online world as unfamiliar and uncertain for all of us.[23]

By focusing on the "digital divide" between levels of access and types of competencies, Jenkins highlights how a well-intentioned public uses the rhetoric surrounding digital natives to obfuscate and reinforce existing inequalities.

The politics surrounding the digital divide date back several decades. In the late 1990s, journalists, academics, and governmental agencies began using the term *digital divide* to describe the gap in access between rich and poor.[24] In its earliest stages of use, the construct referred to a gap in device availability and internet connectivity between the digital "haves and have nots."[25] Activists and politicians rallied to close the gap in access, primarily focusing on a "devices and conduits" approach that looked to provide digitally underprivileged populations with internet-connected computers.[26] Government agencies viewed technology—and the internet in particular—as playing a critical role in economic opportunities. They wanted to ensure "access to the fundamental tools of the digital economy" as a priority investment for the future of the US economy.[27]

As public debates raged over how to address inequality brought about by the digital divide, it soon became clear that access should not be conflated with use. The digital divide soon encompassed discourses surrounding technology skills and media literacy.[28] Scholars and governmental agencies began to argue that access alone mattered little if people didn't know how to use the tools in front of them.[29] As more youth gained access through schools and public institutions, and as a result of the decline in costs of technology, scholars increasingly raised concern about the unevenness of skills, literacy, and "socially meaningful" access.[30]

By 2011, 95 percent of American teenagers had some form of access to the internet, whether at home or at school.[31] What that access looks like and what teens do with that access varies greatly.[32] Concerned about how increased access was prompting the media to declare the digital divide over, Jenkins and his coauthors starting raising concerns over the emerging "participation gap." They highlighted that differential access results in different levels of engagement and participation.[33] For example, a teen who uses a library computer with filtered access for an hour a day has a very different experience with the internet than one who has a smartphone, laptop, and unrestricted connectivity.[34]

I witnessed this phenomenon time and again in my fieldwork. I met teens whose only access to Facebook was on shared computers at a Boys and Girls Club after school. They knew how to get around the site, upload photos, modify privacy settings, and socialize with their friends. At first blush, they looked like sophisticated users. But as I started watching more intently, I realized that their knowledge about how to use technology to meet their own needs was nowhere as sophisticated as those who had their own computers at home and accessed Facebook via their iPhones. The differences weren't noticeable when it came to navigating Facebook for social purposes. They appeared when I watched how both privileged and disadvantaged teens turned to social media to get information and support.

In New York, I watched as a teen girl used her Android phone. She texted and regularly used apps like Twitter and Facebook. Enthusiastically, she showed me how she moved seamlessly between multiple semi-synchronous conversations. But when I asked her about how she used her phone to look things up for school, she let out a deep sigh. She switched over to the browser, opened up Google, and typed in a test query. Then she handed the phone to me, commenting on how long it took for her browser to load a given page. She told me that it was possible to surf the web on her phone, but it was time-consuming and frustrating, so she rarely bothered. She preferred to look things up on the computer at school, but she rarely had that type of access. If she really needed something, she texted her friends to see if anyone knew the answer or had access to a "real" computer. By most measures, she had full internet access through her smartphone, but she was acutely aware of the limitations of that kind of access.

Variations in experience also result in another form of digital inequality: differential levels of skills. For more than a decade, sociologist Eszter Hargittai has surveyed internet users, including youth, about their web skills.[35] She shows that far from being a generational issue, there are significant differences in media literacy and technical skills even within age cohorts. Variation in skills is linked in part to differences in access to computers. On one end of the spectrum, those teens who have their own laptops and smart phones often access the internet wherever they go for everything from fashion advice to homework assignments. At the other end of the spectrum are teens who have limited opportunities to access the internet and then only in highly regulated, filtered contexts like school computer centers or libraries. Not surprisingly, Hargittai found that teens' technological skills are strongly correlated with the quality of their access. Quality of access is, also unsurprisingly, correlated with socioeconomic status. As mentioned earlier, Hargittai argues that many youth, far from being digital natives, are quite digitally naive.[36]

There is little doubt that youth must have access, skills, and media literacy to capitalize on opportunities in a networked society, but focusing on these individual capacities obscures how underlying structural formations shape teens' access to opportunities and information. When information flows through social networks and interaction shapes experience, who you know matters. Youth who are surrounded by highly sophisticated technical peers are far more likely to develop technical skills themselves. In communities where technical wherewithal is neither valued nor normative, teens are far less likely to become digitally savvy. As media scholars Kate Crawford and Penelope Robinson have argued, networks of association and knowledge powerfully affect what information and knowledge people integrate into their lives.[37]

How we picture the issue of digital inequality also has political implications. As communication scholar Dmitry Epstein and his coauthors argue, when society frames the digital divide as a problem of access, we see government and industry as the responsible party for addressing the issue.[38] When society understands the digital divide as a skills issue, we place the onus of learning how to manage on individuals and families. At times, we also invoke educational entities and public institutions to support individual learning, but those conversations rarely include a discussion of government funding. The burden of responsibility shifts depending on how we construct the problem rhetorically and socially. The language we use matters.

Beyond Digital Natives

Most scholars have by now rejected the term digital natives, but the public continues to embrace it. This prompted John Palfrey and Urs Gasser, coauthors of *Born Digital: Understanding the First Generation of Digital Natives*, to suggest that scholars and youth advocates should reclaim the concept and make it more precise.[39] They argue that dismissing the awkward term fails to account for the shifts that are at play because of new technologies. To correct for misconceptions, they offer a description of digital natives that they feel highlights the inequalities discussed in this chapter: "Digital natives share a common global culture that is defined not by age, strictly, but by certain attributes and experiences related to how they interact with information technologies, information itself, one another, and other people and institutions. Those who were not 'born digital' can be just as connected, if not more so, than their younger counterparts. And not everyone born since, say, 1982, happens to be a digital native."[40]

In their writings, Palfrey and Gasser go to great lengths to clarify who is—and who is not—a digital native. They highlight the importance of the emergent participation gap and the challenges brought about as a result of digital inequality. Although their desire to reclaim the term digital native is laudable, it's not clear that many people have recognized the very valid nuance in their argument. More often than not, many people continue to cite Palfrey and Gasser's work as "proof" that all kids are digital natives. Although I respect Palfrey and Gasser's stance, I'm not convinced that the term itself can be reclaimed. Even though they offer a nuanced argument, scholars and journalists continue to point to them while using the term to refer to a whole generation. At this point, the problematic frame of the digital native often undermines efforts to celebrate and critically examine how teens do and do not engage with social media.

I believe that the digital natives rhetoric is worse than inaccurate: it is dangerous. Because of how society has politicized this language, it allows some to eschew responsibility for helping youth and adults navigate a networked world. If we view skills and knowledge as inherently generational, then organized efforts to achieve needed forms of literacy are unnecessary. In other words, a focus on today's youth as digital natives presumes that all we as a society need to do is be patient and wait for a generation of these digital wunderkinds to grow up. A laissez-faire attitude is unlikely to eradicate the inequalities that continue to emerge. Likewise, these attitudes will not empower average youth to be more sophisticated internet participants.

When Marc Prensky popularized the notion of digital natives, he never expected this metaphor to have a significant life, let alone to justify passivity by adults.[41] Instead, he argues, we should be looking to increase "digital wisdom," both in creating empowering tools that enable understanding and in empowering people to use existing tools wisely. Recognizing that technology can be used in both harmful and beneficial ways, Prensky maintains that it is important that we all work to be more thoughtful about our engagement with technology.

Developing wisdom requires active learning. Teens acquire many technological skills through extensive experimentation with social media and curiosity-driven exploration. Because teens turn to these services to socialize with peers, they often gain the skills that are part of informal social learning.[42] However, many of the media literacy skills needed to be digitally savvy require a level of engagement that goes far beyond what the average teen picks up hanging out with friends on Facebook and Twitter. Technical skills, such as the ability to build online spaces, require active cultivation. These skills must be studied deliberately. Teens may develop an intuitive sense for how to navigate social interactions online through casual engagement and experience, but this does not translate to an understanding of why search queries return some content before others. Nor does experience with social media push young people to learn how to build their own systems, versus simply using a social media platform. Teens' social status and position alone do not determine how fluent or informed they are vis-à-vis technology.

Technology will increasingly play an important role in society. Comfort with technology is often a prerequisite for obtaining even the most basic of jobs. Government agencies are increasingly turning to technology to provide services and engage citizens. And many high-status opportunities—from higher education to new forms of employment—expect people to be media literate and technologically advanced. It behooves all of us to move past assumptions about today's youth. Both adults and youth need to develop media literacy and technological skills to be active participants in our information society. Learning is a lifelong process.

8 searching for a public of their own

Not far from my hometown of Lancaster, Pennsylvania, I met a white, middle-class sixteen-year-old named Emily. As she told me about her life and what she liked to do, I couldn't help but feel nostalgic. Although she lived in a different town and went to a different school, so many of her cultural touchstones were familiar to me, including the Turkey Hill convenience stores that dotted the area and Park City, the shopping mall that attracted people for miles around. Emily told me that she loved the mall and attended many school sporting events. But as I probed, I also learned that she didn't particularly care about shopping and that she had never watched a football game or wrestling match in her life, even though she had attended many such events.

For Emily, going to places where her peers gather is a freedom—even if she isn't actually watching the game or buying clothes. When she's out in public, "It's a time when you can just fool around and be free and do whatever you want. It's not fair to be tied down to chores or school. You need that little bit of freedom." Her younger brother prefers hanging out at friends' houses, but Emily would much rather gather in public places because these settings expand the social possibilities. "If you go [out] with your friends, there might be other people you run into that are your friends too. I would say it's more of an opportunity to see more of your friends than just going over to a friend's house. Going over to a friend's house, there might be one friend or maybe three. Whereas going to the mall, it can be seven or twelve." Emily told me that she takes any opportunity possible to gather with friends in public settings. She attends basketball games, track meets, and any other school sports event that her friends might attend. She goes to the movies whenever she can get a ride, even if the film her friends choose doesn't particularly excite her. She wants the opportunity to hang out in the theater before the show.

Emily looks for places where she can hang out, joke around with friends, and simply be herself. Park City is one place that offers her this freedom. That very mall was the go-to place for my peer group as well. Back then, we never had any money to buy anything more luxurious than an Auntie Anne's pretzel, but shopping was never the point. We wanted to go to the mall because the people we knew went there.

Unlike Emily, I was often forbidden from going to Park City. When I was in high school, the local business community had teamed up with the school district to create an alternative high school for students who were not succeeding in traditional schools. They decided to place this experimental school at Park City because that's where so many of the students they were seeking to attract were hanging out. Those kids—and, by extension, the mall—had a bad reputation for violence, truancy, and delinquency more generally. Park City has changed tremendously in the twenty years since that school first opened; it is now considered an upscale establishment with both midrange and high-end brands. Although Emily and her friends meet up at the food court, the presence of teenagers there pales in comparison to what I remember growing up. Whenever I go home, I'm always surprised at how pristine, respectable, and boring Park City feels. As I talked with other teens in the area, I learned that the mall was still seen as dangerous even though it had none of the grime or grit that was present in my teen years. Most teens were allowed to hang out there.

Many of the teens that I met—both in Pennsylvania and elsewhere—craved the freedoms that Emily had. They were desperate for the opportunity to leave their homes to gather with friends. Although not universal, most could attend school functions. Some could get together with friends in public venues on weekends. Yet over and over again and across the country, teens complained to me that they never had enough time, freedom, or ability to meet up with friends when and where they wanted. To make up for this, they turned to social media to create and inhabit networked publics.

The Creation of Networked Publics

The topics addressed in this book often hinge on teens' interest in getting meaningful access to public spaces and their desire to connect to their peers. Rather than fighting to reclaim the places and spaces that earlier cohorts had occupied, many teens have taken a different approach: they've created their own publics. Teens find social media appealing because it allows them access to their friends and provides an opportunity to be a part of a broader public world while still situated physically in their bedrooms. Through social media, they build networks of people and information. As a result, they both participate in and help create networked publics.

As discussed in the Introduction and throughout the book, networked publics serve as publics that both rely on networked technologies and also network people into meaningful imagined communities in new ways. Publics are important, not just for enabling political action, but also for providing a mechanism through which we construct our social world. In essence, publics are the fabric of society.

Through engagement with publics, people develop a sense of others that ideally manifests as tolerance and respect. Although laws provide concrete rules for what is and is not acceptable in a particular jurisdiction, social norms shape most interactions. People develop a sense for what is normative by collectively adjusting their behavior based on what they see in the publics they inhabit and understand. This does not mean that the world is inherently safe or that people always respect their neighbors but that social processes underpinning publics buffer people from hatred by creating common cultural ground.

Teens want access to publics to see and be seen, to socialize, and to feel as if they have the freedoms to explore a world beyond the heavily constrained one shaped by parents and school. By and large, just as society formerly wrote women out of civic life, we now prohibit teenagers from many aspects of public life. Adults justify the exclusion of youth as being for their own good or as a necessary response to their limited experience and cognitive capacity.

Rather than accepting their social position, many teens have clamored to find ways to access and participate in a whole host of publics, from social publics to political ones. Often, they turn to social media and other networked technologies to do so.

What teens do online cannot be separated from their broader desires and interests, attitudes and values. Their relation to networked publics signals their interest in being a part of public life. It does not suggest that they're trying to go virtual or that they're using technology to escape reality. Teens' engagement with social media and other technologies is a way of engaging with their broader social world.

The world that American teens live in is highly circumscribed. Their lives are regulated both by their parents and by institutional forces. Compulsory schooling is a contemporary reality, even if homeschooling provides an alternative. Laws that define when, where, and how they can gather shape teens' activities and mobility. In the same vein, teens' worldviews are influenced by cultural dynamics that underpin American society more generally. They are exposed to media narratives that convey broader cultural values, and they are living within a system that is both consumerist and commercial in nature.

The networked publics that teens inhabit are not public in the sense of being state-run. In fact, most of the public spaces that teens encounter are private, whether at the mall or on Facebook.[1] Their presence and the traces that they leave are often used for commercial interests. They are targets of marketing online, at school, and in most spaces they visit.[2] This trend in American childhood predates the internet, but there is little doubt that it is being reinforced by social media and playing out in networked publics. Rather than critiquing that dynamic, as many excellent scholars have done, this book instead takes it at face value because this is the only world that today's teens know.³ Teens accept this version of networked publics because, however flawed, the spaces and communities provided by social media are what they have available to them in their quest to meaningfully access public life. The commercial worlds that they have access to may not be ideal, but neither is the limited mobility that they experience nor the heavily structured lives that they lead.

To Be Public and To Be in Public

Enamored with Parisian society, French poet Charles Baudelaire documented the public life that unfolded as people strolled along city streets. He wrote of *flâneurs*—individuals who came to the streets not to go anywhere in particular but in order to see and be seen. In Baudelaire's conception, the flâneur is neither fully an exhibitionist nor fully a voyeur at any moment, but a little of both all the time. The flâneur is an intimate part of the city, gaining from both seeing and being seen, performing and watching others.

When teens turn to networked publics, they do so to hang out with friends and be recognized by peers. They share in order to see and be seen. They want to look respectable and interesting, while simultaneously warding off unwanted attention. They choose to share in order to be a part of the public, but how much they share is shaped by how public they want to be. They are, in effect, *digital flâneurs*.

As teens stroll the digital streets, they must contend with aspects of networked technologies that complicate the social dynamics in front of them. The issues of persistence, visibility, spreadability, and searchability that I introduced in the first chapter and addressed throughout the book fundamentally affect their experiences in networked publics. They must negotiate invisible audiences and the collapsing of contexts. They must develop strategies for handling ongoing surveillance and attempts to undermine their agency when they seek to control social situations.

Although most youth are simply trying to be a part of public life, the visibility of their online activities creates tremendous consternation among adults who are uncomfortable with the possibility that teens might share something inappropriate on Instagram or interact with strangers on Twitter. This is where anxieties around online safety and privacy get coupled with broader societal concerns about race and class, sometimes becoming a source of tension. Teens are not ignorant of their parents' fears, but by and large, they see the opportunities presented by participating in public life as far out-weighing the possible consequences they may face.

As teens work through the various issues that emerge around net-worked publics, they must struggle with what it means both to *be* pub-lic and to be *in* public. This often is framed through the language of privacy, and indeed, the tension between being public and being in public comes down to the ability to control the social situation. But the distinction also has to do with how teens relate to public life.

In North Carolina, I met Manu, a seventeen-year-old boy of Indian descent who was active on both Facebook and Twitter. Initially, I assumed that he was using Twitter to create a public presence while keeping Facebook as a more intimate space. I was wrong. Facebook had become so pervasive in his peer group that he felt forced to con-nect with everyone he'd ever met. Twitter was different because Twit-ter had not yet become particularly popular in his community. The difference in audience—and how people on each site responded to his sharing—shaped his understanding of Facebook and Twitter. Whenever Manu posted something on Facebook, he felt that he was forcing everyone he'd ever met to consume it, whereas on Twitter, people opted in when they felt that what he was sharing was interest-ing. As he explained, "I guess Facebook is like yelling it out to a crowd, and then Twitter is just like talking in a room."[4] He posted messages he wanted to broadcast widely on Facebook while sharing whatever intimate thoughts were on his mind on Twitter. Manu's practice contradicts the assumptions then held by adults, who often saw Facebook as a more intimate site than Twitter because of each site's technical affordances and defaults.

What makes a particular site or service more or less public is not necessarily about the design of the system but rather how it is situated within the broader social ecosystem. Although Facebook was initially built to provide an intimate, private alternative to MySpace, Manu's practice reveals how—by becoming the de facto social media site for one billion people—it's often more experientially public than more publicly accessible sites that are not nearly as popular. In this way, the technical architecture of the system matters less than how users understand their relationship to it and how the public perceives any particular site.

The tensions between the technologies that help create networked publics and the publics that are created through networked technologies reveal how the nature of public-ness is actually being remade every day in people's lives. Twitter is not inherently public even if the content is broadly accessible, nor are people's experiences of Facebook private just because the content can be restricted. Both help create networked publics, but the nature of public-ness for teens ends up depending on how the people around them use available tools.

What teens want from being in public—and how they understand publics—varies. Some teens see publics as a site of freedom, and they want to be able to roam free from adult surveillance. Whereas these teens want to be in public, other teens are looking to be public. They use the same technologies that allow them to engage in networked publics to magnify their voices, gather audiences, and connect with others on a large scale.

Some teens who are seeking to be public are enamored by the stories presented by media, including the "reality" of reality TV, the rich narratives of exploratory youth in novels, and the raucous adventures of celebrities. Teens often reference celebrities as individuals who achieve freedom and opportunities by being public. In this way, they blur the lines between being public and being in public.

Long before the internet, there were teens who dreamed of or actively sought out broader engagement and tried to create publics from their own homes. Teens who want to be public often use media or new technologies to do so. In the 1980s and 1990s, some youth turned to pirate radio and homemade magazines, or zines, to connect with others.[5] Even though teen adoption of these technologies was not universal, popular films like *Pump Up the Volume* and *Wayne's World* celebrated these practices and the fun that could be had by being public.

Social media has made being public much more accessible to teens, and many embrace popular technologies to build an audience and contribute their thoughts to the broader cultural ethos. I met teens who had cultivated hundreds of thousands—and even millions—of followers on MySpace, Twitter, YouTube, and Instagram. Some shared homemade videos, fashion commentary, or music they made with their friends. Others posted risqué photos or problematic content in an effort to entice strangers. Their reasons varied, but an interest in attention is common. These teens relish the opportunity to be seen and be part of a broader conversation.

Although some teens are looking for the attention that comes with being public, most teens are simply looking to be in public. Most are focused on what it means to be a part of a broader social world. They want to connect with and participate in culture, both to develop a sense of self and to feel as though they are a part of society. Some even see publics as an opportunity for activism. These teens are looking to actively participate in public life in order to make the world a better place.

When Networked Publics Get Political

Not only has social media enabled new ways of being public and being in public, but these same technologies have been used to reconfigure political publics as we know them.[6] Teens are often eschewed for being apolitical, but some teens are deeply and explicitly political in their activities, both online and off.[7] A networked public is not inherently a political public sphere, but some teens can and do bring their politics to their online engagement and use technology to help them be political.[8]

Around the world, people have leveraged social media and networked technologies to instantiate meaningful political activities.

Using the internet and mobile phones to coordinate and communicate, activists have banded together and engaged different constituencies to resist political regimes.[9] Even the simple act of hanging out online to see and be seen has enormous potential for creating the civic networks that support real-world political engagement.[10] Teens' practices in social media are neither frivolous nor without impact in other parts of public and civic life, whether they are trying to be political or not.

The majority of teens' engagement with networked publics is never expressly political, but there are notable exceptions that often go unacknowledged. In 2005, Congress introduced HR4437, the Border Protection, Anti-Terrorism and Illegal Immigrant Control Act. This bill, directed at undocumented people living in the United States, was rife with measures that would have had serious social justice and humanitarian consequences. Immigration advocates described it as draconian and opposed it. As HR4437 gained traction among anti-immigrant groups, opponents began taking to the streets in protest.

In March 2006, immigrant rights groups organized massive protests through Spanish-speaking media and traditional advocacy networks. Many teen children of undocumented parents felt disconnected from the protests organized by more seasoned activists. They turned to MySpace and used text messaging to coordinate their own public stance.[11]

On March 27, 2006, only a few days after immigrant rights groups hosted a massive protest, thousands of California high school students walked out of school and took to the streets to demand rights on behalf of their families.[12] In Los Angeles alone, more than twenty thousand students marched in protest. Students talked about how the bill represented a form of racist oppression that would permit racial profiling. Others spoke about the fundamental problems with the economic system, about how Mexicans are a critical labor force that is systematically oppressed. Still others described how their parents came to America to give them a chance for a better life. They crafted banners and posters, brought flags to signify the diversity of cultures that people came from, and invoked Cesar Chavez and human rights in their chants.

These teens were doing recognizable political work, despite adults' frequent dismissal of teens as having no civic interests and being otherwise politically disengaged. Were they celebrated? No. Rather than being complimented for their willingness to step forward and take a stance, the students were summarily dismissed.

Public officials and school administrators spoke out against the students' actions and their use of technology for creating a disruptive situation by encouraging fellow students to skip school. They chastised the students for using political issues to justify mass truancy. The press, using the fear-mongering tactics discussed throughout this book, gave the impression that administrators were concerned for students' safety.

In admonishing the students, administrators told the press that the students should return to school, where they could have conversations about immigration in a "productive" way. When Los Angeles mayor Antonio Villaraigosa spoke to the young protesters, he said: "You've come today, you registered your commitment to your families, your opposition to the Sensenbrenner legislation, but it's time to go back to school."[13] His tone was condescending, implying that a day at school was more important than this political act. Some adults invoked Cesar Chavez by telling students that the well-respected civil rights leader would be ashamed of them. The discussions on MySpace painted a different logic to these criticisms as students discussed how schools would be docked anywhere from thirty to fifty dollars in state funding for each student who did not attend class.

The students faced steep consequences for their decision to protest. In some towns, authorities charged them with truancy for participating. Many faced school detention and other punishments. Few adults recognized the teens for their ingenuity in using the tools available to them to engage directly in political action. Activists regularly face punishment for their activities, but these teens weren't even recognized as activists.

Teens' engagement around HR4437 was in many ways a typical protest, but many of the other forms of activism that teens engage in are far less commonplace among adults. Overwhelmingly, public leaders and journalists deem many actions that teens and young adults take in the name of protest as illegitimate. For example, during my fieldwork, I met a handful of teens who proudly associated themselves with Anonymous, an ad hoc collective that initially emerged to mock Scientology and question other powerful institutions. Anonymous' practices and the groups that they affiliate themselves with are a source of significant consternation for powerful adults.

Anonymous is a moniker for a loosely coordinated group of people who share a commitment to challenging powerful entities anonymously. As an entity, Anonymous gained notoriety when people associated with the network engaged in "hacktivist" tactics against the US government and American companies in December 2010.[14] After the nonprofit group WikiLeaks released classified US State Department diplomatic cables, the US government was outraged and put pressure on American companies to stop supporting the organization. Amazon deleted WikiLeaks' account and stopped hosting its content, and Pay-Pal canceled the organization's financial account. The founder of WikiLeaks, Australian citizen Julian Assange, became persona non grata, and the US government initiated a grand jury investigation to indict him. In response, hacktivists sought to bring down the servers of anti-WikiLeaks governmental and corporate entities and otherwise challenge the security of these organizations.

As the incident unfolded, authorities arrested mostly teenagers and twenty-somethings in both the United States and the United Kingdom for their role in challenging authorities using technology.[15] The teens I met who identified themselves as part of Anonymous were not arrested, but many participated in the various political protests that those who used the moniker claimed as Anonymous activities, relishing the Guy Fawkes symbolism and the group's Robin Hood tactics. All the teens I met who were engaged with this movement saw their acts as political protests, even if authorities saw them as anarchic and destructive, terrorists and traitors. These young people saw themselves as political, even if adults did not sanction their approach to political engagement.

Political engagement takes many forms. Although often even less recognized as political, many teens have used the tools of internet culture to express themselves politically. For example, the production and distribution of internet *memes* is a common form of self-expression, but it can also be a form of political speech. Memes start when a particular digital artifact—be it an image, a song, a hashtag, or a video—is juxtaposed with other text or other media to produce a loosely connected collection of media that share a similar base referent.[16] Not only are these artifacts spread online, but people also iterate on them, creating new artifacts.

In the second chapter, I referenced the rise of lolcats, a meme that emerges when people take pictures of cats and add captions using a consistent though not standard English grammar. Many memes, like lolcats, are simply entertaining. Others have more political components. Consider, for example, the Hitler Downfall meme. This meme is based on a video scene from a 2004 German film called *Der Untergang* that depicts Adolf Hitler getting angry with his subordinates. The meme works by people subtitling the German-language film with other possible political and nonpolitical situations that Hitler could be getting upset about. Over the years, these have included the US subprime mortgage debate, the use of the Digital Millennium Copyright Act to silence parodies and memes, the US government's frustration with National Security Administration whistleblower Edward Snowden, and Hitler learning that his Xbox Live account has been banned.[17] This meme mixes commentary with humor, all juxtaposed against a familiar historical reference.

Even though not all Hitler Downfall videos are made by teens—and, in fact, it's not clear how many were—I met numerous teens who had made and shared the videos, as well as a few who had come up with their own. Producing—or even consuming—these videos requires understanding a historical context and developing a rich sense of media literacy. Although, as discussed in the previous chapter, we cannot take teens' technical or media acumen for granted, we must also not ignore that there are youth who are deeply and meaningfully engaged in using the skills they have to help construct publics that are, in fact, political.

Not all teens are politically engaged, and many of the ways in which they do engage in political action are unrecognizable by adults because they take the form of commentary or involve acts of protest adults deem unacceptable. Their activities, controversial as they may be, reveal the more political side of networked publics.

Living in and with Networked Publics

Social media has become an integral part of American society. Today's teens—regardless of their personal levels of participation—are coming of age in an era defined by easy access to information and mediated communication. Innovations in social media will continue to emerge, making possible new interaction forms and complicating social dynamics in interesting ways. The rise of mobile devices is introducing even more challenges, taking the already widespread notion of being "always on" to new levels and creating new pathways for navigating physical spaces. As social media becomes increasingly ubiquitous, the physical and digital will be permanently entangled and blurry. New innovations will introduce new challenges, as people try to reimagine privacy, assert their sense of identity, and renegotiate everyday social dynamics. And if history is any indication, adults are bound to project the same fears and anxieties they have about social media onto whatever new technology captures the imagination of future youth.[18]

Although in this book I describe the dynamics of American youth at a particular time, notably defined by the widespread adoption of social media, the underlying issues are by no means new. In using teen engagement with social media to think about a variety of sociotechnical dynamics, my goal has been to shed light on broader cultural constructs and values that we take for granted. Claims about youth practices can be divisive, particularly when we judge individuals, cohorts, and artifacts through twisted portrayals.

It is easy to make technology the target of our hopes and anxieties. Newness makes it the perfect punching bag. But one of the hardest—

and yet most important—things we as a society must think about in the face of technological change is what has really changed, and what has not. As computer scientist Vint Cerf has said, "The internet is a reflection of our society and that mirror is going to be reflecting what we see. If we do not like what we see in that mirror the problem is not to fix the mirror, we have to fix society."[19] It is much harder to examine broad systemic changes with a critical lens and to place them in historical context than to focus on what is new and disruptive.

Through their experimentation and challenges, today's teens are showcasing some of the complex ways in which technology intersects with society. They don't have all of the answers, but their path through this networked world provides valuable insight into how technology is being integrated into and shaping everyday life.

Teens' struggles to make sense of the networked publics they inhabit—and the ways in which their practices reveal cultural fractures—highlight some of the challenges society faces as technology gets integrated into daily life. At the same time, teens are as they have always been, resilient and creative in repurposing technology to fulfill their desires and goals. When they embrace technology, they are imagining new possibilities, asserting control over their lives, and finding ways to be a part of public life. This can be terrifying for those who are intimidated by youth or nervous for them, but it also reveals that, far from being a distraction, social media is providing a vehicle for teens to take ownership over their lives.

As teens turn to and help create networked publics, they begin to imagine society and their place in it. Through social media, teens reveal their hopes and dreams, struggles and challenges. Not all youth are doing all right, just as not all adults are. Technology makes the struggles youth face visible, but it neither creates nor prevents harmful things from happening even if it can be a tool for both. It simply mirrors and magnifies many aspects of everyday life, good and bad.

Growing up in and being a part of networked publics is complicated. The realities that youth face do not fit into neat utopian or dystopian frames, nor will eliminating technology solve the problems they encounter. Networked publics are here to stay. Rather than resisting technology or fearing what might happen if youth embrace social media, adults should help youth develop the skills and perspective to productively navigate the complications brought about by living in networked publics. Collaboratively, adults and youth can help create a networked world that we all want to live in.

appendix: teen demographics

This appendix provides basic demographic information, interview dates, and social network site use of the teens who are addressed by name or pseudonym in the book. The teens listed here do not represent all 166 teens that I interviewed, nor do they represent all of the teens that I observed. This list is by no means comprehensive but should provide basic information to supplement what is presented in the text.

The information provided about each teen is based on what I know. To protect the confidentiality of teens, I provide only general geographic information. When teens live in or near one of the fifty most populous cities in the United States, I use the city name; otherwise, I use the state name. As much as possible, I use the language that teens used to describe their race, ethnicity, and/or religion. When demographic or cultural information is left unmarked, it's because I did not know and did not dare to guess. Socioeconomic status is left unmarked due to difficulty in consistently marking class across teens. I did not explicitly ask about sexuality, and so that, too, is left unmarked.

Interview date(s) and the dates of comments are given, as are the site(s) that each teen was using at the time of our encounter. Interviews that were conducted by my collaborator, Alice Marwick, are marked as such.

Aaron (15, Texas): white, male, ninth grade, Christian
Interview: March 14, 2007. Active on MySpace without parents' knowledge.

Abigail (17, North Carolina): white, female, twelfth grade, Christian
Interview: October 13, 2010. Active on Facebook; formerly used MySpace.

Alicia (17, North Carolina): white, female, twelfth grade, Christian
Interview: October 10, 2010. Active on Facebook and Twitter; formerly used MySpace.

Allie (17, Indiana): white, female, twelfth grade, Christian
MySpace comments: December 7, 2007. Active on MySpace.

Amy (16, Seattle): biracial black/white, female, tenth grade
Interview: January 20, 2007. Active on MySpace.

Ana-Garcia (15, Los Angeles): biracial Guatemalan/Pakistani, female, tenth grade, Muslim
Interview: March 5, 2007. Active on MySpace.

Anastasia (17, New York): female, twelfth grade
Comments via blog: August 11, 2007. Active primarily on Facebook, but also uses MySpace.

Andrew (17, Nashville): white, male, twelfth grade, Christian
Interview (by Alice): September 30, 2010. Active on 4chan; formerly used Facebook and Twitter.

Anindita (17, Los Angeles): Indian, female, twelfth grade
Interview: February 20, 2007. Active on Facebook and MySpace.

Ashley (14, North Carolina): white, female, ninth grade, Christian
Interview (by Alice): October 13, 2010. Active on Facebook.

Bianca (16, Michigan): white, female, tenth grade
Interview: June 26, 2007. Active on Facebook.

Bly Lauritano-Werner (17, Maine): white, female, twelfth grade
Youth Radio Story: July 24, 2006. Active on Facebook and LiveJournal.

Brooke (15, Nebraska): white, female, ninth grade
Interview: April 17, 2007. Active on Facebook.

Cachi (18, Iowa): Puerto Rican, female, twelfth grade
Interview: April 18, 2007. Active on Facebook, MiGente, and MySpace.

Caleb (17, North Carolina): African American, male, twelfth grade, Christian
Interview (by Alice): October 12, 2010. Active on Facebook and Twitter; formerly used MySpace.

Carmen (17/18, Boston): Hispanic/Argentinean, female, twelfth grade, Catholic
Interview: July 21, 2010. Focus group: August 17, 2011. Active on Facebook and 4chan; formerly used Twitter and MySpace.

Catalina (15, Austin): white, female, tenth grade
Interview: March 14, 2007. Active on Facebook and MySpace.

Chantelle (15, Washington, DC): African American, female, tenth grade, Christian
Interview: November 6, 2010. Active on Facebook; formerly used MySpace.

Chloe (15, Atlanta): white, female, ninth grade, Christian
Interview: May 9, 2009. Active on Facebook.

Christopher (15, Alabama): white, male, between ninth and tenth grade, Christian
Interview: June 27, 2007. Not active on social network sites due to lack of interest.

Corinne (13, Massachusetts): female
Focus Group: November 15, 2007.

Craig Pelletier (17, California): male, twelfth grade
Blog: February 10, 2008. Active on Facebook and MySpace.

Dominic (16, Seattle): white, male, tenth grade
Interview: January 21, 2007. Active on Facebook and MySpace.

Emily (16, Pennsylvania): white, female, tenth grade
Interview: May 5, 2007. Active on Xanga.

Fred (15, Texas): white, male, ninth grade
Interview: March 14, 2007. Not active on social network sites due to parental restrictions.

Heather (16, Iowa): white, female, tenth grade
Interview: April 21, 2007. Active on Facebook, MySpace, and Xanga.

Hunter (14, Washington, DC): African American, male, ninth grade
Interview: November 8, 2010. Active on Facebook.

James (17, Seattle): white with Native American roots, male, eleventh grade
Interview: January 20, 2007. Active on MySpace.

Jenna (17, North Carolina): white, female, twelfth grade, Christian
Interview: October 13, 2010. Active on Facebook; formerly used MySpace.

Jordan (15, Austin): biracial (Mexican and white), female, tenth grade, Catholic
Interview: March 14, 2007. Active on Facebook and MySpace.

Kat (15, Massachusetts): white, female, ninth grade
Interview: June 20, 2007. Active on Facebook; formerly used MySpace.

Kath (17, Maryland): white, female, twelfth grade
Conversation in Colorado: July 2008. Active on Facebook.

Keke (16, Los Angeles): black, female, eleventh grade
Interview: January 12, 2007. Active on MySpace.

Lila (18, Michigan): Asian/Vietnamese, female, between twelfth grade and college
Interview: June 27, 2007. Active on Facebook.

Lilly (16, Kansas): white, female, tenth grade
Interview: April 16, 2007. Active on Facebook and MySpace.

Lolo (15, Los Angeles): Latina/Guatemalan, female, tenth grade
Interview: January 23, 2007. Not active on social network sites due to pressure from ex-boyfriend.

Manu (17, North Carolina): Indian, male, twelfth grade, Hindu
Interview: October 12, 2010. Active on Facebook and Twitter.

Matthew (17, North Carolina): white, male, twelfth grade, Christian
Interview: October 10, 2010. Active on Facebook and Twitter; formerly used MySpace.

Melanie (15, Kansas): white, female, tenth grade
Interview: April 16, 2007. Active on Facebook and MySpace.

Mic (15, Los Angeles): Egyptian, male, tenth grade, Muslim
Interview: January 22, 2007. Not active on social network sites due to parental restrictions.

Mickey (15, Los Angeles): Mexican, male, tenth grade
Interview: January 12, 2007. Active on MySpace.

Mikalah (18, Washington, DC): black, female, eleventh grade
Interview (by Alice): November 7, 2010. Active on MySpace and Facebook.

Mike (15, California): white, male, ninth grade
Conversation: May 2006. Active on Facebook.

Myra (15, Iowa): white, female, ninth grade, Christian
Interview: April 22, 2007. Not active on social network sites due to parental restrictions.

Natalie (15, Seattle): white, female, ninth grade, Christian
Interview: January 20, 2007. Active on MySpace.

Nicholas (16, Kansas): white, male, tenth grade
Interview: April 14, 2007. Active on Facebook and MySpace.

Sabrina (14, Texas): white, female, ninth grade
Interview: March 15, 2007. Active on MySpace.

Samantha (18, Seattle): white, female, twelfth grade, Christian
Interview: January 20, 2007. Active on MySpace.

Sasha (16, Michigan): white, female, tenth grade
Interview: June 26, 2007. Not active on social network sites due to parental restrictions.

Seong (17, Los Angeles): Asian/Korean, female, eleventh grade
Interview: February 20, 2007. Active on Facebook, MySpace, Cyworld, and Xanga.

Serena (16, North Carolina): white, female, eleventh grade, Christian/ Lutheran
Interview: October 14, 2010. Active on Facebook and Twitter; formerly used MySpace.

Shamika (17, Washington, DC): African American, female, eleventh grade, Christian
Interview: November 7, 2010. Active on Facebook and Twitter; formerly used MySpace and Tumblr.

Skyler (18, Colorado): white, female, twelfth grade
Blog post: March 16, 2006. Active on MySpace.

Stan (18, Iowa): white, male, twelfth grade
Interview: April 18, 2007. Active on MySpace.

Summer (15, Michigan): white, female, between ninth and tenth grade, Catholic
Interview: June 27, 2007. Active on MySpace.

Sydnia (15, Washington, DC): tenth grade, black, female
Interview: September 26, 2010. Active on MySpace, Facebook, and Twitter.

Tara (16, Michigan): Asian/Vietnamese, female, between ninth and tenth grade
Interview: June 27, 2007. Active on Facebook and MySpace.

Taylor (15, Boston): white, female, tenth grade
Interview 1: July 26, 2010. Additional conversations: spring 2012. Active on Facebook.

Traviesa (15, Los Angeles): Hispanic, female, ninth grade
Interview: December 5, 2006. Active on MySpace.

Trevor (17, North Carolina): white, male, twelfth grade, Christian
Interview: October 9, 2010. Active on Facebook.

Vicki (15, Atlanta): white, female, ninth grade/homeschooled, Catholic
Interview: May 9, 2009. Active on MySpace, Facebook, and Twitter.

Waffles (17, North Carolina): white, male, twelfth grade, Christian
Interview: October 9, 2010. Active on Facebook.

Wolf (18, Iowa): white, male, twelfth grade
Interview: April 18, 2007. Active on MySpace.

notes

Preface

1. Most names used in this book are pseudonyms. Some pseudonyms are chosen by teens themselves; I chose other pseudonyms to be unique names that maintained cultural and temporal identifiers by using baby name websites that took into account birth year and ethnicity. When I'm quoting from public material, including blog posts and news media interviews, I use the name provided by the teen in that context. The names teens use online may not be their legal names, but I did not seek to verify either way.

2. The interviews and fieldwork conducted from 2010–2011 were done in collaboration with Alice Marwick. Most of these focused on privacy and bullying. I identify the interviews conducted by Alice both in the Appendix and within the text. To learn more about the teens that were interviewed for this book and the methodological approach that informs this book, see http://www.danah.org/itscomplicated/.

Introduction

1. Lenhart, Ling, Campbell, and Purcell, "Teens and Mobile Phones."

2. This book draws on data collected in the United States and refers to cultural references that are particular to American culture. Although many of my arguments have resonance outside the United States, I make no attempt to speak to the cultural practices, norms, or attitudes rooted in other countries. Many scholars have examined young people's mediated practices in other cultural contexts, including Livingstone, *Children and the Internet*; Mesch and Talmud, *Wired Youth*; and Davies and Eynon, *Teenagers and Technology*. In addition, as the directors of the EU Kids Online Project, Sonia Livingstone and Leslie Haddon have created a large network of researchers in Europe to examine children's online practices. They have produced numerous reports, journal articles, and scholarly manuscripts. To learn more, see http://www2.lse.ac.uk/media@lse/research/EUKidsOnline/.

3. To read more about how social media is situated within Web2.0 in light of the rise of social network sites, see Ellison and boyd, "Sociality Through Social Network Sites." In this article, we argue that what makes "social media"

significant as a category is not the various technologies labeled as social media but, rather, the sociotechnical dynamics that unfold as millions of people embrace a variety of technologies available at a particular time and use them to collaborate, share, and socialize.

4. In the introduction to *Hanging Out, Messing Around, and Geeking Out,* Mimi Ito and colleagues (including myself) describe an important tension in online interactions between those that are "interest-driven" and those that are "friendship-driven." Although we use this construct to help describe different youth practices, the same dynamic is at play in terms of how broader media have been adopted. Services like Facebook are primarily friendship-driven while the boards on 4chan are primarily interest-driven. Of course, some major social media services—like LiveJournal and Tumblr—have been adopted for both in ways that often create unique tensions within those sites.

5. Mimi Ito initially used the term *networked publics* in 2008 to "reference a linked set of social, cultural, and technological developments that have accompanied the growing engagement with digitally networked media" (Ito, "Introduction," 2). Although I agree with her framing and believe that the broadness of what she offers has tremendous value, I am trying to add more precision in my usage. To do so, I draw on a broader notion of publics. In employing the concept of "publics," I am purposefully referring to a long strain of scholarly debate and analysis. Much of what I'm nodding toward is rooted in, conversational with, or challenging of Jürgen Habermas's historical analysis of a public sphere as a category of bourgeois society in *Structural Transformation of the Public Sphere* (see also Calhoun, *Habermas and the Public Sphere*). In particular, I subscribe to Nancy Fraser's argument in "Rethinking the Public Sphere" that publics are where identities are enacted, Michael Warner's argument in *Publics and Counterpublics* that counterpublics enable marginalized individuals to create powerful communities in resistance to hegemonic publics, and Sonia Livingstone's recognition in *Audiences and Publics* that publics emerge when audiences come together around shared understandings of the world. To better understand the academic roots of how I understand networked publics, see boyd, "Social Network Sites as Networked Publics."

6. B. Anderson, *Imagined Communities.*

7. The notion of an affordance was popularized by Donald Norman in his book *The Design of Everyday Things*; he used this term to highlight interaction possibilities that were made possible through specific design decisions. While this term has purchase in the field of human-computer interaction, it is regularly critiqued in critical disciplines because it is often used to give agency to the technological artifact without acknowledging the role of the user (see Oliver, "Problem with Affordance"). Although I am aware of the fraught history of this term, it is still a useful construct for addressing the design features with which people must contend.

8. For a discussion on how visibility brought about by new technologies changes the nature of our social and political worlds, see Thompson, "New Visibility."

9. In their 2013 book *Spreadable Media*, Henry Jenkins, Sam Ford, and Josh Green discuss how new technologies can be used by people interested in spreading online content. They argue that this alters the dynamics of media distribution.

10. Coffin, "Consumption, and Images of Women's Desires."

11. Hosokawa, "Walkman Effect."

12. Springhall, *Youth, Popular Culture and Moral Panics.*

13. In Phaedrus, Plato quotes Socrates as paraphrasing an Egyptian god. The relevant excerpts critiquing writing as a medium can be found at: http://www.english.illinois.edu/-people-/faculty/debaron/482/482readings/phaedrus.html.

14. More than a decade before I wrote this book, British media studies scholar David Buckingham wrote *After the Death of Childhood: Growing Up in the Age of Electronic Media* to examine the fears and anxieties that adults had about the effects of media on young people. Many of the issues that he raised in the early days of youth engagement with the internet continue to plague popular discussions about technology and are at the center of the arguments made in this book at a time when new technologies are rehashing old arguments.

15. Science and technology scholars have written extensively about the problems with technological determinism. Langdon Winner makes the case in "Do Artifacts Have Politics?" In the past three decades, much scholarship has focused on how to think about the role of technology in relation to practice. One strain of thinking is referred to as "social constructivism." For a literature review of this approach, see Leonardi, *Car Crashes Without Cars*, chap. 2.

16. To learn more about how various societal anxieties shape teens' lives, see Levine, *Price of Privilege*; and Pope, *Doing School.*

17. For a discussion of how youth build friendships and turn to peers to create a social world that's not just defined by parents, see Bukowski, Newcomb, and Hartup, *The Company They Keep*; Corsaro, *Friendship and Peer Culture in the Early Years*; Pahl, *On Friendship.*

18. In *Last Child in the Woods*, Richard Louv describes how changes in societal norms and the rise of fear have resulted in children being disconnected from nature. His argument is that we must help children get access to nature in order for them to be healthy socially and physically. Although this resonates with me, I've found that teens are primarily using technology as a substitute, often because nature and unregulated space are so challenging for youth.

19. Lewis, "Community Through Exclusion and Illusion."

20. For a historical overview of teens' engagement with and adults' attitudes toward publics, see Valentine, *Public Space and the Culture of Childhood.*

21. Hargittai, "Digital Na(t)ives?"

22. Laura Portwood-Stacer examines media refusal and intentional disengagement from social media in "Media Refusal and Conspicuous Non-Consumption."

23. Ethnography is a qualitative research methodology used by social scientists to understand and document cultural practices. Born out of anthropology—and embraced by many other disciplines—ethnographic work seeks to capture and explain the social meaning behind everyday activities. I do not detail my methodological practices in this book, but for those who are interested in my methods, see boyd, "Making Sense of Teen Life." More details are also available on my website at http://www.danah.org/itscomplicated/. For those who want to learn more about doing ethnographic work with youth, see Best, *Representing Youth*.

24. Throughout this book, I use the term *American* when talking about cultural practices, values, peoples, and norms that are rooted in the United States. I recognize that this is contested and that some scholars prefer to reserve the term American for talking about contexts related to the Americas—including countries in North and South America. I choose to use American in the more narrow sense both because it is the language that my informants use and because there is no notion of United States-ian. When I refer to cultural practices from other countries in the Americas, I use such descriptors as Canadian, Mexican, and Argentinean.

Chapter 1. Identity

1. Paul Willis examined the underlying social dynamics of UK class mobility in *Learning to Labor: How Working Class Kids Get Working Class Jobs*. These ideas were extended and reconsidered in light of an American context by Donna Gaines in *Teenage Wasteland: Suburbia's Dead End Kids*.

2. Rebecca Raby refers to "the great gulf" between adults and adolescents as one of the challenges in truly understanding youth and youth cultural practice. Raby, "Across a Great Gulf?"

3. Marginalized youth are especially vulnerable to being misinterpreted and judged by adults who have no frame for understanding the context in which these teens operate. For example, in her book *Out in the Country: Youth, Media, and Queer Visibility in Rural America*, Mary Gray argues that queer, rural teens need to resolve different conflicted identities when they're both queer and rural. Often, adults who don't experience both of these identities expect teens to focus on one. Rural straight adults believe that sexuality should go unmarked and undiscussed while queer urban adults believe that these youth simply need to leave their rural lives behind. Gray finds that many youth develop innovative ways of resolving conflicted audiences and norms, in spite of adults' assumptions.

4. For a detailed discussion of how context collapse works in networked publics, see Marwick and boyd, "I Tweet Honestly, I Tweet Passionately";

and Vitak, "Impact of Context Collapse and Privacy on Social Network Site Disclosures."

5. For a deeper analysis on how "imagined audience" functions in social media, see Marwick and boyd, "I Tweet Honestly, I Tweet Passionately"; Litt, "Knock, Knock. Who's There?"; Brake, "Shaping the 'Me' in MySpace"; and Baron, "My Best Day."

6. Over the course of this study, Facebook's privacy settings have changed tremendously. This has complicated teens' understanding of how to navigate contexts on Facebook and in social media more generally. For a discussion of how Facebook's privacy settings have changed, see Stutzman, Gross, and Acquisti, "Silent Listeners."

7. Kirschbaum and Kass, "The Switch."

8. Turkle, *Second Self.*

9. Sundén, *Material Virtualities.*

10. Although identity play was commonplace in early online communities, it was not without consequences. The issues of how deception played out during that period are well documented in Stone, *War of Desire and Technology*; and Dibbell, *My Tiny Life.*

11. The dynamics around "real names" and pseudonyms in social media are fraught. Many services, including Facebook and Google Plus, have demanded that users provide their "real name." Other services invite or welcome pseudonyms. For a discussion of the politics of real names in social media, see Hogan, "Pseudonyms and the Rise of the Real-Name Web."

12. In *Hanging Out, Messing Around, and Geeking Out*, Mimi Ito and coauthors (including myself) describe how mediated youth engagement can be understood through a cleavage between friendship-driven practices and those that are interest-driven. Although many youth move between friendship-driven and interest-driven worlds, they often interact with particular genres of media with specific intentions that are organized around one or the other of these approaches. I saw this division throughout my fieldwork.

13. As I mentioned briefly in the Introduction, I approach the study of technology's relation to social practices with a sociotechnical bent, drawing on a broad set of scholarly theories focused on how technology is socially constructed. These theories are often responding to a problematic but pervasive notion that technologies determine practices (a.k.a. "technological determinism"). My analytic approach is heavily influenced by a wide variety of social constructivists, especially the work of Weibe Bijker, Thomas Hughes, and Trevor Pinch. For those who wish to learn more about this analytic approach, see Leonardi, *Car Crashes Without Cars*, chap. 2.

14. To learn more about how identity works in game settings and virtual worlds, see Taylor, *Play Between Worlds*; Boellstorff, *Coming of Age in Second*

Life; Nardi, *My Life as a Night Elf Priest*; and Kendall, *Hanging Out in the Virtual Pub*.

15. Beth Coleman takes up the issue of avatars blurring distinctions between the virtual and the real in *Hello Avatar: Rise of the Networked Generation*.

16. For a journalist's account of 4chan, see Brophy-Warren, "Modest Web Site Is Behind a Bevy of Memes." For more on 4chan as a site of ephemerality and anonymous community practices, see Bernstein et al., "4chan and /b/"; and Knuttila, "User Unknown."

17. For an analysis of the linguistic and cultural practices underpinning lolcats, see Lefler, "I Can Has Thesis?"; and Miltner, "Srsly Phenomenal."

18. For a more in-depth look at Anonymous, see Coleman, "Our Weirdness Is Free"; and Stryker, "Epic Win for Anonymous."

19. In her work on trolls, Whitney Phillips details how participants are socialized into underground anonymous communities through shared language, practices, and in-jokes. See Phillips, "This Is Why We Can't Have Nice Things."

20. The number 69 is often used in teen circles as a crass reference to simultaneous oral sex between two partners.

21. Judith Donath's work on the intersection of identity and deception in online spaces highlights that what appears as deceptive to the viewer may have more strategic signaling purposes. Some signals—such as the demographic information required of major social media sites—are easy to fake. Others, such as photographs with friends, are harder. To learn more, see Donath, "Identity and Deception in the Virtual Community"; and Donath, "Signals in Social Supernets."

22. The first social network sites—including Ryze, Friendster, and MySpace—were designed for networking purposes. (For a history of social network sites, see boyd and Ellison, "Social Network Sites.") As such, these sites' features were created to help users accurately convey who they were to strangers. Users were expected to provide accurate information about their gender, location, tastes, birthday, relationship status, employment, income, etc., so that the site could help them find a date, make a friend, or build a professional relationship. It didn't take long for users to challenge this design intention in an effort to repurpose these sites. When Friendster's users started creating "fake" accounts, the company responded with outrage, shutting down "Fakester" accounts and demanding that users use the site as it was intended. The practice of "configuring" users often results in backlash. (For a more detailed discussion of how this dynamic played out on Friendster, see boyd, "None of This Is Real.") This outraged many early adopters, prompted a mass exodus to other social network sites, including MySpace. Unlike Friendster, MySpace welcomed users to fill out the identity information as they saw fit. In response, many who embraced MySpace—and especially teenagers—had a field day with their profiles.

23. In the 1970s, cultural theorists Angela McRobbie and Jenny Garber described the practice of using media to create personal space as "bedroom culture." Hodkinson and Lincoln are building off of that notion. Hodkinson and Lincoln, "Online Journals as Virtual Bedrooms?"; McRobbie and Garber, "Girls and Subcultures."

24. In *Freaks, Geeks, and Cool Kids: American Teenagers, Schools, and the Culture of Consumption*, Murray Milner Jr. discusses the challenges that young people face as they try to navigate status games among their peers.

25. Goffman, *Presentation of Self in Everyday Life*, 82.

26. Joe Walther et al. discuss how people's practices on social media affect their contacts' impression management processes in "The Role of Friends' Behavior on Evaluations of Individuals' Facebook Profiles."

27. Kirkpatrick, *Facebook Effect*, 199.

28. One perspective of the incident can be found in: Misur, "Old Saybrook High School Makes Privacy Point."

29. Johnston, O'Malley, Bachman, and Schulenberg, *Monitoring the Future*.

30. Teens who are navigating queer identities are often especially aware of the challenges involved in managing different social contexts. Many, but not all, struggle with what it means to be out online while choosing not to expose their sexuality within their physical community. These teens are often framed as being "closeted," but some are simply trying to figure out how to negotiate conflicting identities. In *Out in the Country: Youth, Media, and Queer Visibility in Rural America*, Mary Gray shows how teens use a variety of strategies to address seemingly unresolvable identities of queerness and rurality.

Chapter 2. Privacy

1. Although my data focuses exclusively on American youth, British teens have an almost identical perspective regarding social media and privacy. See Livingstone, "Taking Risky Opportunities in Youthful Content Creation."

2. For example, Kang, "With Quick Click, Teens Part with Online Privacy."

3. Nussbaum, "Say Everything."

4. Studies show that many youth are quite thoughtful about privacy issues. See, e.g., boyd and Hargittai, "Facebook Privacy Settings"; Hoofnagle, King, Li, and Turow, "How Different Are Young Adults from Older Adults?"; and Stutzman, Gross, and Acquisti, "Silent Listeners." This does not mean that they don't share online. Pew's research on teens and privacy reveals how teens navigate both sharing and privacy. See Madden et al., "Teens, Social Media, and Privacy."

5. Kirkpatrick, "Facebook's Zuckerberg Says the Age of Privacy Is Over"; Popkin, "Privacy Is Dead on Facebook"; Johnson, "Privacy No Longer a Social Norm"; Jenkins Jr., "Opinion: Google and the Search for the Future"; Smith, "Google CEO Eric Schmidt's Most Controversial Quotes About Privacy."

6. Leysia Palen and Paul Dourish argue that, contrary to the traditional model of privacy as social withdrawal, privacy (particularly in a networked

world) is actually the result of many concurrent tensions at work. Palen and Dourish, "Unpacking Privacy for a Networked World."

7. Lauritano-Werner, "Effort to Keep an Online Diary Private."

8. Goffman, *Relations in Public.*

9. The dominance of "civil inattention" is so entrenched that multiple mobile phone etiquette studies mention "forced eavesdropping," or being unable to escape others' ostensibly private conversations as a major inconvenience. See Ling, "Mobile Telephones and the Disturbance of the Public Sphere"; and Lipscomb, Totten, Cook, and Lesch, "Cellular Phone Etiquette Among College Students."

10. In reviewing the legal issues surrounding privacy on Facebook, James Grimmelmann describes a variety of reasons that people seek out privacy while using social media. Grimmelmann, "Saving Facebook."

11. The definitions of privacy are numerous. Helen Nissenbaum describes multiple definitions of privacy and groups them based on whether they are normative or descriptive; emphasize access vs. control; or emphasize promoting other values vs. protecting a private realm. Nissenbaum, *Privacy in Context.* From a different direction, Anita Allen defines three types of privacy: physical privacy, informational privacy, and proprietary. Allen, "Coercing Privacy."

12. Gavison, "Privacy and the Limits of the Law."

13. Westin, *Privacy and Freedom,* 7.

14. Solove, *Understanding Privacy.*

15. Nissenbaum, *Privacy in Context.*

16. Although teens may not functionally have agency or social power in relation to their parents, they certainly try valiantly to circumvent surveillance by authority figures. For a review of some techniques teens use, see Marwick, Diaz, and Palfrey, "Youth, Privacy and Reputation" and Marwick and boyd, "Networked Privacy."

17. For the larger cultural impact of celebrity scandals on privacy norms, see Thompson, "Shifting Boundaries of Public and Private Life."

18. Natalya N. Bazarova argues that the seemingly mundane messages that are the stock and trade of social media interaction are actually essential for relational maintenance within these media. Bazarova, "Public Intimacy."

19. Petitcolas, Anderson, and Kuhn, "Information Hiding"; R. Anderson, "History of Steganography."

20. Nathan Jurgenson and P. J. Rey refer to this practice as the "fan dance" of status updates. Jurgenson and Rey, "Comment on Sarah Ford's 'Reconceptualization of Privacy and Publicity.'"

21. The Pew Internet and American Life Project found that 58 percent of teens cloak their messages either through inside jokes or other obscure references, with older teens (62 percent) engaging in this practice more often than younger teens (46 percent). See Madden et al., "Teens, Social Media, and Privacy."

22. Holson, "Text Generation Gap."

23. For a discussion of different privacy practices to manage privacy and publicness, see Lampinen, "Practices of Balancing Privacy and Publicness in Social Network Services."

24. Privacy is, in many ways, a socioeconomic issue. When the state provides social services, intensive scrutiny and surveillance are often normative. Teens who grow up in households in which parents receive welfare or in which child services are involved are accustomed to invasions of privacy. For a discussion of the socioeconomic issues of privacy, see Gilman, "Class Differential in Privacy Law." Likewise, data suggests that black youth take many more measures to obscure their identity and provide fake online information. See Madden et al., "Teens, Social Media, and Privacy."

25. To read more about how different intensive parenting styles intersect with technology, see Nelson, *Parenting Out of Control*; and Clark, *Parent App*.

26. Bernstein and Triger, "Over-Parenting."

27. See Haddon, "Phone in the Home."

28. Heather Armstrong quoted in Rosenberg, *Say Everything*, 265.

29. For a full deconstruction of the "nothing to hide" argument, see Solove, " 'I've Got Nothing to Hide.' "

30. Political dissidents, in particular, have long used strategies to hide in public. This is exemplified in contemporary China, where government censors restrict the kinds of speech people can use and the topics they can discuss. Because of the nature of the Chinese language, citizens often use words that sound similar to their intended word as a way of routing around the censors. For example, the Chinese word for "river crab" sounds a lot like the word for "harmony" or "harmonize," which refers to the government's policy of getting activists to conform. Images are often used instead of text to make it harder for censors to understand what is happening algorithmically. These are just two of the tactics Chinese activists use to counter attempts to control them. An Xiao Mina, an American artist of Chinese descent, has blogged about these practices in "A Curated History of the Grass Mud Horse Song" and "Social Media Street Art."

Chapter 3. Addiction

1. Hafner, "To Deal with Obsession, Some Defriend Facebook."

2. In 2013, the Pew Internet and American Life Project reported that two-thirds of American adults have taken a break from Facebook—or a "Facebook vacation"—because they didn't have time, were bored with the site, found the content unappealing, or grew tired of the gossip and drama. Notably, 8 percent of adults surveyed suggested that they were previously spending too much time on the site and needed to take a break. See Rainie, Smith, and Duggan, "Coming and Going on Facebook." Although it's not clear how common this is among teenagers, many of the teens that I met have similar concerns. Similarly, in her work on media refusal, Laura Portwood-Stacer found that many people

intentionally opt-out of social media. Often, those who decide to quit employ addiction as their frame for describing their decision. See Portwood-Stacer, "Media Refusal and Conspicuous Non-Consumption."

3. C. Stewart, "Obsessed with the Internet"; Fackler, "In Korea, a Boot Camp Cure for Web Obsession."

4. Some psychologists and communication scholars have addressed the issue of TV addiction through the lens of "media effects." This subdiscipline is fraught. For a review on the history of moral panics related to media effects research, see Livingstone, "On the Continuing Problems of Media Effects Research."

5. Csikszentmihalyi, *Flow*.

6. For an account of how gambling machines are designed to enhance flow, see Schüll, *Addiction by Design*. For a discussion of how video games leverage the state of flow, see Cowley, Charles, Black, and Hickey, "Toward an Understanding of Flow in Video Games." For a discussion of the connection between flow and addiction, see Chou and Ting, "Role of Flow Experience in Cyber-Game Addiction."

7. Early in my fieldwork, I asked teenagers whether they ever used a computer that wasn't connected to the internet. One girl furrowed her brow and asked me what would be the point of such a device. A teen boy explained that his home computer collected dust when his mother forgot to pay the internet bill. The public rhetoric suggests that the problem is the technological artifact, but many teens make it very clear that they have no particular interest in the physical device. They're only interested in the opportunities to be social.

8. For an early reference to "addicted to the bottle," see Pittis, *Dr. Radcliffe's Life and Letters*, 31.

9. Zieger, "Terms to Describe Addiction in the Nineteenth Century."

10. Quoted in *Oxford English Dictionary*, s.v. "addiction."

11. World Health Organization, Expert Committee on Drugs Liable to Produce Addiction, *Report on the Second Session, Geneva, 9–14 January 1950*. http://whqlibdoc.who.int/trs/WHO_TRS_21.pdf.

12. Federwisch, "Internet Addiction?" Like Goldman, the American Medical Association (AMA) is often hesitant to label new compulsions as addictions. In 2007, the AMA declined to label "video game addiction" as a disorder even though many rallied for it to be declared one. Psych Central News Editor, "Video Games No Addiction for Now."

13. For example, Jerald J. Block's editorial for the *American Journal of Psychiatry*, titled "Issues for DSM-V: Internet Addiction," cites a variety of studies, primarily in South Korea.

14. The American Library Association maintains a list of books most frequently challenged or banned by schools. In the 1990s, *Go Ask Alice* was listed as number 25 on the list of top 100 books to be banned. American Library Association, "100 Most Frequently Challenged Books: 1990–1999."

15. Gross, "Dad Pays Daughter $200 to Quit Facebook."

16. Llorens, "Tommy Jordan, Dad Who Shot Daughter's Laptop, Says He'd Do It Again"; Jordan, "Facebook Parenting."

17. For an analysis of how physical mobility has changed over multiple generations, see Bird, *Natural Thinking*. For a deeper discussion on the decline of children's access to public spaces and nature, see Valentine, *Public Space and the Culture of Childhood*; and Louv, *Last Child in the Woods*.

18. According to the Bureau of Justice Statistics, violent crime against youth declined 77 percent from 1994 to 2010. http://www.bjs.gov/content/pub/press/vcay9410pr.cfm.

19. For a scholarly discussion of how children have lost access to public spaces, see Valentine, *Public Space and the Culture of Childhood*. For a more popular discussion, see Skenazy, *Free-Range Kids*.

20. Ruefle and Reynolds, "Curfew and Delinquency in Major American Cities."

21. Lyall, "What's the Buzz?"

22. National Center for Safe Routes to School, "How Children Get to School."

23. Mahoney, Larson, and Eccles, *Organized Activities as Contexts of Development*.

24. Pinker, "Mind over Mass Media."

25. Hall, *Adolescence*.

26. For an overview on the Progressive Era, see Pestritto and Atto, *American Progressivism*.

27. For an account of how teenagers were shaped by the various shifts in American policies resulting from Hall's work and adjacent movements, see Hine, *Rise and Fall of the American Teenager*.

28. For an exploration of how the boundaries of various life stages are socially and normatively constructed, see Crawford, *Adult Themes*.

29. Robert Putnam's *Bowling Alone* (2000) is a popular scholarly articulation of the fear that American society has become disconnected. In response, Eric Klinenberg's *Going Solo* (2012) highlights how shifts in household configuration and the rise in people choosing to live alone isn't simply a rejection of sociality, but a byproduct of increasingly social work spaces.

Chapter 4. Danger

1. For examples of media coverage of online predators, see Williams, "MySpace, Facebook Attract Online Predators"; and Poulsen, "MySpace Predator Caught by Code."

2. In the 1990s, before internet usage was mainstream among youth, there was considerable news coverage about the dangers of online sexual predators. See, e.g., Elmer-DeWitt, "Online Erotica."

3. In *The Culture of Fear*, sociologist Barry Glassner provides a detailed account of how American society uses fear to regulate everyday practices. He points out that people are terrible at assessing risk; many fears are connected, not to risk, but to how the media shapes the public's perception of key issues. Eszter Hargittai and I examine the pervasiveness of parental concerns and fears regarding online safety issues in "Connected and Concerned."

4. Some early news reports about the dangers of the internet for youth include: Rovner, "Molesting Children by Computer"; Wetzstein, "Anti-Porn Group Targets On-Line Activities"; and Lennox, "E.mail."

5. One account of how sexual curiosity led to compulsive participation in cybersex is detailed in Kelleher, "With Teens and Internet Sex, Curiosity Can Become Compulsion."

6. Valentine, *Public Space and the Culture of Childhood*.

7. Jahn, "National Youth Rights Association—Analysis of U.S. Curfew Laws"; Favro, "City Mayors."

8. Males and Macallair, "Analysis of Curfew Enforcement and Juvenile Crimes in California."

9. Quoted in Valentine, *Public Space and the Culture of Childhood*, 91.

10. Ibid., 27.

11. Cohen, *Folk Devils and Moral Panics*. For further information on moral panics, see Goode and Ben-Yehuda, *Moral Panics*; and Springhall, *Youth, Popular Culture and Moral Panics*.

12. Jack, *Woman Reader*.

13. For an in-depth exploration on the moral panic surrounding comic books (including the 1954 Senate Subcommittee Hearings into Juvenile Delinquency), see Hadju, *Ten-Cent Plague*.

14. John Springhall details the intersection of teens' media practices and moral panics in *Youth, Popular Culture and Moral Panics*.

15. Finkelhor, "Internet, Youth Safety and the Problem of 'Juvenoia.'"

16. For a discussion of the moral panics surrounding girls' online practices, see Cassell and Cramer, "High Tech or High Risk."

17. For an analysis of the MySpace moral panic, see Marwick, "To Catch a Predator?"

18. Amy Adler critiques the show and presents a more detailed overview of its role in American society in "To Catch a Predator."

19. Henry Jenkins and I wrote a critique of the Deleting Online Predators Act on May 26, 2006, for MIT Talk Tech: http://www.danah.org/papers/MySpaceDOPA.html.

20. In 2007, the attorneys general commissioned an Internet Safety Technical Task Force that was codirected by John Palfrey, Dena Sacco, and myself. As part of that task force, we were asked to consider technical solutions—including age verification technologies—to combat sexual predators. We chose to analyze

existing research and technical interventions and came to the conclusion that age verification would not actually help children who are sexually exploited because the media-driven image of the sexual predator was misleading. Our final report, "Enhancing Child Safety and Online Technologies," can be found online at: http://cyber.law.harvard.edu/pubrelease/isttf/.

21. Lessig, *Code.*

22. In her study of girls' websites, Susannah Stern described a category of "self-conscious site authors" who are aware of (and concerned about) the fact that any information they put online could be used to harm them. Stern, "Expression on Web Home Pages."

23. boyd and Hargittai, "Connected and Concerned."

24. The dynamics of "anxious parenting" are analyzed in Nelson, *Parenting Out of Control*; Stearns, *Anxious Parents*; and Furedi, *Paranoid Parenting.*

25. See Hammel-Zabin, *Conversations with a Pedophile.*

26. For an analysis of how legal policy builds on anxious parenting, see Bernstein and Triger, "Over-Parenting."

27. Snyder and Sickmund, *Juvenile Offenders and Victims: 2006 National Report;* Mitchell, Finkelhor, and Wolak, "Internet and Family and Acquaintance Sexual Abuse"; Finkelhor and Ormrod, "Kidnaping of Juveniles."

28. Finkelhor and Ormrod, "Kidnaping of Juveniles."

29. National Center for Missing and Exploited Children, "CyberTipline: Annual Report Totals"; Calpin, "Child Maltreatment"; Finkelhor and Jones, "Updated Trends in Child Maltreatment, 2006."

30. According to Howard N. Snyder, *Sexual Assault of Young Children as Reported to Law Enforcement* (2000), 84 percent of sexual abuse committed against children under twelve and 71 percent of sexual abuse committed against children age twelve to seventeen are committed in a residence, either the victim's or the perpetrator's. For other data on the trends in sexual abuse, see Jones, Mitchell, and Finkelhor, "Trends in Youth Internet Victimization"; and Shakeshaft, "Educator Sexual Misconduct."

31. Finkelhor, Mitchell, and Wolak, "Online Victimization."

32. Wolak, Mitchell, and Finkelhor, "Online Victimization of Youth."

33. Ybarra, Espelage, and Mitchell, "Co-Occurrence of Internet Harassment and Unwanted Sexual Solicitation Victimization and Perpetration"; Wolak, Finkelhor, and Mitchell, "Is Talking Online to Unknown People Always Risky?"

34. Wolak, Finkelhor, Mitchell, and Ybarra, "Online 'Predators' and Their Victims"; Finkelhor, *Childhood Victimization*; Mitchell, Wolak, and Finkelhor, "Are Blogs Putting Youth at Risk?"; Ybarra and Mitchell, "Prevalence and Frequency of Internet Harassment Instigation."

35. Mitchell, Finkelhor, and Wolak, "Internet and Family and Acquaintance Sexual Abuse."

36. For an in-depth exploration of the tricky nature of adolescent sexual consent and the law, see Hasinoff, "Information, Consent, and Control."

37. Erdely, "Kiki Kannibal."

38. Sexual assault or rape among teens who are in a dating relationship ranges from 3 percent to 23 percent of all females and 2 percent to 4 percent of all males. For more information, see Bergman, "Dating Violence Among High School Students"; Canterbury, Grossman, and Lloyd, "Drinking Behaviors and Lifetime Incidence of Date Rape"; Davis, Peck, and Storment, "Acquaintance Rape and the High School Student"; DeKeseredy and Schwartz, "Locating a History of Some Canadian Women Abuse"; and Vicary, Klingaman, and Harkness, "Risk Factors Associated with Date Rape."

39. Age-discrepant marriages are more frequently associated with non-US populations, lower socioeconomic status, lower educational levels, and certain religions. Although such relationships are common in certain parts of the world, they are often taboo in the United States. For a review of these dynamics, see Berardo, Appel, and Berardo, "Age Dissimilar Marriages."

40. "Mothers Think Teens Were Lured Away by MySpace.com Suitors."

41. Jenkins, "Congressional Testimony on Media Violence."

42. Gaines, *Teenage Wasteland*.

43. The original video can be viewed on YouTube at http://www.youtube.com/watch?v=vOHXGNx-E7E.

44. Wells and Mitchell, "How Do High-Risk Youth Use the Internet?"

45. Wolak, Finkelhor, and Mitchell, "Is Talking Online to Unknown People Always Risky?"; Wells and Mitchell, "How Do High-Risk Youth Use the Internet?"

Chapter 5. Bullying

1. The ideas in this chapter—and much of the data—would not have been possible without help from my collaborator Alice Marwick. For two years, we interviewed teens and worked out numerous ideas about networked youth culture together. The ideas about drama in this chapter are the product of deep collaboration. To read more about our ideas on teen conflict, see Marwick and boyd, "'It's Just Drama'"

2. A literature review produced by the Harvard Berkman Center for the Kinder and Braver World Project found that, although the rates of bullying ranged tremendously depending on how one defined bullying, the bulk of studies suggest that anywhere from 20 percent to 35 percent of youth are bullied offline, a rate that is much higher than the typical online rate. Levy et al., "Bullying in a Networked Era." Studies that compare online and offline bullying consistently show that youth report that bullying happens more frequently and with greater emotional duress at school. See, e.g., Ybarra, Mitchell, and Espelage, "Comparisons of Bully and Unwanted Sexual Experiences."

3. One of the most publicized cases of bullying appearing to prompt teen suicide was that of Phoebe Prince, a fifteen-year-old from Massachusetts, who purportedly killed herself after being tormented by classmates. In response, local prosecutors charged six teenagers with a variety of violations, including statutory rape. Emily Bazelon investigated this case and found that the public narrative obfuscated the serious mental health issues that Prince was experiencing while blaming a group of teens who felt as though they were on the receiving end of Phoebe's abuse. Her excellent documentation and analysis can be found in a three-part series published in *Slate*, "What Really Happened to Phoebe Prince?" She also did a deeper analysis of this case and other teen bully-suicides in her book, *Sticks and Stones*.

4. For a review of the anti-bullying legislation that has been proposed or implemented, see Sacco et al., "Overview of State Anti-Bullying Legislation and Other Related Laws."

5. Based on his research, Dan Olweus created the Olweus Bullying Prevention Program (OBPP), which is now used by many educators. In his scholarly writing, Olweus has described bullying with a variety of words, but the three components listed are generally associated with him and generally used by those implementing OBPP.

6. Ybarra, Mitchell, and Espelage, "Comparisons of Bully and Unwanted Sexual Experiences."

7. Victims of bullying may experience a wide variety of academic, emotional, and social problems, including lower grades, truancy, social anxiety, low self-esteem, suicidal thoughts/behavior, mental health issues, hostility, and delinquency. Perpetrators of bullying behavior are also subject to a series of negative outcomes, including problems in romantic relationships, suicidal thoughts, mental health issues, and drug and alcohol abuse. Many perpetrators are also often victims in other contexts. For a broad literature review on bullying, see Levy et al., "Bullying in a Networked Era." For an empirically grounded analysis of how these dynamics unfold, see Espelage and Swearer, *Bullying in North American Schools*. For a scholarly overview of how technology intersects with other aspects of bullying, see Hinduja and Patchin, *School Climate 2.0*.

8. In their review of Zero Tolerance policies, the American Psychological Association found that not only do highly punitive bullying policies fail to create a better learning environment for students but disruptive students who were removed from school environments as a result of these policies were often exposed to more risk. Skiba et al., "Are Zero Tolerance Policies Effective in the Schools?"

9. Alice Marwick and I document our analysis in great detail in "The Drama!"

10. For an in-depth examination of how heteronormative and homophobic discourses construct adolescent American masculinity, see Pascoe, *Dude, You're a Fag*.

11. Englander, "Digital Self-Harm."

12. Milner, *Freaks, Geeks, and Cool Kids*, 25.

13. Eckert, *Jocks and Burnouts*.

14. Dunbar, *Grooming, Gossip, and the Evolution of Language*.

15. For an overview of the "Star Wars Kid," see the Wikipedia entry: http://en.wikipedia.org/wiki/Star_Wars_Kid.

16. In *Spreadable Media*, Henry Jenkins, Sam Ford, and Josh Green describe the productive value of spreading online content to help create meaning and value in a networked culture. The same practices that they describe can be used to reinforce cultural values and norms at the expense of individuals.

17. The notion of celebrity refers to multiple things. In the colloquial sense, it refers to a famous person (e.g., Lady Gaga is a celebrity). It can also refer to a cultural phenomenon, as in celebrity culture. For scholars, celebrity can be viewed as a process by which people turn into a commodity. To learn more about how celebrity is theorized and conceptualized, see Turner, *Understanding Celebrity*; and David, *Celebrity Culture Reader*.

18. Alice Marwick and I discuss how Twitter is used to enable the practice of celebrity in "To See and Be Seen."

19. Nancy Baym discusses how musicians use technology to engage directly with their fans in "Fans or Friends?"

20. In *Toxic Fame*, Joey Berlin interviews hundreds of celebrities about their experiences with fame. This collection offers a fascinating perspective on the struggles that celebrities face.

21. Terri Senft provides a valuable analysis of microcelebrity and the politics of celebrity in a digital world in *Camgirls*.

22. Wasserman, "How Rebecca Black Became a YouTube Sensation."

23. Rebecca Black discussed her experience with fame on *Primetime Nightline: Celebrity Secrets* in a special episode called "Underage and Famous" on August 10, 2011. For a written description, see Canning, "Rebecca Black."

24. The cultivation of resilience and empathy within teens is seen as key to addressing everyday obstacles, including bullying. See Goldstein and Brooks, *Handbook of Resilience in Children*; Polanin, Espelage, and Pigott, "Meta-Analysis of School-Based Bullying Prevention Programs' Effects."

25. Many of the best programs rely on social emotional learning (SEL) to help people develop the necessary skills to cope with violence, bullying, and other forms of conflict. SEL programs focus on helping people develop empathy and resilience to maintain healthy relationships.

Chapter 6. Inequality

1. The rhetoric used by the US media to suggest that social media could democratize the world took a more magnificent form in January 2011. As citizens throughout the Middle East began challenging authoritarian regimes, the

media described the uprisings of the Arab Spring as being a product of social media. The news media began extolling social media as being the source of the various Middle East revolutions. This narrative has been widely critiqued, but it reveals prevalent notions of how technology can do cultural work to eradicate inequalities and injustices.

2. In *Digitizing Race*, Lisa Nakamura has pointed out that many technological discourses, particularly those involving the digital divide, have envisioned or positioned users of color as technologically limited and/or uninvolved.

3. Briggs and Maverick quoted in Carey, "Technology and Ideology," 160–161.

4. For a discussion of whiteness and photography, see Dyer, "Lighting for Whiteness."

5. Sinclair, "Kinect Has Problems Recognizing Dark-Skinned Users?"

6. Zax, "Siri, Why Can't You Understand Me?"

7. Kendall, "Meaning and Identity in 'Cyberspace'"; Kolko, Nakamura, and Rodman, "Race in Cyberspace."

8. Kolko, Nakamura, and Rodman, "Race in Cyberspace," 4–5.

9. Ethan Zuckerman talks extensively about the "imaginary cosmopolitanism" and the fallacy of social media as an inherently democratizing force in *Rewire*. Although his focus is global in scope, the same issues he highlights internationally also play out domestically. And the challenges that he highlights in describing how adults negotiate differences are also true of teenagers.

10. Warschauer, *Technology and Social Inclusion*; Drori, *Global E-litism*.

11. Steiner, "On the Internet, Nobody Knows You're a Dog."

12. Christopherson, "The Positive and Negative Implications of Anonymity in Internet Social Interactions."

13. The "omgblackpeople" blog was originally hosted on Tumblr, but as of 2013, it is no longer available. The content was reposted on: http://omgblackpeople.wordpress.com/. For a blog post covering the racist tweets surrounding the BET awards, see http://www.blackweb20.com/2009/06/29/bet-awards-dominate-twitter-causes-racist-backlash/#.UVB-flv5ms8.

14. Smith, "Twitter Update 2011."

15. Saraceno, "Swiss Soccer Player Banned from Olympics for Racist Tweet."

16. For an analysis of racism online, see Daniels, *Cyber Racism*; and Nakamura, "Don't Hate the Player, Hate the Game."

17. For a write-up of racist commentary following the casting of *The Hunger Games*, see D. Stewart, "Racist Hunger Games Fans Are Very Disappointed."

18. CoEd Staff, "Alexandra Wallace."

19. Mandell, "Alexandra Wallace, UCLA Student."

20. At times, self-appointed norm protectors seek to regulate online decorum by engaging in digital vigilantism. See Phillips and Miltner, "Internet's Vigilante Shame Army"; and Norton, "Anonymous 101."

21. Eckert, *Jocks and Burnouts*.

22. The tendency for people to downplay racism by talking about how they have friends of different races is so common that it is a frame through which people look at cross-race connections. In the 2012 book *Some of My Best Friends Are Black*, Tanner Colby describes the challenges of racial integration in the United States through four different case studies. In a more comedic treatment of the same issue, comedian Baratunde Thurston dedicates an entire chapter in *How to Be Black* to "how to be the black friend." He offers entertaining advice to black readers on how they can make white people feel comfortable by taking concrete steps to be a "good" black friend.

23. For a discussion of homophily, including how American society is divided along racial and ethnic lines, see McPherson, Smith-Lovin, and Cook, "Birds of a Feather."

24. See Lin, "Inequality in Social Capital."

25. Bonilla-Silva, *Racism Without Racists*.

26. For a more detailed analysis of the division that emerged in the 2006-2007 school year between Facebook and MySpace, see boyd, "White Flight in Networked Publics?" Craig Watkins also documents the racialized tension between these sites in his work on youth and social media. Watkins, *The Young and the Digital*.

27. As Siân Lincoln points out in *Youth Culture and Private Space*, teenagers use whatever platform their friends use, even if they personally prefer other platforms.

28. Black and African American individuals are overrepresented on Twitter compared to their participation online more generally. Scholars have begun analyzing a practice known colloquially as "Black Twitter," referring both to the significant presence of black users as well as how practices and norms in Twitter appear to differ across race lines. See Brock, "From the Blackhand Side"; and Florini, "Tweets, Tweeps, and Signifyin'."

29. Clinton, "Internet Freedom."

30. Scholars and government agencies have pointed out that technology uptake is often dependent on contextual relevance. When it comes to information and communication technologies, people are often more likely to appreciate their value when they see others use them in beneficial ways. If people's personal networks aren't using particular technologies, they often see no reason to use them. See Haddon, "Social Exclusion and Information and Communication Technologies"; and Federal Communications Commission, *National Broadband Plan*.

31. Hargittai, "Digital Reproduction of Inequality."

32. For a sampling of relevant studies on social networks, see Fischer, *To Dwell Among Friends*; Granovetter, "Strength of Weak Ties"; Lin, *Social Capital*; and Wellman, *Networks in the Global Village*.

33. In *Invisible Users*, Jenna Burrell makes the issues of structural inequality especially visible in her study of Ghanaian youth. Although these youth have

access to information technologies, the social networks in which they operate—and the norms that exist in their home communities—complicate their ability to connect successfully and meaningfully with more powerful users.

34. Webster, *Theories of the Information Society*; Webster, "Information and Urban Change"; Garnham, *Information Society Theory as Ideology*.

Chapter 7. Literacy

1. Walz and Brownsberger, "(Real) Virtual Education."

2. Ellen Helsper and Rebecca Eynon have argued, in "Digital Natives," that not only is it misguided to assume that there is a digital knowledge gap between educators and students but it is entirely possible for adults to "become digital natives" through a combination of skill acquisition and interaction with ICT.

3. Barlow, "Declaration of the Independence of Cyberspace."

4. The origin of the concept of "digital natives" is murky. At the same time that John Perry Barlow was penning his manifesto, Doug Rushkoff published *Playing the Future: What We Can Learn from Digital Kids*. While promoting this book, Rushkoff regularly spoke of youth as digital natives. For example, Rushkoff is quoted by Elizabeth Weil in a *Fast Company* article entitled "The Future Is Younger than You Think" as having said, "Kids are natives in a place where most adults are immigrants." Rushkoff and Barlow each told me that he was inspired by the other.

5. Prensky, "Digital Natives, Digital Immigrants."

6. Prensky, "Digital Natives, Digital Immigrants: Origins of the Term."

7. In their report on "Connected Learning," Mimi Ito and coauthors describe how different constituencies should come together to enable new forms of learning through and with technology. This report provides concrete steps that educators can take.

8. Media literacy is a contentious topic. Scholars, policymakers, and educators have long contested its definition, parameters, and pedagogy. Those disputes and discussions will likely continue as the nature of the internet morphs and evolves. For a more in-depth exploration of the debates surrounding media literacy and media literacy education, see Aufderheide, *Media Literacy*; Livingstone, "Media Literacy"; and Hobbs, "Seven Great Debates."

9. The history of media literacy education started in the United Kingdom in 1930s when F. R. Leavis and Denys Thompson published what is considered to be the first instruction manual for teaching about the mass media in schools, *Culture and Environment: The Training of Critical Awareness*. See Buckingham, "Media Education in the UK."

10. In the United States, the media literacy movement started in the 1960s and was spearheaded by John Culkin, who advocated for media education in school curricula. See Moody, "John Culkin."

11. Age, gender, race, and socioeconomic status are all determining factors in whether youth have the opportunity to develop digital literacy skills. For example, children from higher income households are more likely to have access to the latest technology, which means that they will have more opportunity to figure out how to use it, not only from trial-and-error exploration, but from the instruction of their parents and siblings. Furthermore, these children are more likely to have been taught to search for information, as well as to qualify and evaluate it. See Livingstone, Bober, and Helsper, *Internet Literacy Among Children and Young People*; and Hargittai, "Digital Reproduction of Inequality."

12. In his article on "Copy and Paste Literacy," Dan Perkel notes that even though teenagers may know how to engage in "networked discourse" from a social perspective, they still developed technical sensibilities in order to update their MySpace profiles.

13. For a critical examination of how Google—both the company and the search engine—work, see Vaidhyanathan, *Googlization of Everything*.

14. In *Spam*, Finn Bruton details how spammers react to Google's attempt to stop search engine optimizers by developing complex algorithms to manipulate the system. This creates an ongoing battle between the company and those who seek to profit from having their material at the top of the results pages.

15. In "The Relevance of Algorithms," Tarleton Gillespie details the ways in which algorithms have political power.

16. In "The Curious Connection Between Apps for Gay Men and Sex Offenders," Mike Ananny describes the unintended link produced by the algorithm underpinning Android's recommendation system. When Ananny tried to download Grindr, a gay dating site, he was encouraged to also consider downloading a sex offender search site. He wrote this essay to question how such a link was algorithmically produced. Unfortunately, Google did not respond. Instead, the company simply changed the algorithm.

17. Gasser, Cortesi, Malik, and Lee, "From Credibility to Information Quality."

18. Giles, "Special Report."

19. Although educators often dismiss Wikipedia over issues of credibility, they also tend to downplay the educational value of using the service. In "Writing, Citing, and Participatory Media," Andrea Forte and Amy Bruckman found that engaging with wikis was a learning-rich experience for high school students that contributed to both writing and information assessment skills.

20. Texas's undue influence on the US textbook market is discussed in Collins, "How Texas Inflicts Bad Textbooks on Us." For examples of how Texan Christianity shapes textbooks, see Birnbaum, "Historians Speak Out Against Proposed Texas Textbook Changes."

21. See http://en.wikipedia.org/wiki/Wikipedia:List_of_hoaxes_on_Wikipedia.

22. The potential of social media and other recent technologies for helping address issues in information flow and curation—including crowd-sourcing, classification, and cooperation—has been the topic of numerous books in recent years. See Weinberger, *Everything Is Miscellaneous*; Shirky, *Cognitive Surplus*; and Benkler, *Penguin and Leviathan*.

23. Jenkins, "Reconsidering Digital Immigrants."

24. The first official use of the term *digital divide* appeared in a report by the National Telecommunications and Information Administration (NTIA). The NTIA defined the digital divide as the gap between those who had access to a computer and the internet and those who didn't. See NTIA, *Falling Through the Net*.

25. Compaine, *Digital Divide*.

26. Warschauer, *Technology and Social Inclusion*.

27. NTIA, *Falling Through the Net*.

28. For an overview of digital inequality and the various scholarly strands, see Hargittai, "Digital Reproduction of Inequality"; Mossberger, Tolbert, and Stansburgy, *Virtual Inequality*; and Selwyn, "Reconsidering Political and Popular Understandings."

29. Federal Communications Commission, *National Broadband Plan*. See also Eszter Hargittai's work on skill, e.g., DiMaggio, Hargittai, Celeste, and Shafer, "Digital Inequality"; and Hargittai, "Second-Level Digital Divide."

30. Warschauer, *Technology and Social Inclusion*.

31. Lenhart et al., "Teens, Kindness and Cruelty on Social Network Sites."

32. The politics surrounding access for youth are far from straightforward. Christian Sandvig notes, in "Unexpected Outcomes in Digital Divide Policy," that when given unstructured access, young people prefer to play games and use chat, activities that are not considered to be the types of "beneficial" engagement that policymakers had in mind.

33. Jenkins et al., *Confronting the Challenges of Participatory Culture*.

34. The ability to access the internet without restriction is described by Eszter Hargittai as "autonomy of use." Autonomy of use has a significant impact on the depth of engagement and type of benefit that can be gained from internet use. Youth who rely on public sources of access, such as schools or libraries, often face major obstacles that impede their usage and impact, including physical distance, opening hours, and equipment quality and availability. See Hargittai, "Digital Na(t)ives?"

35. Eszter Hargittai's work on the topic of skills can be found at: http://webuse.org/pubs/. Two relevant publications are Hargittai, "Digital Na(t)ives?"; and Hargittai and Hinnant, "Digital Inequality."

36. Hargittai, "Digital Na(t)ives?"

37. Crawford and Robinson, "Beyond Generations and New Media."

38. Epstein, Nisbet, and Gillespie, "Who's Responsible for the Digital Divide?"

39. Palfrey and Gasser, *Born Digital*; Palfrey and Gasser, "Reclaiming an Awkward Term."

40. Gasser and Palfrey's nuanced description of digital natives comes from their answer to the question, "Are all youth digital natives?" here: https://web.archive.org/web/20121122075749/http://blogs.law.harvard.edu/youthandmediaalpha/projects/digital-natives/. They provide a similar explanation in the opening of their book *Born Digital*.

41. Prensky, "Digital Wisdom and Homo Sapiens Digital."

42. *Hanging Out, Messing Around, and Geeking Out* by Mimi Ito et al. provides a more detailed framework for understanding how young people's online activities can lead to tremendous learning opportunities. Many youth approach social media and other technologies as spaces to hang out with their friends, but some start messing around with different technical and media elements—such as those who started learning how to code by exploring ways of creating intricate MySpace pages. When teens become passionate about something, they may turn to social media to geek out, building online communities and drilling down in specialized interests. This book provides a framework for thinking about the various forms of informal learning that can emerge when youth are given the freedom to explore networked settings.

Chapter 8. Searching for a Public of Their Own

1. For an examination of how shopping malls serve as publics, see Matthews, Taylor, Percy-Smith, and Limb, "Unacceptable Flaneur."

2. Two books provide fantastic analyses of the consumer culture that American children inhabit and how it inflects every aspect of their engagement with school, media, and society more generally: Seiter, *Sold Separately*; and Schor, *Born to Buy*.

3. For a broader critique of the commercial side of social media and the privatization of public spaces online, see Scholz, "Market Ideology and the Myths of Web 2.0"; and Lovink, *Networks Without a Cause*.

4. My collaborator, Alice Marwick, and I build off of this case study and detail the dynamics of Twitter and public culture in "Tweeting Teens Can Handle Public Life."

5. Duncombe, *Notes from Underground*; Finders,"Queens and Teen Zines"; Bayerl, "Mags, Zines, and gURLs."

6. In *The Anarchist in the Library*, Siva Vaidhyanathan shows how new technologies erase institutional boundaries, which in turn challenge the political organization of society. Not only are people using new technologies to engage in political acts, but the very architecture of networked publics—and the affordances that underpin them—create new socio-technical configurations that alter the political landscape. In *Communication Power*, Manuel Castells points out that those who control the networks—both technical and social—are often those with the most power.

7. According to Youth and Participatory Politics Survey Project, 41 percent of young people have engaged in at least one act of participatory politics, defined by the project as "interactive, peer-based acts through which individuals and groups seek to exert both voice and influence on issues of public concern." Cohen et al., "New Media and Youth Political Action."

8. Jodi Dean argues that the environments that I'm describing as networked publics cannot serve as political public spheres because of the commercial underpinnings of these systems. Although I respect her argument, I do think that much political work does take place in and through these systems, even if they themselves are not the kinds of ideal publics that enable the public sphere to form. Dean, "Why the Net Is Not a Public Sphere."

9. In *Smart Mobs*, Howard Rheingold describes how activists in the Philippines used technology to spread information and come together politically. As protests were breaking out in Egypt and other parts of the Middle East, people turned to social media for information and to coordinate political resistance. See Tufekci and Wilson, "Social Media and the Decision to Participate in Political Protests."

10. In *The Digital Origins of Dictatorship and Democracy*, Philip Howard discusses how democracy is supported by having a high percentage of the population online, even if they are not directly engaged with political activities. In a paper for the Digital Media and Learning initiative, Joseph Kahne, Nam-Jin Lee, and Jessica Timpany Feezell demonstrated that engagement with nonpolitical online participatory cultures can act as a gateway for behavior that is considered to be more explicitly civic and/or political: volunteering, community problem-solving, protests, and political expression. Kahne, Lee, and Timpany Feezell, "Civic and Political Significance of Online Participatory Cultures among Youth Transitioning to Adulthood."

11. Khokha, "Text Messages, MySpace Roots of Student Protests."

12. Cho and Gorman, "Massive Student Walkout Spreads Across Southland."

13. Leavey, "Los Angeles Students Walk Out in Immigration Reform Protests."

14. For background information on Anonymous, see Coleman, "Our Weirdness Is Free"; Norton, "Anonymous 101"; and Greenberg, "WikiLeaks Supporters Aim Cyberattacks at PayPal."

15. Olson, *We Are Anonymous*.

16. For an in-depth examination of internet memes and the sociopolitical use of memes for humor and cultural commentary, see Shifman, *Memes in Digital Culture*.

17. For an explanation of the Hitler Downfall meme, including other examples, see http://knowyourmeme.com/memes/downfall-hitler-reacts.

18. In his book on the history of the telephone, *America Calling*, Claude Fisher shows how the fears and anxieties discussed throughout this book also played out at the time in which the telephone was first being deployed.

19. Vint Cerf quoted in Ward, "What the Net Did Next."

bibliography

Adler, Amy M. "To Catch a Predator." *Columbia Journal of Gender and Law* 21 (2012): 130.

Allen, Anita L. "Coercing Privacy." *William and Mary Law Review* 40 (1999): 723–757.

American Library Association. "100 Most Frequently Challenged Books: 1990–1999." http://www.ala.org/advocacy/banned/frequentlychallenged/ challengedbydecade/1990_1999.

Ananny, Mike. "The Curious Connection Between Apps for Gay Men and Sex Offenders." *Atlantic*, April 14, 2011.

Anderson, Benedict. *Imagined Communities: Reflections on the Origin and Spread of Nationalism.* New ed. New York: Verso, 2006.

Anderson, Ross. "The History of Steganography." In *Information Hiding*, 1–5. Heidelberg: Springer Berlin, 1996.

Angela. "BET Awards Dominate Twitter, Causes Racist Backlash." *BlackWeb 2.0*, June 29, 2009, http://www.blackweb20.com/2009/06/29/bet-awards- dominate-twitter-causes-racist-backlash/.

Aufderheide, Patricia. *Media Literacy: A Report of the National Leadership Con- ference on Media Literacy.* Washington, DC: Aspen Institute, Communi- cations and Society Program, 1993.

Barlow, John Perry. "A Declaration of the Independence of Cyberspace." February 8, 1996, https://projects.eff.org/~barlow/Declaration-Final.html.

Baron, Naomi. "My Best Day: Managing 'Buddies' and 'Friends.'" In *Always On: Language in an Online and Mobile World*, 71–98. Oxford: Oxford University Press, 2008.

Bayerl, Katherine. "Mags, Zines, and gURLs: The Exploding World of Girls' Publications." *Women's Studies Quarterly* 8, no. 3/4 (2000): 287–292.

Baym, Nancy K. "Fans or Friends? Seeing Audiences as Musicians Do." *Participations* 9 (2012): 286–316.

Bazarova, Natalya N. "Public Intimacy: Disclosure Interpretation and Social Judgments on Facebook." *Journal of Communication* 62 (2012): 815–832.

Bazelon, Emily. *Sticks and Stones: Defeating the Culture of Bullying and Redis- covering the Power of Character and Empathy.* New York: Random House, 2013.

————. "What Really Happened to Phoebe Prince?" *Slate,* July 20, 2010, http://www.slate.com/articles/life/bulle/features/2010/what_really_happened_to_phoebe_prince/could_the_south_hadley_schools_have_done_more.html.

Benkler, Yochai. *The Penguin and the Leviathan: How Cooperation Triumphs over Self-Interest.* New York: Crown, 2011.

Berardo, Felix M., Jeffrey Appel, and Donna H. Berardo. "Age Dissimilar Marriages: Review and Assessment." *Journal of Aging Studies* 7 (1993): 93–106.

Bergman, Libby. "Dating Violence Among High School Students." *Social Work* 37 (1992): 21–27.

Berlin, Joey. *Toxic Fame: Celebrities Speak on Stardom.* Collingdale, PA: Diane Publishing, 1996.

Bernstein, Gaia, and Zvi H. Triger. "Over-Parenting." *University of California–Davis Law Review* 44 (2010): 1221–1279.

Bernstein, Michael S., et al. "4chan and /b/: An Analysis of Anonymity and Ephemerality in a Large Online Community." In *Proceedings of the Fifth International AAAI Conference on Weblogs and Social Media* (2011): 50–57.

Best, Amy, ed. *Representing Youth: Methodological Issues in Critical Youth Studies.* New York: New York University Press, 2007.

Bird, William. *Natural Thinking: A Report by Dr. William Bird, for the Royal Society for the Protection of Birds (RSPB), Investigating the Links Between the Natural Environment, Biodiversity and Mental Health.* 2nd ed. Bedfordshire, UK: RSPB, 2007.

Birnbaum, Michael. "Historians Speak Out Against Proposed Texas Textbook Changes." *Washington Post,* March 18, 2012.

Block, Jerald J. "Issues for DSM-V: Internet Addiction." *American Journal of Psychiatry* 165 (2008): 306–307.

Boellstorff, Tom. *Coming of Age in Second Life: An Anthropologist Explores the Virtually Human.* Princeton, NJ: Princeton University Press, 2008.

Bonilla-Silva, Eduardo. *Racism Without Racists: Color-Blind Racism and the Persistence of Racial Inequality in America.* Lanham, MD: Rowman and Littlefield, 2006.

Bourdieu, Pierre. *Distinction: A Social Critique of the Judgement of Taste.* London: Routledge, 1984.

boyd, danah. "Making Sense of Teen Life: Strategies for Capturing Ethnographic Data in a Networked Era." In *Digital Research Confidential: The Secrets of Studying Behavior Online,* ed. Eszter Hargittai and Christian Sandvig. Cambridge, MA: MIT Press, forthcoming.

————. "None of This Is Real." In *Structures of Participation in Digital Culture,* ed. Joe Karaganis, 132–157. New York: Social Science Research Council, 2008.

————. "Social Network Sites as Networked Publics: Affordances, Dynamics, and Implications." In *A Networked Self: Identity, Community, and Culture on Social Network Sites*, ed. Zizi Papacharissi, 39–58. New York: Routledge, 2011.

————. "White Flight in Networked Publics? How Race and Class Shaped American Teen Engagement with MySpace and Facebook." In *Race After the Internet*, ed. Lisa Nakamura and Peter Chow-White, 203–222. New York: Routledge, 2011.

boyd, danah, and Nicole B. Ellison. "Social Network Sites: Definition, History, and Scholarship." *Journal of Computer-Mediated Communication* 13, no. 1 (2007): article 11, http://onlinelibrary.wiley.com/journal/10.1111/%28I SSN%291083=6101.

boyd, danah, and Eszter Hargittai. "Connected and Concerned: How Parental Concerns About Online Safety Issues Vary." *Policy and Internet* 5, no. 3 (2013): 245–269.

————. "Facebook Privacy Settings: Who Cares?" *First Monday* 15, no. 8 (2010), http://firstmonday.org/article/viewArticle/3086/2589.

Brake, David. "Shaping the 'Me' in MySpace: The Framing of Profiles on a Social Network Site." In *Digital Storytelling, Mediatized Stories: Self-Representations in New Media*, ed. Knut Lundby, 285–300. New York: Peter Lang, 2008.

Briggs, Charles F., and Augustus Maverick. *The Story of the Telegraph and a History of the Great Atlantic Cable.* New York: Rudd and Carleton, 1858.

Brock, André. "From the Blackhand Side: Twitter as a Cultural Conversation." *Journal of Broadcasting and Electronic Media* 56 (2012): 529–549.

Brophy-Warren, Jamin. "Modest Web Site Is Behind a Bevy of Memes." *Wall Street Journal*, July 9, 2008.

Brunton, Finn. *Spam: A Shadow History of the Internet.* Cambridge, MA: MIT Press, 2013.

Buckingham, David. *After the Death of Childhood: Growing Up in the Age of Electronic Media.* Cambridge: Polity, 2000.

————. "Media Education in the UK: Moving beyond Protectionism." *Journal of Communication* 48 (1998): 33–43.

Bukowski, William M., Andrew F. Newcomb, and Willard W. Hartup, eds. *The Company They Keep: Friendship in Childhood and Adolescence.* Cambridge: Cambridge University Press, 1996.

Burrell, Jenna. *Invisible Users: Youth in the Internet Cafes of Urban Ghana.* Cambridge, MA: MIT Press, 2012.

Calhoun, Craig. *Habermas and the Public Sphere.* Cambridge, MA: MIT Press, 1992.

Calpin, Christine M. "Child Maltreatment." US Department of Health and Human Services, http://www.acf.hhs.gov/programs/cb/pubs/cm06/cm06.pdf.

Canning, Andrea. "Rebecca Black, YouTube Sensation Turned Award-Winning Pop Star, Talks About Growing Fame and Harassment." *ABC News*, August 9, 2011, https://web.archive.org/web/20110819090729/http://www.etonline.com/music/113283_Rebecca_Black_Bullied_into_Home schooling/index.html.

Canterbury, R. J., S. J. Grossman, and E. Lloyd. "Drinking Behaviors and Lifetime Incidence of Date Rape Among High School Students upon Entering College." *College Student Journal* 27 (1993): 75–84.

Carey, James W. "Technology and Ideology: The Case of the Telegraph." *Communication as Culture: Essays on Media and Society*. New York: Routledge, 1992.

Carr, Nicholas. *The Shallows: What the Internet Is Doing to Our Brains*. New York: W. W. Norton, 2010.

Cassell, Justine, and Meg Cramer. "High Tech or High Risk: Moral Panics About Girls Online." In *Digital Youth, Innovation, and the Unexpected*, ed. Tara McPherson, 53–76. Cambridge, MA: MIT Press, 2008.

Castells, Manuel. *Communication Power*. New York: Oxford University Press, 2011.

———. *The Rise of the Network Society*. Cambridge, MA: Blackwell, 1996.

Cho, Cynthia H., and Anna Gorman. "Massive Student Walkout Spreads Across Southland." *Los Angeles Times*, March 28, 2006.

Chou, Ting-Jui, and Chih-Chen Ting. "The Role of Flow Experience in Cyber-Game Addiction." *Cyberpsychology and Behavior* 6 (2003): 663–675.

Christopherson, Kimberly M. "The Positive and Negative Implications of Anonymity in Internet Social Interactions: 'On the Internet, Nobody Knows You're a Dog.'" *Computers in Human Behavior* 23 (2007): 3038–3056.

Clark, Lynn Schofield. *The Parent App: Understanding Parents in a Digital Age*. New York: Oxford University Press, 2012.

Clinton, Hillary Rodham. "Internet Freedom." Speech presented at the Newseum, January 21, 2010, http://www.foreignpolicy.com/articles/2010/01/21/internet_freedom.

CoEd Staff. "Alexandra Wallace: Racist UCLA Student's Bikini Photos Revealed." *CoEd Magazine*, March 14, 2011, http://coedmagazine.com/2011/03/14/alexandra-wallace-racist-ucla-students-bikini-photos-revealed-26-pics/.

Coffin, Judith G. "Consumption, and Images of Women's Desires: Selling the Sewing Machine in Late Nineteenth-Century France." *French Historical Studies* 18 (1994): 749–783.

Cohen, Cathy J., et al. "New Media and Youth Political Action." *Youth and Participatory Politics Survey Project, DML Central*, 2012, http://dmlcentral.net/sites/dmlcentral/files/resource_files/ypp_survey_body_cover.pdf.

Cohen, Stanley. *Folk Devils and Moral Panics: The Creation of the Mods and Rockers*. London: MacGibbon and Kee, 1972.

Colby, Tanner. *Some of My Best Friends Are Black*. New York: Viking, 2012.

Coleman, Beth. *Hello Avatar: Rise of the Networked Generation*. Cambridge, MA: MIT Press, 2011.

Coleman, Gabriella. "Our Weirdness Is Free: The Logic of Anonymous— Online Army, Agent of Chaos, and Seeker of Justice." *Triple Canopy*, January 2012, http://canopycanopycanopy.com/15/our_weirdness_is_free.

Collins, Gail. "How Texas Inflicts Bad Textbooks on Us." *New York Review of Books*, June 21, 2012.

Compaine, Benjamin. *The Digital Divide: Facing a Crisis or Creating a Myth?* Cambridge, MA: MIT Press, 2001.

Corsaro, William A. *Friendship and Peer Culture in the Early Years*. Norwood, NJ: Ablex, 1985.

Cowley, Ben, Darryl Charles, Michaela Black, and Ray Hickey. "Toward an Understanding of Flow in Video Games." *Computers in Entertainment* 6, no. 2 (2008): 1–27.

Crawford, Kate. *Adult Themes*. Sydney: Palgrave MacMillan, 2006.

Crawford, Kate, and Penelope Robinson. "Beyond Generations and New Media." In *A Companion to New Media Dynamics*, ed. John Hartley, Jean Burgess, and Axel Bruns, 472–478. Oxford: Blackwell, 2013.

Csikszentmihalyi, Mihaly. *Flow: The Psychology of Optimal Experience*. New York: Harper and Row, 1990.

Daniels, Jessie. *Cyber Racism: White Supremacy Online and the New Attack on Civil Rights*. Lanham, MD: Rowman and Littlefield, 2009.

David, Marshall P. *The Celebrity Culture Reader*. New York: Routledge, 2006.

Davidson, Cathy. *Now You See It*. New York: Penguin, 2011.

Davies, Chris, and Rebecca Eynon. *Teenagers and Technology*. New York: Routledge, 2013.

Davis, Terry C., Gary Q. Peck, and John M. Storment. "Acquaintance Rape and the High School Student." *Journal of Adolescent Health* 14 (1993): 220–224.

Dean, Jodi. "Why the Net Is Not a Public Sphere." *Constellations* 10, no. 1 (2003): 95–112.

DeKeseredy, Walter S., and Martin D. Schwartz. "Locating a History of Some Canadian Woman Abuse in Elementary and High School Dating Relationships." *Humanity and Society* 18, no. 3 (1994): 49–63.

Dibbell, Julian. *My Tiny Life: Crime and Passion in a Virtual World*. New York: Henry Holt, 1999.

DiMaggio, Paul, Eszter Hargittai, Coral Celeste, and Steven Shafer. "Digital Inequality: From Unequal Access to Differentiated Use." In *Social Inequality*, ed. Kathryn M. Neckerman, 355–400. New York: Russell Sage Foundation, 2004.

Donath, Judith S. "Identity and Deception in the Virtual Community." In *Communities in Cyberspace*, ed. Peter Kollock and Marc Smith, 29–59. London: Routledge, 1999.

———. "Signals in Social Supernets." *Journal of Computer-Mediated Communication* 13, no. 1 (2007): article 12, http://onlinelibrary.wiley.com/journal /10.1111/%28ISSN%291083-6101.

Drori, Gili S. *Global E-litism: Digital Technology, Social Inequality, and Transnationality*. New York: Macmillan, 2005.

Dunbar, Robin. *Grooming, Gossip, and the Evolution of Language*. Cambridge, MA: Harvard University Press, 1998.

Duncombe, Stephen. *Notes from Underground: Zines and the Politics of Alternative Culture*. Bloomington, IN: Microcosm, 2008.

Dyer, Richard. "Lighting for Whiteness." In *White*, 89–103. London: Routledge, 1997.

Eckert, Penelope. *Jocks and Burnouts: Social Categories and Identity in High School*. New York: Teachers College Press, 1989.

Ellison, Nicole, and danah boyd. "Sociality Through Social Network Sites." In *The Oxford Handbook of Internet Studies*, ed. William H. Dutton, 151–172. Oxford: Oxford University Press, 2013.

Elmer-DeWitt, Philip. "Online Erotica: On a Screen near You." *Time*, July 3, 1995.

Englander, Elizabeth. "Digital Self-Harm: Frequency, Type, Motivations, and Outcomes." *Report of the Massachusetts Aggression Reduction Center*, June 2012, http://webhost.bridgew.edu/marc/DIGITAL%20SELF%20HARM% 20report.pdf.

Epstein, Dmitry, Erik C. Nisbet, and Tarleton Gillespie. "Who's Responsible for the Digital Divide? Public Perceptions and Policy Implications." *Information Society*, 27, no. 2 (2011): 92–104.

Erdely, Sabrina R. "Kiki Kannibal: The Girl Who Played with Fire." *Rolling Stone*, April 28, 2011.

Espelage, Dorothy L., and Susan M. Swearer. *Bullying in North American Schools*. 2nd ed. New York: Routledge, 2011.

Fackler, Martin. "In Korea, a Boot Camp Cure for Web Obsession." *New York Times*, November 18, 2007.

Favro, Tony. "City Mayors: Youth Curfews in US Cities." City Mayors Society, July 21, 2009, http://www.citymayors.com/society/usa-youth-curfews .html.

Federal Communications Commission. *The National Broadband Plan: Connecting America*. Washington, DC: Federal Communications Commission, 2010.

Federwisch, Anne. "Internet Addiction?" *NurseWeek*, August 8, 1997. Available at: https://archive.today/bKsZ.

Finders, Margaret J. "Queens and Teen Zines: Early Adolescent Females Reading Their Way Toward Adulthood." *Anthropology and Education Quarterly* 27, no. 1 (1996): 71–89.

Finkelhor, David. *Childhood Victimization: Violence, Crime, and Abuse in the Lives of Young People.* New York: Oxford University Press, 2008.

———. "The Internet, Youth Safety and the Problem of 'Juvenoia.'" Crimes Against Children Research Center, University of New Hampshire, January 2011, http://www.unh.edu/ccrc/pdf/Juvenoia%20paper.pdf.

Finkelhor, David, and Lisa Jones. "Updated Trends in Child Maltreatment, 2006." Crimes Against Children Research Center, University of New Hampshire, http://www.unh.edu/ccrc/Trends/index.html.

Finkelhor, David, and Richard Ormrod. "Kidnaping of Juveniles: Patterns from NIBRS." Office of Juvenile Justice and Delinquency Prevention, *Juvenile Justice Bulletin*, June 2000, http://www.unh.edu/ccrc/pdf/kidnaping_of_juveniles.pdf.

Finkelhor, David, Kimberly J. Mitchell, and Janis Wolak. "Online Victimization: A Report on the Nation's Youth." National Center for Missing and Exploited Children, June 2000, http://www.unh.edu/ccrc/pdf/jvq/CV38.pdf.

Fischer, Claude S. *America Calling: A Social History of the Telephone to 1940.* Berkeley: University of California Press, 1992.

———. *To Dwell Among Friends: Personal Networks in Town and City.* Chicago: University of Chicago Press, 1982.

Florini, Sarah. "Tweets, Tweeps, and Signifyin': Communication and Cultural Performance on 'Black Twitter.'" *Television New Media*, March 7, 2013, http://tvn.sagepub.com/content/early/2013/03/07/1527476413480247.

Forte, Andrea, and Amy Bruckman. "Writing, Citing, and Participatory Media: Wikis as Learning Environments in the High School Classroom." *International Journal of Learning and Media* 1, no. 4 (2010): 23–44.

Foucault, Michel. *Discipline and Punish: The Birth of the Prison*, trans. Alan Sheridan. New York: Vintage Books, 1995.

Fraser, Nancy. "Rethinking the Public Sphere: A Contribution to the Critique of Actually Existing Democracy." In *Habermas and the Public Sphere*, ed. Craig Calhoun, 109–142. Cambridge, MA: MIT Press, 1992.

Furedi, Frank. *Paranoid Parenting.* Chicago: Chicago Review, 2002.

Gaines, Donna. *Teenage Wasteland: Suburbia's Dead End Kids.* Chicago: University of Chicago Press, 1998.

Garnham, Nicholas. "Information Society Theory as Ideology." In *The Information Society Reader*, ed. Frank Webster et al., 165–182. New York: Routledge, 2004.

Gasser, Urs, and John Palfrey. "About." *Digital Native*, https://web.archive.org/web/20121122075749/http://blogs.law.harvard.edu/youthandmediaalpha/projects/digital-natives/.

Gasser, Urs, Sandra Cortesi, Momin Malik, and Ashley Lee. "From Credibility to Information Quality." A Report of the Harvard Berkman Center's Youth and Media Project (2012), http://cyber.law.harvard.edu/publications/2012/Youth_Digital_Media_Credibility_Information_Quality.

Gavison, Ruth. "Privacy and the Limits of the Law." *Yale Law Journal* 89 (1980): 421–471.

Giles, Jim. "Special Report: Internet Encyclopaedias Go Head to Head." *Nature* 438 (2005): 900–901.

Gillespie, Tarleton. "The Relevance of Algorithms." In *Media Technologies*, ed. Tarleton Gillespie, Pablo Boczkowski, and Kirsten Foot, 167–194. Cambridge, MA: MIT Press, 2014.

Gilman, Michele Estrin. "The Class Differential in Privacy Law." *Brooklyn Law Review* 77 (2012): 1389–1445.

Glassner, Barry. *The Culture of Fear: Why Americans Are Afraid of the Wrong Things*. New York: Basic Books, 1999.

Goffman, Erving. *The Presentation of Self in Everyday Life*. Garden City, NY: Doubleday, 1959.

———. *Relations in Public*. New York: Harper and Row, 1972.

Gold, Scott. "Student Protests Echo the '60s, but with a High-Tech Buzz." *Los Angeles Times*, March 31, 2006.

Goldstein, Sam, and Robert Brooks, eds. *Handbook of Resilience in Children*. New York: Springer, 2013.

Goode, Erich, and Nachman Ben-Yehuda. *Moral Panics: The Social Construction of Deviance*. 2nd ed. Chichester, UK: John Wiley and Sons, 2009.

Granovetter, Mark. "The Strength of Weak Ties." *American Journal of Sociology* 78 (1973): 1360–1380.

Gray, Mary. *Out in the Country: Youth, Media, and Queer Visibility in Rural America*. New York: New York University Press, 2009.

Greenberg, Andy. "WikiLeaks Supporters Aim Cyberattacks at PayPal." *Forbes*, December 6, 2010, http://www.forbes.com/sites/andygreenberg/2010/12/06/wikileaks-supporters-aim-cyberattacks-at-paypal/.

Grimmelmann, James. "Saving Facebook." *Iowa Law Review* 94 (2009): 1137–1206.

Gross, Doug. "Dad Pays Daughter $200 to Quit Facebook." *CNN*, February 7, 2013, http://www.cnn.com/2013/02/07/tech/social-media/dad-daughter-facebook/index.html?hpt=hp_t4.

Habermas, Jürgen. *The Structural Transformation of the Public Sphere: An Inquiry into a Category of Bourgeois Society*. Cambridge, MA: MIT Press, 1991.

Haddon, Leslie. "The Phone in the Home: Ambiguity, Conflict, and Change." Paper presented at the COST 248 Workshop, "The European Telecom User," 1994.

———. "Social Exclusion and Information and Communication Technologies: Lessons from Studies of Single Parents and the Young Elderly." *New Media and Society* 2 (2000): 387–406.

Hadju, David. *The Ten-Cent Plague: The Great Comic-Book Scare and How It Changed America.* New York: Farrar, Straus and Giroux, 2008.

Hafner, Katie. "To Deal with Obsession, Some Defriend Facebook." *New York Times*, December 21, 2009.

Hall, G. Stanley. *Adolescence.* London: Appleton, 1908.

Hammel-Zabin, Amy. *Conversations with a Pedophile: In the Interest of Our Children.* Fort Lee, NJ: Barricade Books, 2003.

Hargittai, Eszter. "Digital Na(t)ives? Variation in Internet Skills and Uses Among Members of the 'Net Generation.'" *Sociological Inquiry* 80 (2010): 92–113.

———. "The Digital Reproduction of Inequality." In *Social Stratification*, ed. David Grusky, 936–944. Boulder, CO: Westview, 2008.

———. "Second-Level Digital Divide." *First Monday* 7, no. 4 (2002), http://firstmonday.org/issues/issue7 4/hargittai/index.html.

Hargittai, Eszter, and Amanda Hinnant. "Digital Inequality: Differences in Young Adults' Use of the Internet." *Communication Research* 35 (2008): 602–621.

Hasinoff, Amy. "Information, Consent, and Control." In *How to Think About Sexting.* Urbana: University of Illinois Press, forthcoming.

Helsper, Ellen, and Rebecca Eynon. "Digital Natives: Where Is the Evidence?" *British Educational Research Journal* 36 (2010): 503–520.

Hinduja, Sameer, and Justin Patchin. *School Climate 2.0: Preventing Cyberbullying and Sexting One Classroom at a Time.* London: Corwin, 2012.

Hine, Thomas. *The Rise and Fall of the American Teenager.* New York: Perennial, 1999.

"Hoaxes on Wikipedia." *Wikipedia*, http://en.wikipedia.org/wiki/Wikipedia:List_of_hoaxes_on_Wikipedia.

Hobbs, Renee. "The Seven Great Debates in the Media Literacy Movement." *Journal of Communication* 48, no. 1 (1998): 6–32.

Hodkinson, Paul, and Siân Lincoln. "Online Journals as Virtual Bedrooms? Young People, Identity and Personal Space." *Young* 16, no. 1 (2008): 27–46.

Hogan, Bernie. "Pseudonyms and the Rise of the Real-Name Web." In *A Companion to New Media Dynamics*, ed. John Hartley, Jean Burgess, and Axel Bruns, 290–308. Chichester, UK: Blackwell, 2012.

Holson, Laura M. "Text Generation Gap: U R 2 Old (JK)." *New York Times*, March 9, 2008.

Hoofnagle, Chris Jay, Jennifer King, Su Li, and Joseph Turow. "How Different Are Young Adults from Older Adults When It Comes to Information Privacy Attitudes and Policies?" Working paper, April 14, 2010, http://papers.ssrn.com/sol3/papers.cfm?abstract_id=1589864.

Hosokawa, Shuhei. "The Walkman Effect." *Popular Music* 4 (1984): 165–180.

Howard, Philip. *The Digital Origins of Dictatorship and Democracy: Information Technology and Political Islam*. New York: Oxford University Press, 2010.

Ito, Mizuko. "Introduction." In *Networked Publics*, ed. Kazys Varnelis, 1–14. Cambridge, MA: MIT Press, 2008.

Ito, Mizuko, et al. "Connected Learning: An Agenda for Research and Design." DML Research Hub, 2013, http://dmlhub.net/publications/connected-learning-agenda-research-and-design.

———. *Hanging Out, Messing Around, and Geeking Out: Living and Learning with New Media*. Chicago: John D. and Catherine T. MacArthur Foundation, 2008.

Jack, Belinda. *The Woman Reader*. New Haven: Yale University Press, 2012.

Jacobs, Jane. *The Death and Life of Great American Cities*. New York: Random House, 1961.

Jahn, Rich. "National Youth Rights Association—Analysis of U.S. Curfew Laws." http://web.archive.org/web/20110814201121/http://www.youthrights.org/curfewana.php.

Jenkins, Henry. "Congressional Testimony on Media Violence." MIT Communications Forum, September 22, 2004, http://web.mit.edu/comm-forum/papers/jenkins_ct.html.

———. "Reconsidering Digital Immigrants. . . ." *Confessions of an Aca-Fan*, http://henryjenkins.org/2007/12/reconsidering_digital_immigran.html.

Jenkins, Henry, and danah boyd. "Deleting Online Predators Act." MIT Talk Tech, May 26, 2006, http://www.danah.org/papers/MySpaceDOPA.html.

Jenkins, Henry, Sam Ford, and Josh Green. *Spreadable Media*. New York: New York University Press, 2013.

Jenkins, Henry, et al. *Confronting the Challenges of Participatory Culture: Media Education for the 21st Century*. Chicago: John D. and Catherine T. MacArthur Foundation, 2006. Available at: http://mitpress.mit.edu/sites/default/files/titles/free_download/9780262513623_Confronting_the_Challenges.pdf.

Jenkins, Holman W., Jr. "Opinion: Google and the Search for the Future." *Wall Street Journal*, August 14, 2010.

Joerges, Bernward. "Do Politics Have Artefacts?" *Social Studies of Science* 29, no. 3 (1999): 411–431.

Johnson, Bobbie. "Privacy No Longer a Social Norm, Says Facebook Founder." *Guardian*, January 11, 2011.

Johnson, Steven. *Everything Bad Is Good for You: How Today's Popular Culture Is Actually Making Us Smarter*. New York: Riverhead, 2005.

Johnston, Lloyd D., Patrick M. O'Malley, Jerald G. Bachman, and John E. Schulenberg. *Monitoring the Future: National Survey Results on Drug Use, 1975–2009*. Vol. 1: *Secondary School Students*. Bethesda, MD: National Institute on Drug Abuse, 2009.

Jones, Lisa M., Kimberly J. Mitchell, and David Finkelhor. "Trends in Youth Internet Victimization: Findings from Three Youth Internet Safety Surveys, 2000–2010." *Journal of Adolescent Health* 50, no. 2 (2012): 179–186.

Jordan, Tommy. "Facebook Parenting: For the Troubled Teen." *YouTube*, February 8, 2012, http://www.youtube.com/watch?feature=player_embedded&v=kI1ujzRidmU.

Jurgenson, Nathan, and P. J. Rey. "Comment on Sarah Ford's 'Reconceptualization of Privacy and Publicity.'" *Information, Communication and Society* 15, no. 2 (2012): 287–293.

Kahne, Joseph, Nam-Jin Lee, and Jessica Timpany Feezell. "The Civic and Political Significance of Online Participatory Cultures Among Youth Transitioning to Adulthood." Youth and Participatory Politics, DMLcentral Working Papers, 2012, http://dmlcentral.net/sites/dmlcentral/files/resource_files/OnlineParticipatoryCultures.WORKINGPAPERS.pdf.

Kang, Cecilia. "With Quick Click, Teens Part with Online Privacy." *Washington Post*, May 9, 2011, http://www.washingtonpost.com/blogs/post-tech/post/with-quick-click-teens-part-with-online-privacy/2011/05/09/AF5S-NOYG_blog.html.

Kelleher, Kathleen. "With Teens and Internet Sex, Curiosity Can Become Compulsion." *Los Angeles Times*, April 15, 2002.

Kendall, Lori. *Hanging Out in the Virtual Pub*. Berkeley: University of California Press, 2002.

———. "Meaning and Identity in 'Cyberspace': The Performance of Gender, Class, and Race." *Symbolic Interaction* 21, no. 2 (1998): 129–153.

Khokha, Sasha. "Text Messages, MySpace Roots of Student Protests." *NPR*, March 29, 2006, http://www.npr.org/2006/03/29/5309238/text-message-myspace-roots-of-student-protests.

Kirkpatrick, David. *The Facebook Effect*. New York: Simon and Schuster, 2011.

Kirkpatrick, Marshall. "Facebook's Zuckerberg Says the Age of Privacy Is Over." *Read Write Web*, January 9, 2010, http://www.readwriteweb.com/archives/facebooks_zuckerberg_says_the_age_of_privacy_is_ov.php.

Kirschbaum, Bruce, and Sam Kass. "The Switch." *Seinfeld*, season 6, episode 11, aired January 5, 1995, NBC.

Klinenberg, Eric. *Going Solo: The Extraordinary Rise and Surprising Appeal of Living Alone*. New York: Penguin, 2012.

Knuttila, Lee. "User Unknown: 4chan, Anonymity and Contingency." *First Monday* 16, no. 10 (2011), http://firstmonday.org/ojs/index.php/fm/article/view/3665/3055.

Kolko, Beth E., Lisa Nakamura, and Gilbert B. Rodman. "Race in Cyberspace: An Introduction." In *Race in Cyberspace*, ed. Beth E. Kolko, Lisa Nakamura, and Gilbert B. Rodman, 1–14. New York: Routledge, 2000.

Lampinen, Airi. "Practices of Balancing Privacy and Publicness in Social Network Services." In *GROUP '10 Proceedings of the 16th ACM International Conference on Supporting Group Work*, 343–344. New York: ACM, 2010.

Lauritano-Werner, Bly. "The Effort to Keep an Online Diary Private." *NPR*, July 24, 2006, http://www.npr.org/templates/story/story.php?storyId=5579002.

Leavey, Pamela. "Los Angeles Students Walk Out in Immigration Reform Protests." *Democratic Daily*, March 27, 2006, http://blog.thedemocraticdaily.com/?p=2434.

Lefler, Jordan. "I Can Has Thesis? A Linguistic Analysis of Lolspeak." MA thesis, Louisiana State University, 2011.

Lenhart, Amanda, Rich Ling, Scott Campbell, and Kristen Purcell. "Teens and Mobile Phones." Pew Internet and American Life Project, April 20, 2010, http://www.pewinternet.org/Reports/2010/Teens-and-Mobile-Phones.aspx.

Lenhart, Amanda, et al. "Teens, Kindness and Cruelty on Social Network Sites." Pew Internet and American Life Project, November 9, 2011, http://www.pewinternet.org/Reports/2011/Teens-and-social-media.aspx.

Lennox, Graeme. "E.mail: Dangers of Letting Your Kid Date on the Net." *Sunday Mail*, June 4, 2000.

Leonardi, Paul. *Car Crashes Without Cars*. Cambridge, MA: MIT Press, 2012.

Lessig, Lawrence. *Code: Version 2.0*. New York: Basic Books, 2006.

Levine, Madeline. *The Price of Privilege: How Parental Pressure and Material Advantage Are Creating a Generation of Disconnected and Unhappy Kids*. New York: Harper, 2008.

Levy, Nathaniel, et al. "Bullying in a Networked Era: A Literature Review." The Kinder and Braver World Project Research Series, Berkman Center Research Publication No. 2012–17, http://cyber.law.harvard.edu/publications/2012/kbw_bulling_in_a_networked_era.

Lewis, George H. "Community Through Exclusion and Illusion: The Creation of Social Worlds in an American Shopping Mall." *Journal of Popular Culture* 24, no. 2 (1990): 121–136.

Lin, Nan. "Inequality in Social Capital." *Contemporary Sociology* 29, no. 6 (2000): 785–795.

———. *Social Capital: A Theory of Social Structure and Action*. Cambridge: Cambridge University Press, 2002.

Lincoln, Siân. *Youth Culture and Private Space*. London: Palgrave Macmillan, 2012.

Ling, Rich. "Mobile Telephones and the Disturbance of the Public Sphere." *Europe* 115 (2008): 1–17. Available at: http://richardling.com/papers/2004_disturbance_of_social_sphere.pdf.

Lipscomb, Thomas J., Jeff W. Totten, Roy A. Cook, and William Lesch. "Cellular Phone Etiquette Among College Students." *International Journal of Consumer Studies* 31, no. 1 (2007): 46–56.

Litt, Eden. "Knock, Knock. Who's There? The Imagined Audience." *JOBEM* 56 (2012): 330–345.

Livingstone, Sonia. *Audiences and Publics: When Cultural Engagement Matters for the Public Sphere.* Portland, OR: Intellect, 2005.

———. *Children and the Internet.* Cambridge: Polity, 2009.

———. "Media Literacy and the Challenge of New Information and Communication Technologies." *Communication Review* 7 (2004): 3–14.

———. "On the Continuing Problems of Media Effects Research." In *Mass Media and Society*, 2nd ed., ed. J. Curran and M. Gurevitch, 305–324. London: Edward Arnold, 1996.

———. "Taking Risky Opportunities in Youthful Content Creation: Teenagers' Use of Social Networking Sites for Intimacy, Privacy and Self-Expression." *New Media and Society* 10 (2008): 393–411.

Livingstone, Sonia, and Leslie Haddon. *EU Kids Online Project*, http://www2. lse.ac.uk/media@lse/research/EUKidsOnline/.

Livingstone, Sonia, Magdalena Bober, and Ellen Helsper. *Internet Literacy Among Children and Young People: Findings from the UK Children Go Online Project.* London: LSE Research Online, 2005. Available at: http:// eprints.lse.ac.uk/archive/00000397.

Llorens, Ileana. "Tommy Jordan, Dad Who Shot Daughter's Laptop, Says He'd Do It Again." *Huffington Post*, February 14, 2012, http://www.huffington-post.com/2012/02/14/dad-shot-daughters-laptop-would-do-it-again_n_1276243.html.

Louv, Richard. *Last Child in the Woods: Saving Our Children from Nature-Deficit Disorder.* Chapel Hill, NC: Algonquin Books, 2005.

Lovink, Geert. *Networks Without a Cause: A Critique of Social Media.* Cambridge: Polity, 2011.

Lyall, Sarah. "What's the Buzz? Rowdy Teenagers Don't Want to Hear It." *New York Times*, November 29, 2005.

Madden, Mary, et al. "Teens, Social Media, and Privacy." Pew Internet and American Life Project, May 21, 2013, http://www.pewinternet.org/ Reports/2013/Teens-Social-Media-And-Privacy.aspx.

Mahoney, Joseph L., Reed W. Larson, and Jacquelynne S. Eccles. *Organized Activities as Contexts of Development: Extracurricular Activities, After School and Community Programs.* Mahway, NJ: Lawrence Erlbaum, 2005.

Males, Mike, and Dan Macallair. "An Analysis of Curfew Enforcement and Juvenile Crimes in California." *Western Criminology Review* 1, no. 2 (1999). Available at: http://wcr.sonoma.edu/v1n2/males.html.

Mandell, Nina. "Alexandra Wallace, UCLA Student Who Created Offensive Viral Video, Withdrawing from School." *NYDailyNews.com*, March 19, 2011, http://nydailynews.com/news/national/alexandra-wallace-ucla-student-created-offensive-viral-video-withdrawing-school-article-1.119105.

Marwick, Alice. *Status Update: Celebrity, Publicity, and Branding in the Social Media Age*. New Haven: Yale University Press, 2013.

———. "To Catch a Predator? The MySpace Moral Panic." *First Monday* 13, no. 6 (2008), http://firstmonday.org/htbin/cgiwrap/bin/ojs/index.php/fm/article/view/2152/1966.

Marwick, Alice, and danah boyd. "'It's Just Drama': Teen Perspectives on Conflict and Aggression in a Networked Era." *Journal of Youth Studies* 17, no. 9 (2014): 1187–1204.

———. "Networked Privacy: How Teenagers Negotiate context in Social Media." *New Media & Society* 16, no. 7 (2014): 1051–1067.

———. "I Tweet Honestly, I Tweet Passionately: Twitter Users, Context Collapse, and the Imagined Audience." *New Media and Society* 13 (2011): 114–133.

———. "To See and Be Seen: Celebrity Practice on Twitter." *Convergence* 17, no. 2 (2011): 139–158.

———. "Tweeting Teens Can Handle Public Life." *Guardian*, February 15, 2011.

Marwick, Alice, Diego Murgia Diaz, and John Palfrey. "Youth, Privacy and Reputation (Literature Review)." The Kinder and Braver World Project Research Series, Berkman Center Research Publication No. 2010-5, http://papers.ssrn.com/sol3/papers.cfm?abstract_id=1588163.

Matthews, Hugh, Mark Taylor, Barry Percy-Smith, and Melanie Limb. "The Unacceptable Flaneur: The Shopping Mall as a Teenage Hangout." *Childhood* 7, no. 3 (2000): 279–294.

McPherson, Miller, Lynn Smith-Lovin, and James M. Cook. "Birds of a Feather: Homophily in Social Networks." *Annual Review of Sociology* 27 (2001): 415–444.

McRobbie, Angela, and Jenny Garber. "Girls and Subcultures." In *Resistance Through Rituals: Youth Subcultures in Post-War Britain*, ed. Stuart Hall and Tony Jefferson, 209–222. New York: Routledge, 1976.

Mesch, Gustavo, and Ilan Talmud. *Wired Youth: The Social World of Adolescence in the Information Age*. East Sussex, UK: Routledge, 2010.

Meyrowitz, Joshua. *No Sense of Place: The Impact of Electronic Media on Social Behavior*. New York: Oxford University Press, 1985.

Milner, Murray, Jr. *Freaks, Geeks, and Cool Kids: American Teenagers, Schools, and the Culture of Consumption*. New York: Routledge, 2004.

Miltner, Kate. "Srsly Phenomenal: An Investigation into the Appeal of LOL-Cats." MSc diss., London School of Economics and Political Science, 2011.

Mina, An Xiao. "A Curated History of the Grass Mud Horse Song." *88 Bar*, February 27, 2012, http://www.88-bar.com/2012/02/a-curated-history-of-the-grass-mud-horse-song/.

———. "Social Media Street Art: Censorship, China's Political Memes and the Cute Cat Theory." *An Xiao Studio*, December 28, 2011, http://anxiaostudio.com/2011/12/28/social-media-street-art-censorship-chinas-political-memes-and-the-cute-cat-theory/.

Misur, Susan. "Old Saybrook High School Makes Privacy Point; Some Per-
turbed When Real Students Shown in Social-Media Slide Show." *New
Haven Register*, April 10, 2011.

Mitchell, Kimberly, David Finkelhor, and Janis Wolak. "The Internet and
Family and Acquaintance Sexual Abuse." *Child Maltreatment* 10, no. 1
(2005): 49–60.

Mitchell, Kimberly J., Janis Wolak, and David Finkelhor. "Are Blogs Putting
Youth at Risk for Online Sexual Solicitation or Harassment?" *Child Abuse
and Neglect* 32 (2008): 277–294.

Moody, Kate. "John Culkin: The Man Who Invented Media Literacy." *Center
for Media Literacy*, http://www.medialit.org/reading-room/john-culkin-
sj-man-who-invented-media-literacy-1928-1993.

Mossberger, Karen, Caroline J. Tolbert, and Mary Stansburgy. *Virtual Inequality: Beyond the Digital Divide*. Washington, DC: Georgetown University
Press, 2003.

"Mothers Think Teens Were Lured Away by MySpace.com Suitors." *NBC4.TV*,
February 26, 2006, https://web.archive.org/web/20060811085939/http://
www.nbc4.tv/news/7473070/detail.html.

Nakamura, Lisa. *Digitizing Race: Visual Cultures of the Internet*. Minneapolis:
University of Minnesota Press, 2008.

———. "Don't Hate the Player, Hate the Game: The Racialization of Labor in
World of Warcraft." *Critical Studies in Media Communication* 26, no. 2
(2009): 128–144.

Nardi, Bonnie. *My Life as a Night Elf Priest: An Anthropological Account of
World of Warcraft*. Ann Arbor, MI: University of Michigan Press, 2010.

National Center for Missing and Exploited Children. "CyberTipline: Annual
Report Totals by Incident Type." http://www.cybertipline.com/en_US/
archive/documents/CyberTiplineReportTotals.pdf.

National Center for Safe Routes to School. "How Children Get to School:
School Travel Patterns from 1969 to 2009." November 2011, http://www.
saferoutesinfo.org/sites/default/files/resources/NHTS_school_travel_
report_2011_0.pdf.

National Telecommunications and Information Administration. *Falling
Through the Net: Defining the Digital Divide*. Washington, DC: US
Department of Commerce, 1999.

Nelson, Margaret K. *Parenting Out of Control: Anxious Parents in Uncertain
Times*. New York: New York University Press, 2010.

Nissenbaum, Helen. *Privacy in Context: Technology, Policy, and the Integrity of
Social Life*. Palo Alto, CA: Stanford University Press, 2010.

Norman, Donald. *The Design of Everyday Things*. New York: Basic Books,
1988.

Norton, Quinn. "Anonymous 101: Introduction to the Lulz." *Wired*, November
8, 2011, http://www.wired.com/threatlevel/2011/11/anonymous-101/.

Nussbaum, Emily. "Say Everything." *New York Magazine*, February 12, 2007.

Oliver, Martin. "The Problem with Affordance." *E-Learning* 2 (2005): 402–413.

Olson, Parmy. *We Are Anonymous: Inside the Hacker World of LulzSec, Anonymous, and the Global Cyber Insurgency*. Boston: Little, Brown, 2012.

Olweus, Dan, Sue Limber, and Sharon Mihalic. "Blueprints for Violence Prevention: Book Nine—Bullying Prevention Program." Bureau of Justice Assistance, 1999, http://www.ncjrs.gov/App/publications/abstract.aspx?ID=174202.

OMG Black People. http://omgblackpeople.wordpress.com/.

Pahl, Ray. *On Friendship*. Cambridge: Polity, 2000.

Palen, Leysia, and Paul Dourish. "Unpacking Privacy for a Networked World." In *Proceedings of the SIGCHI Conference on Human Factors in Computing Systems*, 129–136. New York: ACM, 2003.

Palfrey, John, and Urs Gasser. *Born Digital: Understanding the First Generation of Digital Natives*. New York: Basic Books, 2010.

———. "Reclaiming an Awkward Term: What We Might Learn from 'Digital Natives.'" In *Deconstructing Digital Natives: Young People, Technology and New Literacies*, ed. Michael Thomas, 186–204. New York: Routledge, 2011.

Pariser, Eli. *The Filter Bubble: What the Internet Is Hiding from You*. New York: Penguin, 2011.

Pascoe, C. J. *Dude, You're a Fag: Masculinity and Sexuality in High School*. Berkeley: University of California Press, 2011.

Perkel, Dan. "Copy and Paste Literacy? Literacy Practices in the Production of a MySpace Profile." In *Informal Learning and Digital Media: Constructions, Contexts, Consequences*, ed. Kirsten Drotner, Hans Siggard Jensen, and Kim Schroeder, 203–224. Newcastle, UK: Cambridge Scholars Press, 2006.

Pestritto, Ronald J., and William J. Atto, eds. *American Progressivism: A Reader*. Lanham, MD: Lexington Books, 2008.

Petitcolas, Fabian A. P., Ross J. Anderson, and Markus G. Kuhn. "Information Hiding: A Survey." In *Proceedings of the IEEE* 87 (1999): 1062–1078.

Phillips, Whitney. "This Is Why We Can't Have Nice Things: The Origins, Evolution and Cultural Embeddedness of Online Trolling." PhD diss., University of Oregon, 2012.

Phillips, Whitney, and Kate Miltner. "The Internet's Vigilante Shame Army." *Awl*, December 19, 2012, http://www.theawl.com/2012/12/the-internets-vigilante-shame-army.

Pinker, Steven. "Mind over Mass Media." *New York Times*, June 1, 2010.

Pittis, William. *Dr. Radcliffe's Life and Letters*. London, 1716.

Plato. *Phaedrus*. Trans. Harold N. Fowler. Cambridge, MA: Harvard University Press, 1925.

Polanin, Joshua R., Dorothy L. Espelage, and Therese D. Pigott. "A Meta-Analysis of School-Based Bullying Prevention Programs' Effects on Bystander Intervention Behavior and Empathy Attitude." *School Psychology Review* 4 (2012): 47–65.

Pope, Denise Clark. *Doing School: How We Are Creating a Generation of Stressed-Out, Materialistic, and Miseducated Students*. New Haven: Yale University Press, 2003.

Popkin, Helen A. S. "Privacy Is Dead on Facebook; Get over It." *MSNBC*, January 1, 2010, http://www.msnbc.msn.com/id/34825225/ns/technology_and_science-tech_and_gadgets/t/privacy-dead-facebook-get-over-it/.

Portwood-Stacer, Laura. "Media Refusal and Conspicuous Non-Consumption: The Performative and Political Dimensions of Facebook Abstention." *New Media and Society*, December 5, 2012, doi:10.1177/1461444812465139.

Poulsen, Kevin. "MySpace Predator Caught by Code." *Wired*, October 16, 2006, http://www.wired.com/science/discoveries/news/2006/10/71948.

Prensky, Marc. "Digital Natives, Digital Immigrants." *On the Horizon* 9 (2001), http://www.marcprensky.com/writing/Prensky%20-%20Digital%20Natives,%20Digital%20Immigrants%20-%20Part1.pdf.

———. "Digital Natives, Digital Immigrants: Origins of the Term." Marc Prensky's Weblog, June 12, 2006, http://www.marcprensky.com/blog/archives/000045.html.

———. "Digital Wisdom and Homo Sapiens Digital." In *Deconstructing Digital Natives: Young People, Technology and New Literacies*, ed. Michael Thomas, 15–29. New York: Routledge, 2011.

Psych Central News Editor. "Video Games No Addiction for Now." *Psych Central*, August 20, 2007, http://psychcentral.com/news/2007/06/26/video-games-no-addiction-for-now.

Putnam, Robert D. *Bowling Alone*. New York: Simon and Schuster, 2001.

Raby, Rebecca. "Across a Great Gulf? Conducting Research with Adolescents." In *Representing Youth: Methodological Issues in Critical Youth Studies*, ed. Amy L. Best, 39–59. New York: New York University Press, 2007.

Rainie, Lee, Aaron Smith, and Maeve Duggan. "Coming and Going on Facebook." Pew Internet and American Life Project, February 5, 2013, http://www.pewinternet.org/Reports/2013/Coming-and-going-on-facebook.aspx.

Rheingold, Howard. *Smart Mobs: The Next Social Revolution*. Cambridge, MA: Perseus, 2002.

Rosenberg, Scott. *Say Everything: How Blogging Began, What It's Becoming, and Why It Matters*. New York: Crown, 2009.

Rovner, Sandy. "Molesting Children by Computer." *Washington Post*, August 2, 1994.

Ruefle, William, and Kenneth Reynolds. "Curfew and Delinquency in Major American Cities." *Crime and Delinquency* 41 (1995): 347–363.

Rushkoff, Douglas. *Playing the Future: What We Can Learn from Digital Kids.* New York: Penguin, 1996.

Sacco, Dena T., et al. "An Overview of State Anti-Bullying Legislation and Other Related Laws." The Kinder and Braver World Project Research Series, February 13, 2012, http://cyber.law.harvard.edu/sites/cyber.law.harvard.edu/files/State_Anti_bullying_Legislation_Overview_0.pdf.

Sandvig, Christian. "Unexpected Outcomes in Digital Divide Policy: What Children Really Do in the Public Library." In *Communications Policy in Transition: The Internet and Beyond*, ed. Benjamin M. Compaine and Shane Greenstein, 265–293. Cambridge, MA: MIT Press, 2001.

Saraceno, Jon. "Swiss Soccer Player Banned from Olympics for Racist Tweet." *USA Today*, July 30, 2102, http://www.usatoday.com/sports/olympics/london/soccer/story/2012-07-30/swiss-athlete-banned-michel-morganella-olympics/56591966/1.

Scholz, Trebor. "Market Ideology and the Myths of Web 2.0." *First Monday* 13, no. 3 (2008), http://firstmonday.org/ojs/index.php/fm/article/view/2138/1945.

Schor, Juliet B. *Born to Buy: The Commercialized Child and the New Consumer Culture.* New York: Scribner, 2005.

Schüll, Natasha Dow. *Addiction by Design: Machine Gambling in Las Vegas.* Princeton, NJ: Princeton University Press, 2012.

Seiter, Ellen. *Sold Separately: Children and Parents in Consumer Culture.* New Brunswick, NJ: Rutgers University Press, 1995.

Selwyn, Neil. "Reconsidering Political and Popular Understandings of the Digital Divide." *New Media and Society* 6, no. 3 (2004): 341–362.

Senft, Theresa M. *Camgirls: Celebrity and Community in the Age of Social Networks.* New York: Peter Lang, 2008.

Shakeshaft, Charol. "Educator Sexual Misconduct: A Synthesis of Existing Literature." US Department of Education, Office of the Under Secretary, Policy and Programs Studies Service, Doc. #2004–09, 2004.

Shifman, Limor. *Memes in Digital Culture.* Cambridge, MA: MIT Press, 2013.

Shirky, Clay. *Cognitive Surplus: Creativity and Generosity in a Connected Age.* New York: Penguin, 2010.

Sinclair, Brendan. "Kinect Has Problems Recognizing Dark-Skinned Users?" *Gamespot*, November 3, 2010, http://www.gamespot.com/news/kinect-has-problems-recognizing-dark-skinned-users-6283514.

Skenazy, Lenore. *Free-Range Kids: How to Raise Safe, Self Reliant Children.* San Francisco: Wiley, 2009.

Skiba, Russell, et al. "Are Zero Tolerance Policies Effective in the Schools? An Evidentiary Review and Recommendations." *American Psychologist* 63 (2008): 852–862.

Smith, Aaron. "Twitter Update 2011." Pew Internet and American Life Project, June 1, 2011, http://pewresearch.org/pubs/2007/twitter-users-cell-phone-2011-demographics.

Smith, Catherine. "Google CEO Eric Schmidt's Most Controversial Quotes About Privacy." *Huffington Post*, November 4, 2010, http://www.huffingtonpost.com/2010/11/04/google-ceo-eric-schmidt-privacy_n_776924.html#s170420.

Snyder, H. N. *Sexual Assault of Young Children as Reported to Law Enforcement: Victim, Incident, and Offender Characteristics*. US Department of Justice, Office of Justice Programs, Bureau of Justice Statistics, 2000, http://www.bjs.gov/content/pub/pdf/saycrle.pdf.

Snyder, Howard N., and Melissa Sickmund. *Juvenile Offenders and Victims: 2006 National Report*. US Department of Justice, Office of Justice Programs, Office of Juvenile Justice and Delinquency Prevention, March 2006, http://www.ojjdp.gov/mcd/pdf/212906.pdf.

Solove, Daniel J. " 'I've Got Nothing to Hide' and Other Misunderstandings of Privacy." *San Diego Law Review* 44 (2007): 745–772.

———. *Understanding Privacy*. Cambridge, MA: Harvard University Press, 2008.

Springhall, John. *Youth, Popular Culture and Moral Panics: Penny Gaffs to Gangsta-Rap, 1830–1996*. New York: St. Martin's, 1998.

"Star Wars Kid." *Wikipedia*, http://en.wikipedia.org/wiki/Star_Wars_Kid.

Stearns, Peter M. *Anxious Parents: A History of Modern Childrearing in America*. New York: New York University Press, 2003.

Steiner, Peter. "On the Internet, Nobody Knows You're a Dog." Cartoon, *New Yorker*, July 5, 1993.

Stern, Susannah. "Adolescent Girls' Expression on Web Home Pages: Spirited, Somber, and Self-Centered." In *Growing Up Online: Young People and Digital Technologies*, ed. Sandra Weber and Shanly Dixon, 159–180. New York: Palgrave Macmillan, 2007.

Stewart, Christopher S. "Obsessed with the Internet: A Tale from China." *Wired*, January 13, 2010, http://www.wired.com/magazine/2010/01/ff_internetaddiction/.

Stewart, Dodai. "Racist Hunger Games Fans Are Very Disappointed." *Jezebel*, March 26, 2012, http://jezebel.com/5896408/racist-hunger-games-fans-dont-care-how-much-money-the-movie-made.

Stone, Allucquère Rosanne. *The War of Desire and Technology at the Close of the Mechanical Age*. Cambridge, MA: MIT Press, 1995.

Stryker, Cole. *Epic Win for Anonymous: How 4chan's Army Conquered the Web*. New York: Overlook Duckworth, 2011.

Stutzman, Fred, Ralph Gross, and Alessandro Acquisti. "Silent Listeners: The Evolution of Privacy and Disclosure on Facebook." *Journal of Privacy and Confidentiality* 4, no. 2 (2012): 7–41.

Sundén, Jenny. *Material Virtualities: Approaching Online Textual Embodiment.* New York: Peter Lang, 2003.

Tatum, Beverly Daniel. *Why Are All the Black Kids Sitting Together in the Cafeteria?* New York: Basic Books, 1997.

Taylor, T. L. *Play Between Worlds: Exploring Online Game Culture.* Cambridge, MA: MIT Press, 2006.

Thompson, John B. "The New Visibility." *Theory, Culture and Society* 22, no. 6 (2005): 31–51.

———. "Shifting Boundaries of Public and Private Life." *Theory, Culture and Society* 28, no. 4 (2011): 49–70.

Thurston, Baratunde. *How to Be Black.* New York: HarperCollins, 2012.

Todd, Amanda. "My Story: Struggling, Bullying, Suicide, Self Harm." *YouTube,* September 7, 2012, http://www.youtube.com/watch?v=vOHXGNx-E7E.

Tufekci, Zeynep, and Christopher Wilson. "Social Media and the Decision to Participate in Political Protests: Observations from Tahrir Square." *International Journal of Communication* 62, no. 2 (2012): 363–379.

Turkle, Sherry. *Life on the Screen: Identity in the Age of the Internet.* New York: Simon and Schuster, 1995.

———. *The Second Self: Computers and the Human Spirit.* New York: Simon and Schuster, 1984.

Turner, Graeme. *Understanding Celebrity.* Thousand Oaks, CA: Sage, 2004.

Vaidhyanathan, Siva. *The Anarchist in the Library: How the Clash Between Freedom and Control Is Hacking the Real World and Crashing the System.* New York: Basic Books, 2005.

———. *The Googlization of Everything (and Why We Should Worry).* Berkeley: University of California Press, 2011.

Valentine, Gill. *Public Space and the Culture of Childhood.* Hants, UK: Ashgate, 2004.

Vicary, Judith R., Linda R. Klingaman, and William L. Harkness. "Risk Factors Associated with Date Rape and Sexual Assault of Adolescent Girls." *Journal of Adolescence* 18 (1995): 289–306.

Vitak, Jessica. "The Impact of Context Collapse and Privacy on Social Network Site Disclosures." *Journal of Broadcasting and Electronic Media* 56 (2012): 451–470.

Walther, Joseph B., et al. "The Role of Friends' Behavior on Evaluations of Individuals' Facebook Profiles: Are We Known by the Company We Keep?" *Human Communication Research* 34 (2008): 28–49.

Walz, Marty, and Will Brownsberger. "A (Real) Virtual Education." *Boston Globe,* September 8, 2010.

Ward, Mark. "What the Net Did Next." *BBC News,* January 1, 2004, http://news.bbc.co.uk/2/hi/technology/3292043.stm.

Warner, Michael. *Publics and Counterpublics*. Brooklyn, NY: Zone Press, 2005.

Warschauer, Marc. *Technology and Social Inclusion: Rethinking the Digital Divide*. Cambridge, MA: MIT Press, 2003.

Wasserman, Todd. "How Rebecca Black Became a YouTube Sensation." *Mashable*, March 16, 2001, http://mashable.com/2011/03/16/rebecca-black-youtube/.

Watkins, Craig S. *The Young and the Digital: What the Migration to Social Network Sites, Games, and Anytime, Anywhere Media Means for Our Future*. Boston: Beacon, 2009.

Webster, Frank. "Information and Urban Change: Manuel Castells." In *Manuel Castells*, vol. 2, ed. Frank Webster and Basil Dimitriou, 15–39. London: Sage, 2004.

———. *Theories of the Information Society*. 2nd ed. New York: Routledge, 2002.

Weil, Elizabeth. "The Future Is Younger than You Think." *Fast Company*, April–May 1997.

Weinberger, David. *Everything Is Miscellaneous: The Power of the New Digital Disorder*. New York: Holt, 2007.

Wellman, Barry. *Networks in the Global Village: Life in Contemporary Communities*. Boulder, CO: Westview, 1999.

Wells, Melissa, and Kimberly J. Mitchell. "How Do High-Risk Youth Use the Internet? Characteristics and Implications for Prevention." *Child Maltreatment* 13, no. 3 (2008): 227–234.

Westin, Alan F. *Privacy and Freedom*. New York: Atheneum, 1967.

Wetzstein, Cheryl. "Anti-Porn Group Targets On-Line Activities: Modem Can Bring Smut Home to Kids." *Washington Times*, June 8, 1995.

White, Nicole, and Janet L. Lauritsen. *Violent Crime Against Youth, 1994–2010*. Bureau of Justice Statistics, NCJ 240106, 2012, http://www.bjs.gov/content/pub/press/vcay9410pr.cfm.

Wilkinson, Jamie, and Brad Kim. "Downfall/Hitler Reacts." *Know Your Meme*, 2008, http://knowyourmeme.com/memes/downfall-hitler-reacts.

Williams, Pete. "MySpace, Facebook Attract Online Predators." *NBC News*, February 3, 2006, http://www.nbcnews.com/id/11165576/#.UVMiRRzvt8E.

Willis, Paul. *Learning to Labor: How Working Class Kids Get Working Class Jobs*. New York: Columbia University Press, 1981.

Winner, Langdon. "Do Artifacts Have Politics?" *Daedalus* 109, no. 1 (1980): 120–136.

Wolak, Janis, David Finkelhor, and Kimberly Mitchell. "Is Talking Online to Unknown People Always Risky? Distinguishing Online Interaction Styles in a National Sample of Youth Internet Users." *CyberPsychology and Behavior* 11, no. 3 (2008): 340–343.

Wolak, Janis, Kimberly Mitchell, and David Finkelhor. "Online Victimization of Youth: Five Years Later." National Center for Missing and Exploited Children, #07-06-025, 2006. Available at: http://www.unh.edu/ccrc/pdf/CV138.pdf.

Wolak, Janis, David Finkelhor, Kimberly Mitchell, and Michele Ybarra. "Online 'Predators' and Their Victims: Myths, Realities, and Implications for Prevention and Treatment." *American Psychologist* 63 (2008): 111–128.

Wong, Jimmy. "Ching Chong! Asians in the Library Song (Response to Alexandra Wallace)." *YouTube*, March 15, 2011, http://www.youtube.com/watch?v=zulEMWj3sVA.

World Health Organization. Expert Committee on Drugs Liable to Produce Addiction. *Report on the Second Session, Geneva, 9–14 January 1950*. Technical Report Series No. 21. Geneva: World Health Organization, 1950. Available at: http://whqlibdoc.who.int/trs/WHO_TRS_21.pdf/.

Ybarra, Michele, and Kimberly J. Mitchell. "Prevalence and Frequency of Internet Harassment Instigation: Implications for Adolescent Health." *Journal of Adolescent Health* 41 (2007): 189–195.

Ybarra, Michele, Dorothy L. Espelage, and Kimberly J. Mitchell. "The Co-Occurrence of Internet Harassment and Unwanted Sexual Solicitation Victimization and Perpetration: Associations with Psychosocial Indicators." *Journal of Adolescent Health* 41 (2007): S31—S41.

Ybarra, Michele, Kimberly J. Mitchell, and Dorothy L. Espelage. "Comparisons of Bully and Unwanted Sexual Experiences Online and Offline Among a National Sample of Youth." In *Complementary Pediatrics*, ed. Öner Özdemir, 203–216. New York: InTech, 2012.

Zax, David. "Siri, Why Can't You Understand Me?" *Fast Company*, December 7, 2011, http://www.fastcompany.com/1799374/siri-why-cant-you-understand-me.

Zieger, Susan. "Terms to Describe Addiction in the Nineteenth Century." *Victorian Web*, September 7, 2002, http://www.victorianweb.org/science/addiction/terms.htm.

Zinn, Howard. *A People's History of the United States: 1492–Present*. New York: HarperCollins, 2003.

Zuckerman, Ethan. *Rewire: Digital Cosmopolitans in the Age of Connection*. New York: W. W. Norton, 2013.

acknowledgments

As exciting as it is to produce a monograph, the very notion of a book being the product of a single person is laughable. So many people helped me create this work, and I am forever grateful for their tremendous advice, support, and editorial efforts.

Long ago, in a land far away, this book began as a dissertation. In 2003, I started collecting data about social network sites, which led me to asking questions about youth practices. This project evolved over time and I have been blessed to be a part of numerous collaborative efforts that helped guide me along the way. When the MacArthur Foundation helped initiate what would become the Digital Media & Learning community, I was lucky enough to be a part of the first massive ethnographic digital youth project. I am indebted to the MacArthur Foundation for funding much of this project and am especially thankful to John Seely Brown and Connie Yowell for their ongoing commitment to my research. It was a blessing to embark on this project surrounded by a community of like-minded scholars working on similar studies. The twenty-eight-person Digital Youth team assembled by Mimi Ito, Peter Lyman, and Michael Carter provided the ideal intellectual space for working out the puzzles in my dissertation. I am especially grateful for long conversations and debates with Becky Herr-Stephenson, Heather Horst, CJ Pascoe, and Dan Perkel.

This project began at the University of California, Berkeley, and I'm grateful for all of the wonderful support I received there. In particular, my dissertation committee—Mimi Ito, Cori Hayden, Jenna Burrell, and Anno Saxenian—helped me realize my ideas into a thesis respectable enough to earn a lollipop. I couldn't have made it through without them, especially after my beloved adviser—Peter Lyman—lost his battle with brain cancer. I am grateful for the entire School of Information faculty who supported me along the way, especially Marc Davis and Nancy Van House.

After finishing my PhD, I embarked on a new set of fieldwork with the best collaborator imaginable: Alice Marwick. Together, we toured the south talking with teens and embedding ourselves in youth culture. This collaboration enhanced my thinking more than I can say. Two chapters in particular—privacy and bullying—would not have been possible without her brilliant insights. Alice helped me rethink many of my assumptions and challenged me to push myself theoretically.

As I started processing the data, numerous research assistants helped me track down literature and keep things organized, including Sam Jackson, Ann Murray, Alex Leavitt, Heather Casteel, and Benjamin Gleason. Others patiently helped me organize my thoughts. My colleagues at Harvard's Berkman Center for Internet and Society helped me stay on track by providing a book club structure. In particular, I wish to thank Judith Donath, Eszter Hargittai, Colin Maclay, Doc Searls, David Weinberger, and Ethan Zuckerman for hours of shared misery and joy.

Doree Shafrir helped me rip out the dissertation language and restructure the material into a book. When I got lost and confused in my own writing, Quinn Norton stepped in to serve as my literary trainer and editorial dominatrix, helping me whip my disorganized thoughts into prose that someone might want to read. And Kate Miltner helped me ground my arguments and fill in gaps in logic.

When I turned to friends and colleagues for feedback, I was overwhelmed by their willingness to read and critique what I wrote. In particular, I wish to acknowledge the amazing feedback offered at different stages from Mark Ackerman, Ronen Barzel, Geof Bowker, Elizabeth Churchill, Beth Coleman, Jessie Daniels, Cathy Davidson, Judith Donath, Nicole Ellison, Megan Finn, Jen Jack Gieseking,

Elizabeth Goodman, Germaine Halegoua, Eszter Hargittai, Bernie Hogan, Mimi Ito, Henry Jenkins, Airi Lampinen, Amanda Lenhart, Jessa Lingel, Nalini Kotamraju, Eden Litt, Mary Madden, Alice Marwick, John Palfrey, CJ Pascoe, Jillian Powers, Hannah Rohde, Adrienne Russell, Jason Schultz, Clay Shirky, Christo Sims, TL Taylor, David Weinberger, Sarita Yardi, Michele Ybarra, and Ethan Zuckerman. Their insights and challenges helped make this book stronger.

Throughout this journey, my editors at Yale University Press—Alison Mackeen and Joe Calamia—provided ongoing guidance to help make this a coherent manuscript. The Yale University Press team helped me go from scribbled Word documents to a proper book. And my agents at ICM (first Kate Lee and then Kristine Dahl) and Leigh Bureau (notably, Wes Neff) helped me develop my voice and imagine how this book could reach an audience.

Outside the process of producing the book itself, I have been lucky enough to have a series of mentors who have helped me intellectually and strategically. In particular, I'm grateful to Andy van Dam, Judith Donath, Henry Jenkins, Genevieve Bell, Mimi Ito, Peter Lyman, John Palfrey, and Jennifer Chayes for their ongoing advice and support. I'm especially thankful for Mimi Ito, who helped guide me through this project at every turn, and to my beloved adviser Peter, who took a bet on me. Outside of academia, I have been fortunate to have many mentors, bosses, and advocates in industry who have opened doors and helped me understand the technical side of social media. I'm especially grateful to Tom Anderson, Adam Bosworth, Lili Cheng, Cory Doctorow, Caterina Fake, Reid Hoffman, Bradley Horowitz, Joi Ito, Craig Newmark, Tim O'Reilly, Ray Ozzie, Marc Pincus, Ian Rogers, Linda Stone, Jeff Weiner, and Evan Williams.

After finishing graduate school, I have been fortunate to find an intellectual home at Microsoft Research (MSR). At MSR, I have been surrounded by phenomenal scholars who have pushed me to think deeply. In particular, I want to thank Alice Marwick, Mike Ananny, Andrés Monroy-Hernández, Megan Finn, Nancy Baym, Kate Crawford, and Mary Gray—as well as a stream of amazing interns and visitors—for their ongoing collaboration and advice. I am also grateful for the loose collection of folks who have come in and out of MSR to collaborate with me and the rest of the Social Media Collective. And I am deeply thankful for the mathematicians and computer scientists who welcomed me with open arms. Jennifer Chayes, Christian Borgs, and Rick Rashid, in particular, have been more supportive than I ever thought imaginable. MSR provided me with an intellectual home to do research and showed me how powerful constructing a healthy intellectual community can be for enabling innovation and critical thought.

Over the years, I have been fortunate enough to participate in numerous professional networks that have enriched me and supported me in different ways. Conferences, workshops, book clubs, and salons have enabled me to think deeply with diverse scholars. And I'm deeply, deeply, deeply grateful to the countless unnamed friends, scholars, peers, and colleagues who have supported and challenged me over the years. I can't imagine having done this project without their love, support, and laughter.

This project wouldn't have been possible without the hundreds of teens who took the time to talk to me and provide feedback. I'm also thankful to their parents for letting me talk with them and to the teachers, librarians, religious leaders, afterschool project coordinators, and community members who introduced me to them. Although I cannot name all of these wonderful people without undermining the anonymity of the teens I met, I am deeply grateful for their willingness to help me pursue this research. I am also thankful to the various technology creators and engineers who helped me gain access to data or walked me through practices that they were seeing on their services. This perspective, though not always visible in the manuscript, helped me better map teens' practices.

No project of this scale and duration is possible without the support of family. I am eternally grateful for my mother, Kathryn, who has been willing to stand behind me even as I stayed in school long after she imagined necessary; my brother, Ryan, who always managed to roll his eyes at his big sister's insanity in a way that brought a smile to my face; and my cousins Trevor and Julie for making sure I was OK even when I was out causing trouble. I am also deeply indebted to my grandparents Dick and Rita, who have been an inspiration for as long as I can remember.

Last and most important, I have been lucky enough to have the best partner by my side during this process. Midway through my dissertation fieldwork, I met my soulmate. Gilad has bounced around the world with me, keeping me calm and asking me strange questions about my peculiar country. He has supported me through thick and thin and been there for me in ways that I can't even express. As I finish this book, our child is growing inside of me. Together, we are both looking forward to watching Ziv embrace a whole host of new-fangled technologies in years to come.

index

MySpace (*Continued*)
 inserted code in profiles, 182; intended audience and, 29–30; internet addiction and, 79–80; limited mobility of teens and, 90–91; number of followers on, 206; political activities and, 207, 208; privacy settings, 32; profile as identity performance, 43–47; as public space, 21; racism online and, 164, 167–171
"My Story: Struggling, Bullying, Suicide, Self Harm" (Amanda Todd YouTube video), 123

Nakamura, Lisa, 158, 237n2
National Center for Missing and Exploited Children, 111
Native Americans, 189
networked publics, 4, 28, 98, 205, 211–213, 222n5; anxiety about sexual predators and, 104; context collapses and, 31; creation of, 201–203; identity work in, 36–43; politicization of, 206–211, 243n8; privacy in, 59, 60, 69; significance of, 8–14; visibility to adults, 57
"news junkies," 92, 108
Nissenbaum, Helen, 60, 228n11
Norman, Donald, 222n7
No Sense of Place (Meyrowitz), 31
nostalgia, 16, 26, 199
notaracistbut.com, 161–162
novels, addiction narrative and, 105
Now You See It (Davidson), 93
Nussbaum, Emily, 55–56

Obama, Barack, 156
obesity, 88
Olweus, Dan, 131–132, 138, 235n5
"omgblackpeople" blog, 161, 237n13
One Direction (boy band), 40
Ostrenga, Kirsten "Kiki," 114–116, 117
Out in the Country (Gray), 224n3, 227n30

Palfrey, John, 196
parents, 2, 33–34, 44, 125; abductions by

noncustodial parents, 118; anxiety about sexual predators and, 100–101, 109–110, 118–120; bullying and, 134; cell phone calls to children, 3; cooperative, 21; gossip cycle and, 69; online profiles created by, 58; privacy settings and, 32; restrictions on freedom of teens, 84–90, 96–99; teens' privacy and, 47, 54, 70–74; values projected onto children, 17–18
Pariser, Eli, 186
"participation gap," 193
pedophiles, 103, 109
peer groups, 40, 100, 136, 137, 200
People's History of the United States, A (Zinn), 189–190
Perkel, Dan, 240n12
Perry, Katy, 151
persistence, of online content, 11, 13, 61, 203
Phillips, Whitney, 226n19
photo sharing, 33
Pinker, Steven, 92–93
pirate radio, 205
Playing the Future (Rushkoff), 178, 239n4
Poole, Chris, 42
pornography, 103
Portwood-Stacer, Laura, 229–230n2
pranking, 137, 139, 140, 141
pregnancy, teenage, 103
Prensky, Marc, 179, 197
Presentation of Self in Everyday Life, The (Goffman), 47–48
Presley, Elvis, 105
Prince, Phoebe, 235n3
privacy, 8, 19, 50–51, 125, 193; celebrity culture and, 150; conflicting norms of, 57–59; control of social situation and, 59–61; definitions of, 59, 228n11; identity performance and, 47; as process, 74–76; public-by-default framework and, 61–65; publicity in interplay with, 57, 204, 227–228n6; settings on social media, 32, 225n6; surveillance and, 70–74, 229n24; teens' attitudes toward, 54–57, 227n4

Progressive Era, 94
propaganda, 239n10
pseudonyms, 38, 225n11
public-by-default framework, 61–65
public spaces, 18–19, 20, 54, 155, 201;
  civil inattention and, 58; legal
  restrictions on teens' access to,
  103–104, 106; parental restrictions on
  access to, 87; privately owned, 202;
  sharing in, 56
Pump Up the Volume (film), 206
punking, 137, 139, 140, 141
punk subculture, 2
Putnam, Robert, 231n29

Raby, Rebecca, 224n2
race, 2, 37, 86, 160; in cyberspace, 158;
  gang culture and, 154–156
Race in Cyberspace (Kolko, Nakamura,
  and Rodman), 158
racism, 24, 238n22; Facebook versus
  MySpace in racial divide, 167–171; in
  a networked age, 160–163; racial
  profiling, 207; segregation in everyday
  life, 163–166
radio, 31
rape and rapists: in dating relationships,
  115–116, 234n38; fears about abduction
  and, 110, 113, 114, 118–120; statutory
  rape, 113–114, 115, 116. *See also* sexual
  predators
Reagan, Nancy, 125
"reality" TV shows, 19, 147, 205
Reefer Madness (film, 1938), 82
"Rehab" (Amy Winehouse song), 83
Rheingold, Howard, 243n9
Rise of the Network Society, The
  (Castells), 173
Robinson, Penelope, 195
Rodman, Gilbert, 158
Rolling Stone magazine, 114, 115
rumors, 13, 129, 131–132, 135, 137,
  142–143
Runescape, 100
Rushkoff, Doug, 239n4
Ryze, 226n22

Schmidt, Eric, 56
searchability, 11, 12, 13, 33, 203
search engine optimization, 184
search engines, 12, 13
Second Life, 41
Seinfeld (TV show), 36
self-expression, 8
self-harm, digital, 141
self-presentation, 17, 30, 48, 50
Senft, Terri, 150, 236n21
sexual abuse, reality of, 110–111,
  233n30
sexuality, 2, 14, 103, 224n3; bullying
  and, 134–135; moral panics over, 105;
  queer identity, 52, 227n30; unhealthy
  sexual encounters, 114–118, 234n38
sexual predators, 22, 24, 100–102, 127,
  231n2; abductions, 118–120; everyday
  life and fear of, 107–110; foundation
  of fears about, 102–107; myth of
  online predators, 110–114
Shallows, The (Carr), 92
shaming, public, 146
siblings, 47, 73, 86, 141
Sidekick smartphone, 171
Siri (Apple voice recognition software),
  158
Skins (TV show), 82
Skype, 38
Slabyk, John, 15
slut shaming, 24, 52
Smart Mobs (Rheingold), 243n9
smartphones, 3, 80, 171, 194
Snapchat, 26, 27, 64
Snowden, Edward, 210
Snyder, Howard N., 233n30
social media, 4, 206, 211–213; addiction
  to, 91; celebrity culture and, 149;
  death of privacy and, 56; definition
  of, 6–8; hopes and fears attached to,
  15; identity performance on, 44; as
  moving landscape, 27; persistence
  and, 11; polarized views of, 24; as
  public spaces, 20; social divisions
  and, 171–175; sociality reclaimed
  through, 95

interaction with strangers on, 204;
interest-driven communities on, 39,
40; number of followers on, 206;
participation in public life and, 10;
privacy settings, 32; as public space,
21; race and, 171, 238n28; social
context and, 41; streaming content
on, 32

Untergang, Der (film), 210
Usenet, 7

Vaidhyanathan, Siva, 242n6
Valentine, Gill, 103, 105
vampire tales, 117, 118
video games, 35, 55, 80
Villaraigosa, Antonio, 208
viral videos, 145
visibility, potential audience and, 11,
12, 203

Walkman music player, 14
Wallace, Alexandra, 162–163
"wangstas," 168
Wayne's World (film), 206
Web 2.0, 6
Weil, Elizabeth, 239n4
Wells, Melissa, 124
Westin, Alan, 59
West, Kanye, 17
whites, 2, 33–34, 63, 68, 77, 128; cell
phone brands used by, 3; Facebook

versus MySpace and, 167–171; racism
in networked age and, 162–163
*Why Are All the Black Kids Sitting
Together in the Cafeteria?* (Tarum), 166
Whyville, 41
WikiLeaks, 209
Wikipedia, 180, 183, 186–192, 240n19
Willis, Paul, 30
Winehouse, Amy, 83
Winner, Langdon, 157, 223n15
Wong, Jimmy, 162
World of Warcraft, 41, 42, 162
"Writing, Citing, and Participatory
Media" (Forte and Bruckman),
240n19

Xanga, 8

Yankovic, Weird Al, 146
Young, Kimberly, 77
youth culture, 28, 39, 82
Youth Culture and Private Space
(Lincoln), 238n27
Youth Radio, 57
YouTube, 13, 85, 123, 132; celebrity
culture and, 149; number of followers
on, 206; racism and, 162

zines (homemade magazines), 205
Zinn, Howard, 189
Zuckerberg, Mark, 50, 56
Zuckerman, Ethan, 237n9